Conversations with William Styron

Literary Conversations Series

Peggy Whitman Prenshaw,
General Editor

Conversations
with William Styron

Edited by
James L. W. West III

French Interviews Translated by
W. Pierre Jacoebee

Foreword by William Styron

University Press of Mississippi
Jackson & London

Books by William Styron

Lie Down in Darkness. Indianapolis: Bobbs-Merrill, 1951.
The Long March. New York: Random House—Modern Library Paperback, 1956.
Set This House on Fire. New York: Random House, 1960.
The Confessions of Nat Turner. New York: Random House, 1967.
In the Clap Shack. New York: Random House, 1973.
Sophie's Choice. New York: Random House, 1979.
This Quiet Dust and Other Writings. New York: Random House, 1982.

Copyright © 1985 by the University Press of Mississippi
All rights reserved
Manufactured in the United States of America

88 87 86 85   4 3 2 1

Library of Congress Cataloging in Publication Data

Styron, William, 1925–
    Conversations with William Styron.

    (Literary conversations series)
    Bibliography: p.
    Includes index.
    1. Styron, William, 1925–   —Interviews.
2. Novelists, American—20th century—Interviews.
I. West, James L. W.   II. Series
PS3569.T9Z463   1985   813'.54 [B]   85-7556
ISBN 0-87805-260-7
ISBN 0-87805-261-5 (pbk.)

Contents

Foreword   *William Styron*   vii

Introduction   viii

Chronology   xii

Talk with William Styron   *David Dempsey*   3

William Styron   *John K. Hutchens*   6

The Art of Fiction V: William Styron   *Peter Matthiessen*
and *George Plimpton*   8

A Visit with William Styron   *Hubert Juin*   20

Interview   *Madeleine Chapsal*   23

The Prey of the Critics   *Annie Brierre*   28

Meet the Professor   *William Blackburn, William Styron,
Reynolds Price, Mac Hyman, Fred Chappell*   32

Two Writers Talk It Over   *James Jones* and *William Styron*   40

A Conversation with William Styron   *Jack Griffin, Jerry Homsy,
Gene Stelzig*   49

An Interview with William Styron   *Robert Canzoneri*
and *Page Stegner*   66

William Styron   *Alice Rewald*   80

The Confessions of William Styron   *C. Vann Woodward*
and *R. W. B. Lewis*   83

William Styron on *The Confessions of Nat Turner:* A Yale Lit
Interview   *Douglas Barzelay* and *Robert Sussman*   93

Portrait of a Man Reading   *Charles Monaghan*   109

The Uses of History in Fiction   *Ralph Ellison, William Styron,
Robert Penn Warren, C. Vann Woodward*   114

Intolerable America   *Michel Salomon*   145

The Editor Interviews William Styron   *Philip Rahv*   151

Conversation: Arthur Miller and William Styron   *Rust Hills*   162

An Interview with William Styron   *Ben Forkner*
    and *Gilbert Schricke*   190

A Bibliographer's Interview with William Styron
    James L. W. West III   203

An Interview with William Styron   *Michael West*   217

Creators on Creating: William Styron   *Hilary Mills*   234

Why I Wrote *Sophie's Choice*   *Michel Braudeau*   243

William Styron   *Stephen Lewis*   256

William Styron: The Confessions of a Southern Writer
    Georgann Eubanks   265

Index   276

Foreword

Writers should perhaps make it a rule not to give interviews; however, they do seem to be inevitable. As James West points out in his introduction to this volume, Faulkner's interviews were often intentionally wily and deceptive but he did talk to enough interviewers to fill a book—demonstrating that only the most fanatically hermetic writer (Salinger, perhaps, or Pynchon) seems to be able to escape the literary inquisitor. Generally speaking, only two motives have lain behind my willingness to grant interviews. A certain amiable garrulousness, part of my southern background, is to blame for a great deal of this. Often, when approached by people who seem capable of asking interesting questions (and most of the interviewers in this book fall into such a category) I have found myself responding at length out of the sheer pleasure of the intellectual interchange that ensued. Some people are chronically withdrawn but most of us, if we are honest about it, like to hear ourselves talk, and when the questions are provocative the dialogue can sometimes get quite exciting. My other motive for talking publicly at such length comes (as Mr. West points out correctly) from a frequent desire to set the record straight. My work has been "controversial" more often than I might have wished, sometimes perplexing and infuriating readers and driving certain commentators to imprudent and occasionally false conclusions. In a number of interviews, therefore, I have merely tried to restore a little balance. I hope that somewhere between the extremes of talkativeness and those areas that might appear merely didactic the reader will find a reasonable measure of entertainment.

William Styron
Roxbury, Connecticut
10 April 1985

Introduction

In March 1958, while visiting at Princeton University, William Faulkner was interviewed three separate times by three different interviewers over a two-day period. At the beginning of each session, Faulkner gave each interviewer three pieces of information about himself: his place of birth, his date of birth, and the original spelling of his surname. To each interviewer he deliberately gave two of these items incorrectly, but to no two interviewers did he give the same two pieces of misinformation.

Most students of modern American literature are familiar with Faulkner's attitude toward interviewers, his resentment of their intrusions into his private life. It is not surprising that he misled the three interviewers in Princeton in this way, nor is it suprising that in interview sessions throughout his career he sometimes feigned ignorance or forgetfulness. His implied message was that if people wanted to know about him, they had only to read his fiction. The published interview, for Faulkner, was an effort to substitute chat for *écriture*, an exercise which elevated mere talk to the level of literary artifact. He therefore resisted the interview process and on occasion even subverted it.[1]

Faulkner's attitude toward interviews has influenced American writers of the generations that have followed him, and many of these authors have developed what they must take to be a facsimile of his stance—a deliberate coyness, a tendency toward obfuscation, a conscious (though perhaps less than genuine) hostility to the interviewing process. William Styron has fortunately not adopted such an attitude. He has lived in a time more thoroughly saturated with print and broadcast media than was Faulkner's, and, unlike Faulkner, he has been accustomed to the presence of interviewers from the earliest days of his career. He has not always welcomed their visits, but over the years he has become of necessity a patient and cooperative interview subject, at ease in question-and-answer sessions. He has learned to use interviews much as Vladimir Nabokov used them—as occasions on which to respond publicly to important questions about his writing and thinking.

Styron may well be the most frequently interviewed writer of his generation: at last count, almost one hundred interviews with him had appeared since publication of *Lie Down in Darkness,* his first novel, in 1951.[2] Inevitably the numerous interviewers have asked many of the same questions. They have repeatedly urged Styron to talk about himself as a "southern" writer in the tradition of Faulkner and Thomas Wolfe, to comment on his attitude toward book reviewers, to answer attacks on *The Confessions of Nat Turner* by black militants, to state his beliefs about the novel vs. history, and to respond to critics who have doubted his qualifications for writing about the Holocaust. Styron has developed standard responses to these questions; what he said for publication in 1968 during the controversy over *Nat Turner,* for example, he is still saying in 1985. I had therefore feared that a collection of Styron's interviews would contain much repetition—valuable, of course, in showing the consistency of his public statements over time but repetitive all the same. It has been good to discover that one can assemble a collection of Styron's interviews in which there is not a great amount of overlapping. There are many interviews from which to choose, and fortunately there have been knowledgeable, well-prepared questioners who have avoided familiar territory and have approached Styron on fresh ground. One senses, in such sessions, that Styron has been pleased to engage in intellectual give-and-take rather than to deliver new versions of his familiar responses. It is these atypical interviews that I have sought out for this collection. I have, to be sure, included the best of the other kind: Styron's *Yale Lit* interview in which he responds to militant black critics, for example, and the famous symposium at the 1968 Southern Historical Association meeting in New Orleans during which he referred to one Negro heckler as his *"bête noire."* But by and large, I have preferred diversity of subject matter over public pronouncement, a policy which should make this volume the more useful to critics and teachers of Styron's work.

Included in this collection are translations of six French-language interviews with Styron, all published originally in Paris periodicals. Styron's literary reputation has been high in France since the appearance of Maurice-Edgar Coindreau's translation of *Set This House on Fire* there in 1962.[3] In general, French interviewers have avoided the stock questions with rather more success than have their American counterparts; as a result, these French interviewers have elicited some valuable responses from Styron.

Several of the items published here appeared originally in established literary reviews, while others are reprinted from less well-known sources. The only criterion governing inclusion has been the quality of the interview. One of the better items in this book, for example, is the interview conducted by three University of Pennsylvania students and published in their undergraduate literary magazine in 1965. The students—Jack Griffin, Jerry Homsy, and Gene Stelzig—were well prepared and inquisitive, not only about Styron's writings but about literature and the literary vocation. One sees Styron, in this session, in the unaccustomed role of teacher, explaining novelistic techniques to these young men and revealing to them some of the conditions under which he works.

The term "interview" has been interpreted loosely here. Some of the items in this volume are not true interviews; they might be referred to more accurately as symposia or recorded conversations. Styron's discussions with many of his contemporaries have been taped, both for publication and for broadcast, and transcriptions of several of these sessions have been included in this volume. When one reads this collection, one therefore has the opportunity of being present at conversations between Styron and fellow authors Reynolds Price, Mac Hyman, Fred Chappell, James Jones, Ralph Ellison, Robert Penn Warren, and Arthur Miller. Important historians and literary critics such as C. Vann Woodward, R. W. B. Lewis, and Philip Rahv are also represented.

A volume such as this one must be used with circumspection. These are all serious interviews, well above the level of talk-show chatter, but they are still only interviews. One cannot hold an author responsible for what he says in an interview in quite the same way one holds him accountable for what he writes and publishes. Nevertheless, this book should be valuable both as a series of glimpses into Styron's character and as an index to his thinking at various moments during his career.

Unless otherwise indicated, all interviews in this collection are republished from their source texts without substantive emendation. All
texts are uncut; ellipsis points are printed only when they appear in
the original texts. Obvious typographical errors have been corrected
and a few missing punctuation marks silently supplied. The source
text is always cited at the head of the interview; the exact date on
which the interview was conducted is given when that date is known.
Many interviews are prefaced, in their original appearances, by short
notes identifying Styron and sketching in the highlights of his literary
career. When these headnotes also contain significant information
about the circumstances under which the interview took place, they
are reproduced. Otherwise they are not included. In a few interviews,
prefixes have been added to identify speakers.

French interviews were rendered into English initially by my col-
league W. Pierre Jacoebee. He and I then collaborated in smoothing
and clarifying the translated texts. By Styron's own testimony, these
interviews were all originally conducted in English and translated into
French for publication. Jacoebee and I have therefore felt at liberty to
translate freely and expressively in an effort to capture what we believe to be the essence of Styron's responses.

JLWW III
January 1985

1. For further discussion of Faulkner's attitude toward interviews, see the introduction to
Lion in the Garden: Interviews with William Faulkner, 1926–1962, ed. James B. Meriwether
and Michael Millgate (New York: Random House, 1968).

2. For a listing of the interviews through 1976, see Section I of James L. W. West III, *William
Styron: A Descriptive Bibliography* (Boston: G. K. Hall, 1977).

3. See Melvin J. Friedman, "William Styron and the *Nouveau Roman,*" and Valarie M.
Arms, "William Styron in France," in *Critical Essays on William Styron,* ed. Arthur D. Casciato
and James L. W. West III (Boston: G. K. Hall, 1982).

Chronology

1925 William Clark Styron, Jr., is born on 11 June; he is the only child of William Clark Styron and Pauline Margaret Abraham.

1939 Pauline Styron dies on 20 July.

1940–42 Styron attends Christchurch, an Episcopal boys' school on the Rappahannock River near Urbanna, Virginia.

1942–43 Styron is a student at Davidson College; he pledges Phi Delta Theta and writes for the school newspaper and literary magazine. He enlists in the Marine Corps during the spring of 1943.

1943–44 As a student at Duke University in the Navy's V-12 program, Styron comes under the influence of William Blackburn. He leaves Duke late in 1944 for Marine training camp at Parris Island; while there he is incarcerated in a V. D. ward with a case of trench mouth, incorrectly diagnosed as syphilis.

1945 Styron moves from Parris Island to officer training school in May and is later commissioned. He serves as a guard at the Naval Disciplinary Barracks on Hart's Island in New York harbor; he is discharged from the Marines late in the year.

1946 In March, Styron returns to Duke to begin finishing requirements for his degree; he travels to Trieste and back on a cattle boat and attends Bread Loaf Writers Conference at Middlebury during the summer.

1947 Styron competes unsuccessfully for a Rhodes Scholarship in February; he graduates from Duke and begins work in New York City as an associate editor at Whittlesey House, a division of McGraw-Hill. He enrolls in Hiram Haydn's class in fiction writing at the New School for Social Research. He is fired from McGraw-Hill in October; he works on *Lie Down in Darkness,* then entitled "Inheritance of Night."

1948 Styron signs a contract for a novel with Crown Publishers in January; he moves to Durham in July and there revises and expands the opening sections of "Inheritance." In September he acquires a literary agent, Elizabeth McKee.

1949 He visits New York in January; by mid-March he has abandoned his novel. He moves to a rooming house in Brooklyn and begins work again on the novel, now titled *Lie Down in Darkness.*

1950 Styron writes steadily on his novel while living, for a time, at Valley Cottage, a village near Nyack, New York. He returns to New York City in May and continues work on his manuscript.

1951 Early in 1951, Styron is recalled into the Marines for the Korean War. Haydn has his induction postponed in order that he can complete his novel. The manuscript is finished by early April; some sexually explicit material is later excised at the insistence of Bobbs-Merrill, now Styron's publisher. Styron reenters the Marines that summer; he goes on a forced march at Camp Lejeune and is given a medical discharge for eye trouble in the late summer. *Lie Down in Darkness* is published on 10 September.

1952 Styron wins the *Prix de Rome* for *Lie Down in Darkness.* He sails to Europe in the spring; he tours England and Denmark, then stays for a time in Paris, where he writes "Long March" in June and July. He associates with the *Paris Review* group and helps launch the first issue of that journal. He begins thinking about a novel on Nat Turner. Styron moves to the American Academy in Rome early in October; he renews his acquaintance with Rose Burgunder.

1953 "Long March" appears in the February issue of *discovery. Lie Down in Darkness* is published in a French translation that same month. Styron and Rose Burgunder marry in Rome on 4 May; they spend the summer and fall in Ravello. Styron works on a novella about his experiences as a prison guard and finishes 7,000 words before aborting the manuscript.

1954 The Styrons settle in Roxbury, Connecticut, in October. Styron begins work on *Set This House on Fire,* which he will finish late in 1959.

1955 Susanna Styron is born on 25 February.

1956 The first separate edition of *The Long March* is published by Random House in the Modern Library on 29 October.

1957 *The Long March* is included in *The Best Short Stories of World War II,* edited by Charles A. Fenton.

1958 Paola Styron is born on 13 March.

1959 Thomas Styron is born on 4 August.

1960 *Set This House on Fire* is published on 4 May, the Styrons' seventh wedding anniversary.

1961 Styron begins work on *The Confessions of Nat Turner*. He publishes "Mrs. Aadland's Little Girl, Beverly" in *Esquire* in November.

1962 "As He Lay Dead, a Bitter Grief," Styron's account of William Faulkner's funeral, is published in *Life* on 20 July. Maurice-Edgar Coindreau's translation of *Set This House on Fire* is published by Gallimard in February. Styron's "The Death-in-Life of Benjamin Reid" appears in *Esquire* that same month.

1963 Gallimard publishes a French translation of *The Long March* in May and reissues the French text of *Lie Down in Darkness* in July.

1964 Styron is elected an Honorary Fellow of Silliman College, Yale University, in April. The Styrons buy a house in Vineyard Haven, Massachusetts, on Martha's Vineyard, in August.

1965 "This Quiet Dust" appears in *Harper's* in April.

1966 Styron is inducted into the American Academy of Arts and Letters and the National Institute of Arts and Letters on 25 May. Alexandra Styron is born on 28 October.

1967 *The Confessions of Nat Turner* is published by Random House on 9 October. The novel is also distributed by both Book-of-the-Month Club and Literary Guild.

1968 Styron receives the Pulitzer Prize for *Nat Turner*. He attends the Democratic National Convention in Chicago during the summer and publishes "In the Jungle" in the *New York Review of Books* on 26 September. *William Styron's Nat Turner: Ten Black Writers Respond* is published by Beacon Press.

1969 Coindreau's translation of *The Confessions of Nat Turner* is published by Gallimard in January. Styron begins work on "The Way of the Warrior."

1970 Styron receives the Howells Medal for Fiction on 26 May, from the American Academy of Arts and Letters.

1972 *In the Clap Shack* premieres 15 December at the Yale Repertory Theatre. Styron contributes an article on Nat Turner to the *Encyclopedia Britannica*, 1972 edn.; it is dropped from subsequent editions.

1973 Random House publishes *In the Clap Shack* on 15 June. With John Phillips, Styron publishes "Dead!" in the December issue of *Esquire*. *Lie Down in Darkness* is named to the Agrégation list in France. Styron abandons work on "The Way of the Warrior" and begins a manuscript entitled "Sophie's Choice: A Memory."

1974 He lectures at several French universities in April in connection with the appearance of *Lie Down in Darkness* on the Agrégation list.

1975 Styron delivers the commencement address at Christchurch School, 24 May. He continues to work on *Sophie's Choice*.

1976 "William Styron in Mid-Career," an exhibition of manuscripts, editions, and other materials, is mounted at Duke University during March and April.

1977 Styron publishes "A Friend's Farewell to James Jones" in *New York*, 6 June.

1978 William C. Styron, Sr., dies in August in Southbury, Connecticut.

1979 *Sophie's Choice* is published on 11 June, Styron's fifty-fourth birthday; Random House gives a publication party at the River Cafe in Brooklyn.

1980 The Styron Scholarships are established at Christopher Newport College in Newport News. *Sophie's Choice* wins the first American Book Award for Fiction.

1981 Styron delivers the commencement address at Duke in May. In July he attends the inauguration of François Mitterrand by invitation; he publishes an account entitled "A Leader Who Prefers Writers to Politicians" in the *Boston Globe*, 26 July. In August, Styron actively opposes the establishment of a Nixon Library at Duke.

1982 Styron begins work on a novel which will incorporate most of his work on "The Way of the Warrior." *This Quiet Dust and Other Writings* is published on 30 November. The movie version of *Sophie's Choice* premieres in December.

1983 In February, Styron lobbies in Congress on behalf of a bill which will allow authors to make tax deductible donations of their manuscripts to nonprofit institutions. He delivers the convocation address at the University of Virginia on 14 October.

1984 In May, Styron attends an Amnesty International conference in
Tokyo and later visits Okinawa. He is named a Commander in the
Order of Arts and Letters in France in October.

(For a biographical sketch, see "William Styron in Mid-Career," in *Critical Essays on
William Styron,* ed. Arthur D. Casciato and James L. W. West III [Boston: G. K. Hall,
1982], pp. 1–10).

Conversations with William Styron

Talk with William Styron

David Dempsey / 1951

From the *New York Times Book Review,* 9 September 1951,
p. 27. Copyright © 1951 by The New York Times Company.
Reprinted by permission.

It is an occasion for comment—some might even say rejoicing—
when a novel with a Southern locale is not about the South. "Lie
Down in Darkness," by William Styron, is such a book—at least the
26-year-old Virginia author intended it to be, although he is willing to
concede that the critics might not agree with him.

"I wanted to write a novel that has more than regional implications. I wanted to avoid the ancestral theme, too—the peculiar, in-
bred and perverse types that Faulkner, Caldwell and other Southern
writers have dealt in. At the same time I didn't want to exploit the old
idea of wreckage and defeat as a peculiarly Southern phenomenon.
Elements of this are in the book, but they're part of the people rather
than the place. I like to think that my story could have happened in
Massachusetts just as well as in Virginia."

Styron had obviously picked himself a big order, being at once a
Southerner and not a Southerner. Isn't that a section of the country
that doesn't allow for divided loyalties? "It's true, you can't escape
your background," he admitted. "But I've tried to keep mine an in-
tangible feeling. Influences? Well, I grew up on Wolfe—I don't regard
him quite as highly as I once did—and I read Caldwell, Robert Penn
Warren and Eudora Welty. Capote is very impressive, too, but he has
a little less to say." With all this in his bloodstream would it be fair to
say that perhaps he hadn't detached himself from the Southern mystique as much as he thought? "Well, not exactly. The influences are
pretty indefinite at this point. Faulkner was the hardest to shake off.
The early parts of my novel were so imbued with his style that I had
to go back and rewrite them completely. His characters wouldn't be
great if they weren't Southern. Mine will have to stand or fall as
individuals."

There were compensating forces, too, Mr. Styron made it plain—

3

Joyce was one; in the historical sense, Mark Twain. "Hands down, he's the best writer we have produced." As for the Virginia school—Glasgow and Cabell notably—Mr. Styron confessed to ignorance. "I've read one or two books by them—I intend to do better when I have the time. To tell the truth, I haven't read much fiction at all in the last three years."

He spent three years writing "Lie Down in Darkness," most of that time in the North (Nyack, N.Y., and West Eighty-eighth Street, Manhattan). It's the only professional writing he's ever done, even though he was briefly employed here by a book publisher. A couple of short stories in college anthologies convinced him that that form wasn't conducive to what—from a look at the novel—is obviously a rather sprawling talent.

Born in Newport News, Va., he was educated at a prep school in Middlesex County and graduated from Duke University in 1947. Part of his college days were as a V-12 student while he was in the Marine Corps, which took him as far as a naval prison (as a guard, to be sure). He was called back again last year, turning the MS of his book over to the publishers the same day he went into uniform. As a kind of getting out present, when he was separated last month, Bobbs-Merrill presented him with an advance copy. "It was nice timing," he said.

Styron's plans for the future are admittedly vague. He'd like to write a play and take a trip to Europe—no connection—and then do a short novel dealing with the Reserves: that's an aspect of military life writers have not touched on. "I'm not overwhelmed by the idea of writing, though—Valery once said that it bored him, but that he had to go on with it. I think a lot of writers must feel that way. It's a mission. I don't want to sound pompous, but a book is something that should be approached with high seriousness. It helps you discover something about yourself. A novel should educate the author as well as the reader."

Did it work that way with "Darkness"? Well, yes—the book was begun without any preconceived theme or plan. "That came out as I went along. I had only a vague idea of the plot, although I knew in general what I wanted to say. I trust my instinct . . . I managed to stay one jump ahead of myself all the way through, but that's all. No scale models or notebooks like Sinclair Lewis used—nothing like that."

The theme? It was more or less inherent in the material. "I wanted to tell the story of four tragically fated people, one of them the innocent victim of the others. It was important to me that I write about this thing, but I can't tell you why. I didn't conceive it, directly at any rate, as a contemporary statement of any kind. The symbols are there, I suppose, but to me the important thing was the story."

William Styron

John K. Hutchens / 1951

From the *New York Herald Tribune Book Review*, 9 September 1951, p. 2.

He got to work on his first novel, William Styron said, six months after a New York publisher fired him for tossing balloons out of the window of an office in the McGraw-Hill Building where he presumably was working as an associate editor. If the publisher remembers Mr. Styron by name or face, he may as well learn also that the novel is "Lie Down in Darkness."

That beginning was made in the summer of 1948, and for about a year "Lie Down" did not go well. What happened, Mr. Styron went on to say, was that he was imitating William Faulkner. He stopped for six months, then started all over, "chopping out the Faulkner mood and building up the story in careful scenes" toward the long soliloquy with which it concludes. He had planned that soliloquy from the first, but hadn't known how to get there. Even when he knew, the progress was "extremely painful." About 150 words a day, he said— "Sometimes it was a matter of finding the right word, but more often of feeling what I wanted to say or just sitting there and thinking." From first to last, then, about two-and-a-half years, or about a tenth of his life. He was twenty-six last June.

Most of that time he has spent in Virginia in the neighborhood of his native Newport News, but his book, though its setting is Virginia, avoids specific, recognizable personalities, he said, predicting no local uproar down there. He would be going South again? He hasn't decided if he is interested in writing more about Virginia. He has, in fact, no immediate plans, not the vaguest idea of what he will attempt next.

He was well along at Duke University (A.B. '47) before he thought much about writing at all—"some fragments of short stories, none of which were much good." Through his 'teens he read nothing much, though at twenty he plunged into Faulkner and Joyce, whose influence upon himself he recognizes and hopes he has assimilated into his own style. In the case of Faulkner, especially, he admitted, "the rhetorical influence was overwhelming.". . . Before Duke, there were two and a half years in the Marines, during which he did not get overseas, ending the war as a Naval prison guard. (He re-entered the Marines last May was honorably discharged for poor eyesight.) "No picturesque jobs, and I have hardly been anywhere except to Italy, where I went in 1946 with U.N.R.R.A., taking care of cows. It was a gay tour, and I'd like to go back," he said in the soft Virginia voice that stops this side of a Southern accent.

The first person to spot the Styron talent was Hiram Haydn, now his editor at Bobbs-Merrill. Mr. Haydn was then, as now, conducting a course in the novel at the New School for Social Research. He read some of Mr. Styron's prose and asked, "How would you like to write a novel? I'll give you an option. . . ." Mr. Styron pondered, came up with a general idea for a story about "a girl who gets in a lot of trouble." At first he really had no more in mind than that, and the flashback technique he wanted to use, he said.

"A hybrid Virginian," he calls himself, his father having come from North Carolina, his mother from Western Pennsylvania. He is grateful especially to his father, an engineer, for the understanding the parent has shown for his son's ambition.

The Art of Fiction V: William Styron

Peter Matthiessen and George Plimpton / 1954

From the *Paris Review*, 2 (Spring 1954), 42–57; republished in
Writers at Work: The Paris Review Interviews, 1st series, ed.
Malcolm Cowley (New York: Viking, 1958), pp. 268–82. Copyright © 1957, 1958 by The Paris Review, Inc. Reprinted by
permission of Viking Penguin Inc. and the interviewers.

William Styron was interviewed in Paris, in early autumn,
at Patricks, a café on the Boulevard Montparnasse which
has little to distinguish it from its neighbors—the Dome,
the Rotonde, Le Chapelain—except a faintly better
brand of coffee. Across the Boulevard from the café and
its sidewalk tables, a red poster portrays a skeletal family.
They are behind bars, and the caption reads: TAKE YOUR
VACATION IN HAPPY RUSSIA. The lower part of the poster has
been ripped and scarred and plastered with stickers
shouting: LES AMÉRICANS EN AMÉRIQUE! U.S. GO HOME! An
adjoining poster advertises carbonated water. PERRIER! it
sings. L'EAU QUI FAIT PSCHITT! The sun reflects strongly off
their vivid colors, and Styron, shading his eyes, peers
down into his coffee. He is a young man of good appearance, though not this afternoon; he is a little paler than is
healthy in this quiet hour when the denizens of the quarter lie hiding, their weak night eyes insulted by the light.

Interviewers: You were about to tell us when you started to write.

Styron: What? Oh, yes. Write. I figure I must have been about
thirteen. I wrote an imitation Conrad thing, "Typhoon and the Tor
Bay" it was called, you know, a ship's hold swarming with crazy
Chinks. I think I had some sharks in there too. I gave it the full treatment.

Interviewers: And how did you happen to start? That is, why did
you want to write?

Styron: I wish I knew. I wanted to express myself, I guess. But after "Typhoon and the Tor Bay" I didn't give writing another thought until I went to Duke University and landed in a creative writing course under William Blackburn. He was the one who got me started.

Interviewers: What value has the creative writing course for young writers?

Styron: It gives them a start, I suppose. But it can be an awful waste of time. Look at those people who go back year after year to summer writers' conferences, you get so you can pick them out a mile away. A writing course can only give you a start, and help a little. It can't teach writing. The professor should weed out the good from the bad, cull them like a farmer, and not encourage the ones who haven't got something. At one school I know in New York which has a lot of writing courses there are a couple of teachers who moon in the most disgusting way over the poorest, most talentless writers, giving false hope where there shouldn't be any hope at all. Regularly they put out dreary little anthologies, the quality of which would chill your blood. It's a ruinous business, a waste of paper and time, and such teachers should be abolished.

Interviewers: The average teacher can't teach anything about technique or style?

Styron: Well, he can teach you something in matters of technique. You know—don't tell a story from two points of view and that sort of thing. But I don't think even the most conscientious and astute teachers can teach anything about style. Styles come only after long, hard practice and writing.

Interviewers: Do you enjoy writing?

Styron: I certainly don't. I get a fine warm feeling when I'm doing well, but that pleasure is pretty much negated by the pain of getting started each day. Let's face it, writing is hell.

Interviewers: How many pages do you turn out each day?

Styron: When I'm writing steadily—that is, when I'm involved in a project which I'm really interested in, one of those rare pieces which has a foreseeable end—I average two-and-a-half or three pages a day, longhand on yellow sheets. I spend about five hours at it, of which very little is spent actually writing. I try to get a feeling of what's going on in the story before I put it down on paper, but actually most of this breaking-in period is one long, fantastic daydream, in which I think about anything but the work at hand. I can't turn out slews of stuff each day. I wish I could. I seem to have some neurotic need to perfect each paragraph—each sentence, even—as I go along.

Interviewers: And what time of the day do you find best for working?

Styron: The afternoon. I like to stay up late at night and get drunk and sleep late. I wish I could break the habit but I can't. The afternoon is the only time I have left and I try to use it to the best advantage, with a hangover.

Interviewers: Do you use a notebook?

Styron: No, I don't feel the need for it. I've tried, but it does no good, since I've never used what I've written down. I think the use of a notebook depends upon the individual.

Interviewers: Do you find you need seclusion?

Styron: I find it's difficult to write in complete isolation. I think it would be hard for me on a South Sea island or in the Maine woods. I like company and entertainment, people around. The actual process of writing, though, demands complete, noiseless privacy, without even music; a baby howling two blocks away will drive me nuts.

Interviewers: Does your emotional state have any bearing on your work?

Styron: I guess like everybody I'm emotionally fouled up most of the time, but I find I do better when I'm relatively placid. It's hard to say, though. If writers had to wait until their precious psyches were completely serene there wouldn't be much writing done. Actually—though I don't take advantage of the fact as much as I should—I find that I'm simply the happiest, the placidest, *when* I'm writing, and so I suppose that that, for me, is the final answer. When I'm writing I find it's the only time that I feel completely self-possessed, even when the writing itself is not going too well. It's fine therapy for people who are perpetually scared of nameless threats as I am most of the time—for jittery people. Besides, I've discovered that when I'm not writing I'm prone to developing certain nervous tics, and hypochondria. Writing alleviates those quite a bit. I think I resist change more than most people. I dislike traveling, like to stay settled. When I first came to Paris all I could think about was going home, home to the old James River. One of these days I expect to inherit a peanut farm. Go back home and farm them old peanuts and be real old Southern whisky gentry.

Interviewers: Your novel was linked to the Southern school of fiction. Do you think the critics were justified in doing this?

Styron: No, frankly, I don't consider myself in the Southern school, whatever that is. *Lie Down in Darkness,* or most of it, was set in the South, but I don't care if I never write about the South again, really. Only certain things in the book are particularly Southern. I used leitmotivs—the Negroes, for example—that run throughout the book, but I would like to believe that my people would have behaved the way they did anywhere. The girl, Peyton, for instance, didn't have to come from Virginia. She would have wound up jumping from a window no matter where she came from. Critics are always linking writers to "schools." If they couldn't link people to schools, they'd die. When what they condescendingly call "a genuinely fresh talent" arrives on the scene, the critics rarely try to point out what makes him fresh or genuine but concentrate instead on how he behaves in accordance with their preconceived notion of what school he belongs to.

Interviewers: You don't find that it's true of most of the so-called Southern novels that the reactions of their characters are universal?

Styron: Look, I don't mean to repudiate my Southern background completely, but I don't believe that the South alone produces "universal" literature. That universal quality comes far more from a single writer's mind and his individual spirit than from his background. Faulkner's a writer of extraordinary stature more because of the great breadth of his vision than because he happened to be born in Mississippi. All you have to do is read one issue of the *Times Book Review* to see how much junk comes out regularly from south of the Mason-Dixon line, along with the good stuff. I have to admit, though, that the South has a definite literary tradition, which is the reason it probably produces a better quality of writing, proportionately. Perhaps it's just true that Faulkner, if he had been born in, say, Pasadena, might very well still have had that universal quality of mind, but instead of writing *Light in August* he would have gone into television or written universal ads for Jantzen bathing suits.

Interviewers: Well, why do you think this Southern tradition exists at all?

Styron: Well, first, there's that old heritage of Biblical rhetoric and story-telling. Then the South simply provides such wonderful material. Take, for instance, the conflict between the ordered Protestant tradition, the fundamentalism based on the Old Testament, and the twentieth century—movies, cars, television. The poetic juxtapositions you find in this conflict—a crazy colored preacher howling those tremendously moving verses from Isaiah 40, while riding around in a maroon Packard. It's wonderful stuff and comparatively new, too, which is perhaps why the renaissance of Southern writing coincided with these last few decades of the machine age. If Faulkner had written in the 1880s he would have been writing, no doubt, safely within the tradition, but his novels would have been genteel novels, like those of George Washington Cable or Thomas Nelson Page. In fact, the modern South is such powerful material that the author runs the danger of capturing the local color and feeling that's enough. He gets so bemused by decaying mansions that he forgets to populate them with people. I'm beginning to feel that it's a good idea for writers who come from the South, at least some of them, to break away a little from all them magnolias.

Interviewers: You refer a number of times to Faulkner. Even though you don't think of yourself as a "Southern" writer, would you say that he influenced you?

Styron: I would certainly say so. I'd say I had been influenced as much, though, by Joyce and Flaubert. Old Joyce and Flaubert have influenced me stylistically, given me arrows, but then a lot of the contemporary works I've read have influenced me as a craftsman. Dos Passos, Scott Fitzgerald, both have been valuable in teaching me how to write the novel, but not many of these modern people have contributed much to my *emotional* climate. Joyce comes closest, but the strong influences are out of the past—the Bible, Marlowe, Blake, Shakespeare. As for Flaubert, *Madame Bovary* is one of the few novels that moves me in every way, not only in its style, but in its total communicability, like the effect of good poetry. What I really mean is that a great book should leave you with many experiences, and slightly exhausted at the end. You live several lives while reading it. Its writer should, too. Without condescending, he should be conscious of himself as a reader, and while he's writing it he should be able to step outside of it from time to time and say to himself, "Now if I were just *reading* this book, would I like this part here?" I have the feeling that that's what Flaubert did—maybe too much, though, finally, in books like *Sentimental Education.*

Interviewers: While we're skirting this question, do you think Faulkner's experiments with time in *The Sound and the Fury* are justified?

Styron: Justified? Yes, I do.

Interviewers: Successful, then?

Styron: No, I don't think so. Faulkner doesn't give enough help to the reader. I'm all for the complexity of Faulkner, but not for the confusion. That goes for Joyce, too. All that fabulously beautiful poetry in the last part of *Finnegans Wake* is pretty much lost to the world simply because not many people are ever going to put up with the chaos that precedes it. As for *The Sound and the Fury,* I think it succeeds in spite of itself. Faulkner often simply stays too damn intense for too long a time. It ends up being great stuff, somehow, though, and the marvel is how it could be so wonderful being pitched for so long in that one high, prolonged, delirious key.

Interviewers: Was the problem of time development acute in the writing of *Lie Down in Darkness?*

Styron: Well, the book started with the man, Loftis, standing at the station with the hearse, waiting for the body of his daughter to arrive from up North. I wanted to give him density, but all the tragedy in his life had happened in the past. So the problem was to get into the past, and this man's tragedy, without breaking the story. It stumped me for a whole year. Then it finally occurred to me to use separate moments in time, four or five long dramatic scenes revolving around the daughter, Peyton, at different stages in her life. The business of the progression of time seems to me one of the most difficult problems a novelist has to cope with.

Interviewers: Did you prefigure the novel? How much was planned when you started?

Styron: Very little. I knew about Loftis and all his domestic troubles. I had the funeral. I had the girl in mind, and her suicide in Harlem. I thought I knew why, too, But that's all I had.

Interviewers: Did you start with emphasis on character or story?

Styron: Character, definitely. And by character I mean a person drawn full-round, not a caricature. E. M. Forster refers to "flat" and

"round" characters. I try to make all of mine round. It takes an ex-
trovert like Dickens to make flat characters come alive. But story as
such has been neglected by today's introverted writers. Story and
character should grow together; I think I'm lucky so far in that in
practically everything I've tried to write these two elements have
grown together. They must, to give an impression of life being lived,
just because each man's life is a story, if you'll pardon the cliché. I
used to spend a lot of time worrying over word order, trying to create
beautiful passages. I still believe in the value of a handsome style. I
appreciate the sensibility which can produce a nice turn of phrase,
like Scott Fitzgerald. But I'm not interested any more in turning out
something shimmering and impressionistic—Southern, if you will—
full of word-pictures, damn Dixie baby-talk, and that sort of thing. I
guess I just get more and more interested in people. And story.

Interviewers: Are your characters real-life or imaginary?

Styron: I don't know if that's answerable. I really think frankly,
though, that most of my characters come closer to being entirely
imaginary than the other way round. Maybe that's because they all
seem to end up, finally, closer to being like myself than like people
I've actually observed. I sometimes feel that the characters I've
created are not much more than sort of projected facets of myself,
and I believe that a lot of fictional characters have been created that
way.

Interviewers: How far removed must you be from your subject
matter?

Styron: Pretty far. I don't think people can write immediately, and
well, about an experience emotionally close to them. I have a feeling,
for example, that I won't be able to write about all the time I've spent
in Europe until I get back to America.

Interviewers: Do you feel yourself to be in competition with other
writers?

Styron: No, I don't. "Some of my best friends are writers." In
America there seems to be an idea that writing is one big cat-and-dog
fight between the various practitioners of the craft. Got to hole up in
the woods. Me, I'm a farmer, I don't know no writers. Hate writers.
That sort of thing. I think that just as in everything else writers can be
too cozy and cliquish and end up nervous and incestuous and
scratching each other's backs. In London once I was at a party where

everything was so literary and famous and intimate that if the place had suddenly been blown up by dynamite it would have demolished the flower of British letters. But I think that writers in the U.S. could stand a bit more of the attitude that prevailed in France in the last century. Flaubert and Maupassant, Victor Hugo and Musset, they didn't suffer from knowing each other. Turgenev knew Gogol. Chekhov knew Tolstoi and Andreiev, and Gorki knew all three. I think it was Henry James who said of Hawthorne that he might have been even better than he was if he had occasionally communicated a little bit more with others working at the same sort of thing. A lot of this philosophy of isolation in America is a dreary pose. I'm not advocating a Writers' Supper Club on Waverly Place, just for chums in the business, or a union, or anything like that, but I do think that writers in America might somehow benefit by the attitude that, what the hell, we're all in this together, instead of all my pals are bartenders on Third Avenue. As a matter of fact, I do have a pal who's a bartender on Third Avenue, but he's a part-time writer on the side.

Interviewers: In general, what do you think of critics, since they are a subject which must be close to a writer's heart?

Styron: From the writer's point of view, critics should be ignored, although it's hard not to do what they suggest. I think it's unfortunate to have critics for friends. Suppose you write something that stinks, what are they going to say in a review? Say it stinks? So if they're honest they do, and if you were friends you're still friends, but the knowledge of your lousy writing and their articulate admission of it will be always something between the two of you, like the knowledge between a man and his wife of some shady adultery. I know very few critics, but I usually read their reviews. Bad notices always give me a sense of humility, or perhaps humiliation, even when there's a tone of envy or sour grapes or even ignorance in them, but they don't help me much. When *Lie Down in Darkness* came out, my hometown paper scraped up the local literary figure to review the book, a guy who'd written something on hydraulics, I think, and he came to the conclusion that I was a decadent writer. Styron is a decadent writer, he said, because he writes a line like "the sea sucking at the shore," when for that depraved bit he should have substituted "the waves lapping at the shore." Probably his hydraulic background. No, I'm afraid I don't think much of critics for the most part, although I have to admit that some of them have so far treated me quite kindly. Look, there's only one person a writer should listen to, pay any attention to. It's not any damn critic. It's the reader. And that doesn't mean any compromise or sell-out. The writer must criticize his own work as a reader. Every day I pick up the story or whatever it is I've been working on and read it through. If I enjoy it as a reader then I know I'm getting along all right.

Interviewers: In your preface to the first issue of this magazine you speak of there being signs in the air that this generation can and will produce literature to rank with that of any other generation. What are these signs? And do you consider yourself, perhaps, a spokesman for this new generation?

Styron: What the hell is a spokesman, anyway? I hate the idea of spokesmen. Everybody, especially the young ones, in the writing game jockeying into position to give a name for a generation. I must confess that I was guilty of that in the preface, too. But don't you think it's tiresome, really, all these so-called spokesmen trumpeting around, elbowing one another out of the way to see who'll be the first to give a new and original name to twenty-five million people: the Beat Generation, or the Silent Generation, and God knows what-all? I think the damn generation should be let alone. And that goes for the eternal idea of competition—whether the team of new writers can beat the team of Dos Passos, Faulkner, Fitzgerald, and Hemingway. As I read in a review not long ago, by some fellow reviewing an anthology of new writing which had just that sort of proprietary essay in it and which compared the new writers with the ones of the twenties, the reviewer said, in effect, what the hell, there's plenty of *Lebensraum* and *Liebestraum* for everybody.

Interviewers: But you *did* say, in the preface, just what we were speaking of—that this generation can and will—

Styron *(interrupting):* Yes, can and will produce literature equal to that of any other generation, especially that of the twenties. It was probably rash to say, but I don't see any reason to recant. For instance, I think those "signs in the air" are apparent from just three first novels, those being *From Here to Eternity, The Naked and the Dead,* and *Other Voices, Other Rooms.* It's true that a first novel is far from a fair standard with which to judge a writer's potential future output, but aren't those three novels far superior to the first novels of

Dos Passos, Faulkner, and Fitzgerald? In fact I think one of those novels—*The Naked and the Dead*—is so good by itself that it can stand up respectably well with the *mature* work of any of those writers of the twenties. But there I go again, talking in competition with the older boys. Anyway, I think that a lot of the younger writers around today are stuffed with talent. A lot of them, it's true, are shameless and terrible self-promoters—mainly the members of what a friend of mine calls "the fairy axis"—but they'll drop by the wayside and don't count for much anyway. The others, including the ones I've mentioned, plus people like Salinger and Carson McCullers and Hortense Calisher—all those have done, and will go on doing, fine work, unless somebody drops an atom bomb on them, or they get locked up in jail by Velde and that highly cultured crowd.

Interviewers: Speaking of atom bombs and Representative Velde, among other such contemporary items, do you think—as some people have been saying—that the young writer today works at a greater disadvantage than those of preceding—uh—generations?

Styron: Hell no, I don't. Writers ever since writing began have had problems, and the main problem narrows down to just one word—life. Certainly this might be an age of so-called faithlessness and despair we live in, but the new writers haven't cornered any market on faithlessness and despair, any more than Dostoevski or Marlowe or Sophocles did. Every age has its terrible aches and pains, its peculiar new horrors, and every writer since the beginning of time, just like other people, has been afflicted by what that same friend of mine calls "the fleas of life"—you know, colds, hangovers, bills, sprained ankles, and little nuisances of one sort or another. *They* are the constants of life, at the core of life, along with nice little delights that come along every now and then. Dostoevski had them and Marlowe had them and we all have them, and they're a hell of a lot more invariable than nuclear fission or the Revocation of the Edict of Nantes. So is Love invariable, and Unrequited Love, and Death and Insult and Hilarity. Mark Twain was as baffled and appalled by Darwin's theories as anyone else, and those theories seemed as monstrous to the Victorians as atomic energy, but he still wrote about riverboats and old Hannibal, Missouri. No, I don't think the writer today is any worse off than at any other time. It's true that in Russia he might as well be dead and that in Youngstown, Ohio, that famous

police chief, whatever his name is, has taken to inspecting and ban-
ning books. But in America he can still write practically anything he
pleases, so long as it isn't libelous or pornographic. Also in America
he certainly doesn't have to starve, and there are few writers so economically strapped that they can't turn out work regularly. In fact, a
couple of young writers—and good writers—are damn near mil-
lionaires.

Interviewers: Then you believe in success for a writer? Financial,
that is, as well as critical?

Styron: I sure do. I certainly have sympathy for a writer who
hasn't made enough to live comfortably—comfortably, I mean, not
necessarily lavishly—because I've been colossally impoverished at
times, but impoverished writers remind me of Somerset Maugham's
remark about multilingual people. He admired them, he said, but did
not find that their condition made them necessarily wise.

Interviewers: But getting back to the original point—in *Lie Down
in Darkness* didn't your heroine commit suicide on the day the atom
bomb was dropped on Hiroshima? This seems to us to be a little bit
more than fortuitous symbolism, and perhaps to indicate a sense of
that inescapable and overpowering despair of our age which you just
denied was our peculiar lot.

Styron: That was just gilding the lily. If I were writing the same
thing now I'd leave that out and have her jump on the Fourth of July.
Really, I'm not trying to be rosy about things like the atom bomb and
war and the failure of the Presbyterian Church. Those things are awful. All I'm trying to say is that those things don't alter one bit a
writer's fundamental problems, which are Love, Requited and Unrequited, Insult, et cetera.

Interviewers: Then you believe that young writers today have no
cause to be morbid and depressing, which is a charge so often
leveled at them by the critics?

Styron: Certainly they do. They have a perfect right to be anything they honestly are, but I'd like to risk saying that a great deal of
this morbidity and depression doesn't arise so much from political
conditions, or the threat of war, or the atom bomb, as from the
terrific increase of the scientific knowledge which has come to us
about the human self—Freud, that is, abnormal psychology, and all
the new psychiatric wisdom. My God, think of how morbid and de-

pressing Dostoevski would have been if he could have gotten hold of some of the juicy work of Dr. Wilhelm Stekel, say *Sadism and Masochism.* What people like John Webster and, say, Hieronymus Bosch felt intuitively about some of the keen horrors which lurk in the human mind, we now have neatly catalogued and clinically described by Krafft-Ebing and the Menningers and Karen Horney, and they're available to any fifteen-year-old with a pass-card to the New York Public Library. I don't say that this new knowledge is *the* cause of the so-called morbidity and gloom, but I do think it has contributed to a new trend toward the introspective in fiction. And when you get an eminent journal like *Time* magazine complaining, as it often has, that to the young writers of today life seems short on rewards and that what they write is a product of their own neuroses, in its silly way the magazine is merely stating the status quo and obvious truth. The good writing of any age has always been the product of *someone's* neurosis, and we'd have a mighty dull literature if all the writers that came along were a bunch of happy chuckleheads.

Interviewers: To sort of round this out, we'd like to ask finally what might sound like a rather obvious question. That is, what should be the purpose of a young writer? Should he, for instance, be *engagé,* not concerned as much with the story aspects of the novel as with the problems of the contemporary world?

Styron: It seems to me that only a great satirist can tackle the world problems and articulate them. Most writers write simply out of some strong interior need, and that I think is the answer. A great writer, writing out of this need, will give substance to and perhaps even explain all the problems of the world without even knowing it, until a scholar comes along a hundred years after he's dead and digs up some symbols. The purpose of a young writer is to write, and he shouldn't drink too much. He shouldn't think that after he's written one book he's God Almighty and air all his immature opinions in pompous interviews. Let's have another cognac and go up to Le Chapelain.

A Visit with William Styron
Hubert Juin / 1962

From *Les Lettres Françaises*, 1–7 March 1962, p. 5.

William Styron is a tall young man with a serious mien and an athletic bearing. He obviously lives in the country. A sports lover perhaps. He was born in Newport News, Virginia, in 1925. *Set This House on Fire* (translated by M. E. Coindreau and prefaced by Michel Butor) is his third novel. For his first novel, *Lie Down in Darkness,* which appeared in 1951, he received the *Prix de Rome* from the American Academy of Arts and Letters. A French version of that novel was published by Del Duca. In 1953 Styron published *The Long March* in America.

HJ: What is it about?

WS: It's a rather short narrative about war.

HJ: Is it an autobiographical work?

WS: Everything is autobiographical, more or less. So is *The Long March.* Let's say it's semi-autobiographical.

HJ: You have lived in Italy for a long time and it could be said that the presence of Italy in your work (as in *Set This House on Fire*) is enormously important.

WS: That is true. I think that Italy, the Italy of the area of Naples, is an integral part of what I have written. You cannot separate *Set This House on Fire* from this locale, from the presence of that particular Italian climate.

HJ: In the opening pages of *Set This House on Fire* I notice that you include, as an epigraph, a long quotation from a sermon by John Donne. May I ask the reason for including this particular quotation or, more precisely, its meaning for a reader who is beginning the novel?

WS: As I see it, Donne's text illustrates what I am attempting to describe; the idea developed in his sermon is that of the body and the soul tormented by the absence of God.

HJ: Must one conclude, then, that there is a metaphysical "climate" in your book, or at least an underlying metaphysical idea?

WS: Yes, indeed. My characters, the location in which the plot develops and then unravels—all that is, in the final analysis, the mask of a very precise metaphysical comedy.

HJ: When I read you I cannot help thinking about Faulkner.

WS: A certain resemblance does exist. And if you are thinking more precisely about *Light in August* or *Sanctuary,* the resemblance appears to be deep and undeniable.

HJ: I notice that you speak of resemblance between Faulkner and you and not of Faulkner's influence.

WS: You know, all books from the South have this same resemblance. They are all metaphysical comedies, and all are concerned with roots and being uprooted. Moreover, all deal with transgression, sin, and guilt.

HJ: How do you explain this?

WS: So far as guilt is concerned, the racial problem both gives and incarnates that feeling. This guilt of the South, as it is lived in the South, can also be found in *Set This House on Fire.* As for this interplay of rooting and uprooting (such a tragic interplay), you must understand that, in the United States, there are roots only in the South. Old southern traditions do exist.

HJ: Is the opposition between North and South still that strong?

WS: Yes and no! Currently the South is becoming day by day more like the North.

HJ: Let us talk about the novelist's art, yours. How did you develop the technique used in *Set This House on Fire?*

WS: Actually I wanted to see if I could write a book in the first person narrative, then pass to the third person so that it does not seem abnormal to the reader.

HJ: It is as if you began the novel not trusting yourself.

WS: A writer must set a goal and undertake difficult tasks for himself. And when he reaches his goal—if he succeeds—this creates a muted and invisible tension throughout the work, elusive to the reader, but ever present.

HJ: On reading your fiction, one also has the impression that the concept of time plays an important role in the way you apprehend the world or, if you prefer, in the metaphysical comedy through which the world reveals itself.

WS: I have tried to turn time upside down, that is to say, to go backwards, but I never want to lose control of time or sight of the aim pursued.

HJ: Please explain.

WS: A man tries, in vain, to remember.

HJ: I imagine the experience you are talking about is far removed from the Proustian endeavor.

WS: Absolutely. The man in *Set This House on Fire* is trying to glue himself back together, to put himself back together, to recollect himself if you wish.

HJ: In your books, then, it is not fictional time that is discontinuous?

WS: No. No, it's consciousness that's discontinuous.

HJ: So much for time in fiction. Now, your novel takes place in different points in space. Does space in fiction represent a particularly demanding problem for you?

WS: Not at all. Not in the sense that Thomas Wolfe understood it, for instance. All things considered, there is no original experience of space in *Set This House on Fire*. There are places, which is quite a different matter.

HJ: Yes, I understand: places that are like so many squares on a chessboard.

WS: Yes, but which are also like so many clues surrounding the uprooted hero. Italy dominates everything else and completes the uprooting.

HJ: We have spoken a great deal about a metaphysical comedy. Could we not also speak of a critique of civilization?

WS: Yes, the critique of contemporary civilization is extremely important in *Set This House on Fire*. If you wish, it rests within the very character of Mason. He is the typical American, materialistic and without history. Yes, he does represent, embody, the critique. Moreover, American readers were not deceived. Many do not forgive me for it.

William Styron is the very model of the conscientious author. He meditated on this particular work for a long time, then carefully and lucidly perfected it. He says, "In the main it was an enormous work of elucidation, of bringing to light, even of laying bare."

When he returns home, William Styron will continue working on his next novel. Its subject is the only slave rebellion to have taken place in the South, in 1831 to be precise.

Interview

Madeleine Chapsal / 1962

From *L'Express*, 8 March 1962, pp. 26–27. Partial English text published in *Newport News Daily Press*, 27 May 1962, p. 4D. There is a translation in Scrapbook II of the Styron Papers, Manuscript Department, Perkins Library, Duke University. The original French text has been reprinted in *Quinze Ecrivains: Entretiens* (Paris: Rene Julliard, 1963), pp. 173–81. Reprinted by permission.

Express: William Styron, your novel *Set This House on Fire* has just been published in France and has received extensive notice. Aside from that, the French know nothing about you, yet you are very well known in the United States. How does the American public see you?

WS: That's precisely what I'd like to know! But I don't . . . writers never know those things about themselves. I can only say that *Set This House on Fire* was very badly received by American critics, though that didn't prevent it from becoming a bestseller.

Express: How do you explain this?

WS: Whatever I published was bound to arouse public attention.

Express: Why is that?

WS: Because my first book, *Lie Down in Darkness,* published in the United States ten years ago, was a great success. That was enough to make me a well known author. Incidentally, *Lie Down in Darkness* continues to sell regularly. It was also published in France in 1953 by Del Duca, but it went unnoticed then; Gallimard is going to try to reissue it. Since *Lie Down in Darkness* I had only published a short novel about the Korean War, *The Long March*—Gallimard is also going to publish it. That's why *Set This House on Fire,* my second large-scale work, was eagerly awaited by the readers who had liked *Lie Down in Darkness.* I'm telling you this since you ask, but you are going to find me lacking in modesty.

Express: Not at all! Unfortunately we are much too ignorant about the new American literature. We have just discovered Salinger, now we are discovering Styron, and no one can speak about him better than you. What was the subject of your first book?

WS: It's the story of a young woman who commits suicide. It takes place in the South.

Express: It has been said that you had been influenced by Faulkner. Would you agree?

WS: I believe that I was indeed influenced by Faulkner in *Lie Down in Darkness.* All writers, at first, come under the influence of someone, but I think that, as far as Faulkner and I are concerned, it's over.

Express: Why were American critics hard on *Set This House on Fire?*

WS: Writers do not readily accept the opinions of critics. Writers always think that critics are unjust to them, that they don't understand them. Still I must admit to having been surprised by the violence of the onslaught which greeted *Set This House on Fire.* They said everything: that it was an unbelievable and stupid story, a pile of trash and nonsense, and even that it was a "dirty" book.

Express: I have read *Set This House on Fire,* and indeed you don't mince words. It is a vehement critique of some aspects of American society. And, from what I have heard, American society does not very much like to be criticized.

WS: Probably I won't tell you anything you don't already know by saying that American society is an overly optimistic society. Except for the Civil War, it has never known tragedy and horror on its own soil. Incidentally, this Civil War business has been somewhat overplayed, but it's the only war we have known. There is a terrible difference between sending regiments to fight abroad, even if many men are killed, and being invaded like so many European populations have been, seeing civilians massacred, discovering concentration camps and having to face the horrors that have been yours for centuries. Therefore, it is more difficult for America than for Europe to conceive of tragedy. Americans do not like being told that people can be unbalanced, desperate, sometimes corrupt, that life can be horrible. We have a cliché to express their will to optimism: they want to see life as "a bowl of cherries." And they reject any tragic representation of life, not realizing that this representation can be a catharsis, that to accept a tragic picture of life on the artistic level can indeed free one from the horror so that one may enjoy life more.

Express: You have said that your book was charged with being not only tragic but also "dirty." It is true that you touch on all of your subjects, and on sexual matters in particular, with a freedom which must not be common in puritanical America.

WS: Personally, I don't find my book offensive in the least. Critics have refused to see one thing: that I was attempting to delve deeply into the problem I was faced with in the case of two characters, Cass and Mason, and that I was trying to find the reason why Cass murdered Mason. This proved to be very difficult. Never again will I write a book with such a complicated plot! I had to retrace the entire history of these two men, completely analyze their personalities, and I could not exclude the sexual elements.

Express: You said that the plot of *Set This House on Fire* is complicated; the manner in which it develops, as an investigation and successive hypotheses about the truth, is strikingly similar to some French literary experiments known as the *nouveau roman*. Moreover, Michel Butor wrote a preface to your novel. Do you have any ties with the French *nouveau roman?*

WS: I had not met Michel Butor before last week. I had only read one of his works, *A Change of Mind,* and am now reading *Mobile,* his book about America which, by the way, I find brilliant though strange. (I am considering translating it myself into English.) I have not read the other authors. If I should fall under the influence of the French *nouveau roman* it would have to be in my future books. But I must say that some of the great critics have pointed out that *Set This House on Fire* was not so much an American as a European novel, which would explain why it was so poorly understood by run-of-the-mill critics.

Express: You divide critics into two categories?

WS: It's very clear-cut in America. On the one hand you have those critics who write for the newspapers and weeklies and who, with few exceptions, are inferior in cultivation and intelligence to their French counterparts. It is about those I was speaking earlier. They wring the neck—sometimes definitively—of any book which strays from the mainstream. On the other hand, you have the critics who write for the reviews—two, three, six months after the book's publication—which does not always allow them to catch the errors of the others. They are, I believe, among the greatest literary critics in the world.

Express: Can you give us a few names?

WS: Edmund Wilson, who henceforth will write only essays. Allen Tate, Granville Hicks of the *Saturday Review,* Maxwell Geismar of the *New York Times,* Philip Rahv of the *Partisan Review.*

Express: What is the social status of a writer in the United States?

WS: Difficult. You cannot imagine it here in France where a writer is esteemed, respected as such, and feels himself necessary to the intellectual life of his country at all times. But in America a writer is much less well accepted. He is not really despised, but he is regarded with suspicion. People wonder what this guy, who stays in his room to write, may be good for. Most of them never read what he writes. In comparison with Europe, very little is read in the United States. It seems to Americans that writing novels is a relatively easy way of making money! (Of course I don't speak about educated circles, but of the country in general.) In terms of respect from his neighbors, I believe that, in America, a writer rates well below a doctor and even comes after a politician.

Express: His this situation not changed lately?

WS: You mean since Kennedy came to power? It is true that Kennedy, an intelligent and thoughtful man, does not have the disdain for intellectuals characteristic of his predecessor. But the mere fact that we notice it and feel the need to say, "Eisenhower did not like intellectuals, Kennedy does," proves how unsure we are of ourselves and our status. What good are we on a national level? It's a question we should not have to ask ourselves.

Express: Where do you live in the United States?

WS: In Roxbury, Connecticut. It's a two-hour drive from New York. I live on a farm, surrounded by woods, with my wife and three children.

Express: Aren't you somewhat isolated?

WS: From what? Literary circles as you conceive of them in London and Paris have not existed in America, at least not up to now. Writers who live in New York are very rare. America is a vast country. It has shrunk a bit lately thanks to the acceleration in, and multiplication of, the means of communication, but it remains large.

Express: Do you know your contemporaries? Do you know Faulkner, Salinger?

WS: I have never laid eyes on Salinger. As for Faulkner, I saw him once, only once. It's a question I have never considered. Whom do I know among my colleagues? I have just received a list which appeared in the *Saturday Review*. It gives the titles of twelve books by contemporary writers, books which, according to a group of professors in California, may become classics.

Express: I see that you are listed.

WS: Which of them do I know? Salinger? No. Arthur Miller? He lives five miles from my house in Roxbury. I've never met him, never. Faulkner? As I have said, I saw him once.

Express: What was the occasion?

WS: We have the same publisher, and one day when we were in New York at the same time our publisher had the good idea of inviting us both to lunch. It was very nice. Faulkner is a charming man. Tennessee Williams? I don't know him, but I shook his hand once. Saul Bellow? I shook his hand once. Hemingway? I never saw him. Robert Lowell? An excellent poet. I met him a few times at dinner parties. T. S. Eliot? I never saw him. Wallace Stevens? He was an old man. He died. I know Richard Wilbur slightly and hope to get to know him better. Robert Penn Warren? Yes, I know him. He is the only one I know well, I mean as a friend. So you see there are not many. Yet I don't consider myself to be an unusual case. When it comes to being acquainted with my peers, I can even consider myself above average. Yes, writers are rather isolated in America. It's not like here in France, where I have the impression that everybody knows everyone else in the literary world and is a member of the same club. It must be very pleasant! Well, perhaps.

The Prey of the Critics
Annie Brierre / 1962

From *Les Nouvelles littéraires*, 22 March 1962, p. 8.

Lie Down in Darkness appeared over ten years ago. Not only did the novel receive the *Prix de Rome* for literature but it placed William Styron immediately among the foremost American writers of his generation. Therefore, as soon as his second novel, *Set This House on Fire*, was announced, European publishers vied for the translation rights even before having read it.

The slim fiery-eyed young man of former days has matured: his face is fuller, his appearance more imposing. Today he is married to a slender, radiant woman from Baltimore. They have three children.

Lie Down in Darkness was greeted by a chorus of praise, but *Set This House on Fire* has been the object of harsh criticism in English-speaking countries. It may be because this latest work, richer and denser, does not make for easy reading. Under the sky of Amalfi, drunken brawls and debaucheries succeed each other. The protagonists are Mason Flagg, a young American millionaire, and Cass Kinsolving, a drunk and scruffy painter. Beyond this deceptive decor, Styron wanted to draw an allegory of the American condition. That is what Michel Butor showed in the penetrating preface he wrote to the novel, translated into French by Maurice Coindreau.

Along with the translator and the author of the preface, William Styron is now before me and will answer some of the questions raised by his book.

AB: Michel Butor's preface seems to me remarkable. Do you find it faithful to the spirit of your book, William Styron?

WS: Completely. And Butor was the only critic to discover the importance of the myth of Oedipus in the book.

AB: What is the importance of the guilt complex upon which he insists when discussing the black slaves transported from Africa to

America? I always thought that in the United States, mystical inspiration comes above all else.

WS: The two are inseparable. In the South, Christian doctrine teaches you to love your neighbor. But you have only to open your front door to see how this instruction is being applied. Therefore any southerner is bound to suffer from a guilt complex.

A.B.: You have said that a true writer must not belong to any literary school. Do you feel independent?

WS: I think of myself as independent. But perhaps one day I'll see myself as associated with some school, in spite of myself. I don't think schools are created by the writers themselves, but writers can be united in a kind of brotherhood, by thought currents or by forms of expression.

AB: Are there now in the United States any writers who could be compared to the writers of the "New Wave"?

WS: I believe the Beatniks would be very flattered by the comparison, but they don't succeed. They would like to be able to create a new form. Unfortunately for them, what they are doing is very much like what was done in 1925.

MC: Absolutely.

WS: I don't believe there is any resemblance whatever between the New Wave and the Beats. Interestingly, moreover, each country has its own *esprit*. A writer like Jack Kerouac is of no great significance. At best he is an example of the slightly "mad" type, like most Beatniks anyway, but I believe his work to be neither interesting nor of any lasting effect.

MC: Yet I advised that it be published in France, for purely historical reasons.

MB: As representative of a movement that cannot be ignored, but nothing else.

AB: William Styron, your ideas, your ideals, are extremely important to you when you write a novel. Why, then, don't you write essays?

WS: But I do write essays. Two in the past three months have been published in *Esquire,* among them one on capital punishment. But the essay has a smaller readership in America than in France.

AB: Ten years ago you believed in the necessity of religious or spiritual aspirations. You also spoke to me then of the influence of

Flaubert and Faulkner on your literary development. And you said that an age has only the literature it deserves, and if it is a dark and dismal age, its literature will be as well. Generally speaking, has your thinking changed?

WS: I believe that a writer is born with a certain vision of life and that this vision does not change in its basics. The best example of self-betrayal by a writer is Dos Passos, who eventually allowed his political opinions to alter his vision of life. Everything he wrote afterwards is worthless. When propaganda triumphs over art, there is no art left.

AB: William Styron, you used to hate critics?

WS: I still do! Whoever they may be, even the kindest.

AB: All English and American writers suffer from a lack of respect in their own countries. Is that also your opinion, Maurice Coindreau?

MC: It is undeniable that an appearance by Faulkner makes less of a public impression in New York than in Paris.

AB: Harold Nicholson went so far as to tell me that in England even a bank clerk was looking at him suspiciously whereas, had he been French, he would have been called *"Maître"!*

WS: Still, Nicholson was raised to the nobility. It's something that can happen only in England, and it must be quite pleasant to be a baronet! But here, I believe, is the difference between France and America. If a foreign writer acquires a certain reputation in the United States, he will be given a warm welcome, while American writers are not treated with the same respect unless they become movie stars like Hemingway.

AB: An excellent critic, writing in the *Saturday Review,* has compared *Set This House on Fire* to Faulkner's *Light in August* and *Absalom, Absalom!*

WS: I scarcely see any resemblance. And if there has been any influence, it is a subconscious and rather distant one.

MB: Still there is some similarity with *Absalom* in the way the story appears little by little through the dialogue.

AB: You told me once that Dos Passos and Fitzgerald contributed in the creation of your emotional climate.

WS: Fitzgerald, yes. Dos Passos less strongly.

AB: What are you working on now?

WS: On a historical novel about a rebellion by blacks. Adapting my first two books for the screen has also kept me very busy.

AB: You told me once that you could work only in complete silence, that a child crying in a house some distance from yours drove you mad.

WS: It's true. And you wonder how I managed with my three children in the next room? Well I shouted louder than they. I screamed, and everything went all right.

AB: You are leaving us soon, I believe.

WS: I'm leaving Paris for Italy and Germany tomorrow. But we'll meet again in April. They always talk about April in Paris. I want to see it, and I'll spend the entire month here.

Meet the Professor

William Blackburn, William Styron, Reynolds Price,
Mac Hyman, Fred Chappell / 1963

Transcription of an ABC radio program broadcast 3 February
1963; text first published in the *Mississippi Quarterly*, 31 (Fall
1978), 605–14. Reprinted by permission.

William Blackburn was a member of the Department of
English at Duke University from 1926 until 1969. A
Rhodes Scholar with a Ph.D. from Yale, Blackburn taught
Elizabethan and seventeenth-century literature and pub-
lished research on Thomas Carlyle, Matthew Arnold, and
Joseph Conrad. He is best remembered, though, as a
teacher of creative writing. Blackburn's English 103 is not
so well known as George Pierce Baker's English 47 at
Harvard (Baker's pupils included Eugene O'Neill and
Thomas Wolfe), but Blackburn was nevertheless quite
successful as a tutor of aspiring writers. The apprentice
efforts of his students were collected in three volumes—
One and Twenty: Duke Narrative and Verse, 1924–1945;
*Under Twenty-five: Duke Narrative and Verse, 1945–
1962*; and *A Duke Miscellany*.

On 3 February 1963, Blackburn and four of his best-
known pupils—William Styron, Mac Hyman, Reynolds
Price, and Fred Chappell—were featured on a program
called *Meet the Professor*. The program, part of a series
sponsored by the American Association for Higher Education and broadcast over ABC radio and television,
brought together prominent teachers with their former
students. A transcription of the five-way conversation is
published below.

The format of *Meet the Professor* should be explained.
The program began with a commentator introducing
Blackburn and his former students. Attention then shifted
to the conversation, already in progress. From time to
time, Blackburn's voice was cut in over the conversation
to give background data about the writer who was speaking at that moment. Blackburn's comments, though

lengthy, tell us nothing new about any one of the four writers. These comments have not been included in the transcription below. Too, Blackburn's comments were spliced into the middle of remarks being made by the writers, so that several passages are truncated in the sound track. These few fragmentary remarks, meaning-less in abbreviated form, have been removed from the transcription. All cuts are indicated by four ellipsis points. A videotape of the entire program is in the Blackburn collection at the Manuscript Department, Perkins Library, Duke University.

As we pick up the conversation, the participants are discussing compositions which they wrote, as under-graduates, in Blackburn's classes.

August J. Nigro
James L. W. West III

Blackburn: Fred, you wrote a sketch, perhaps your first one, which I am running in *Under Twenty-five,* about a little boy and girl, brother and sister, walking through a very cold wintry evening.* I believe your novel grew out of that first sketch, in a way. I'm not asking you *how* it did, of course, but is that a fact?

Chappell: Well, it did. It was a very short sketch. It was only nine hundred words, I think—one page. I wrote it as a one-page sketch and I started thinking about it. The thing gathered more and more energy until it wasn't something made up after a while. It became something I remembered really happening. After a while it gathered to this sketch. And there just happened to be enough energy to make a novel out of it.

Blackburn: Mac, could you remember your first paper?

Hyman: Oh yeah. It was strictly Hemingway stuff. At that time, I was reading Hemingway. And so I handed it in and I kept waiting for you to read the thing. Nothing was right except Hemingway to me at

---

*"January," in *Under Twenty-five: Duke Narrative and Verse, 1945–1962,* ed. William Black-burn (Durham: Duke Univ. Press, 1963), pp. 191–193.

the time. So I kept waiting it out. I'd been looking for somebody to help me write, and I thought to myself, "Well, if he doesn't like this, I'm just going to quit the class tomorrow and go to another place!"

Blackburn: Either/or ethic.

Chappell: An ultimatum!

Blackburn: I was wondering if this business of steeping yourself in a contemporary writer, or *any* writer, is one way of making great progress as a young writer. The old saying is that you always crawl up on somebody's back anyhow in this life. Do you feel that reading Hemingway, steeping yourself in Hemingway, did you good?

Hyman: Well, I don't know. I think it took me about a year or two to unlearn a lot of things I had learned—that I *thought* I had learned. Sooner or later, you are going to have to throw the rules out. But I do think it helps you, it gives you something to be going on—a point of view, at least, that maybe is not your own, and you are trying to find your own.

. . . .

Styron: I wonder if a very young person has really absorbed enough experience to encompass the idea of a novel. It's a tentative beginning in a short story; it's probably the logical extension of the essay or the composition. The novel is a rather formidable undertaking for somebody who's still trying his wings, so to speak.

Price: The short story also makes a young writer aware, makes him attentive to the whole texture of a given experience, so that he has to notice it in *great* detail.

. . . .

Chappell: The thing you don't get from short stories is balancing the masses of material.

Styron: Also, a novel does involve a tremendous adventure and a multiplicity of characters. I still feel, at least if my own experience is any guide, that when you are of college age, you probably haven't really had enough experience to encompass all of these characters that you eventually project into a novel.

Price: Well, you've probably had it, but you haven't got the understanding to deal with it.

Chappell: Maybe just can't write English well enough. That's a great deal of the problem. How much experience do you have to have to write a novel?

Styron: I don't know. That's one of the thorniest questions. I think it was Hemingway who said something to the effect that all the experience needed to write a novel a man had accumulated before he was twenty-five years old. That's quite arbitrary and you can take it for what it's worth. But I think there's something to it. But I do think that one has to wait until a period, let us say, being arbitrary, after twenty-five, before you can make use of that experience in the novel form.

Hyman: That's probably because Hemingway wrote his first book after he was twenty-five.

Price: Well, you don't have to have any experience at all. Emily Brontë just sat there in the vicarage.

Styron: Oh no. She had plenty of experience.

Price: Of course, it was interior.

Styron: You're right.

Price: She was a genius. If you are going to write *Wuthering Heights,* you don't have to get out and go be a hobo or anything. You don't have to be a gypsy to know what it's like to be Heathcliff. You just have to be Emily Brontë.

Styron: But at the same time you have to have lived. How many novels do we have from people who are eighteen years old, twenty years old?

Price: Precious few, right?

Styron: None. The idea of experience is certainly apposite and completely important to the idea of a novel. I do think that there *is* something to what Hemingway says in that after this age—let us say it's twenty-five—you have absorbed so much that from then on, you could sit in a room somewhere.

Hyman: One thing he means, too, is the fact that after you have begun writing, you might become more conscious of the experience *as* experience. Therefore, it is not as strong inside. It is not something that you automatically just pick up. It's something you observe, when looking at it.

Chappell: It doesn't have the same effect as experience. You can't go and look for certain types of experience and have them, and come home and write them up.

Price: That's very sad, because too many people do that!

Blackburn: I'm always asking this question, or rather, quoting

Jane Austen to the effect that she wished she had read more and written less in her younger years. I'm wondering if this is not another way of saying what you gentlemen have said: that one can hardly hope to write anything worth reading until one is twenty-five or so.

Chappell: Well, you've read a great deal more too by that time. It's not that you've got more experience.

. . . .

Chappell: Have you ever heard a student say he is afraid to read a certain author because it might influence him too much?

Blackburn: Oh yes, of course.

Price: It's a real fear at times.

Styron: Yes, but I don't think it makes much difference at an early age. It's healthy to even imitate because you immerse yourself—immerse yourself deeply. We all can recall the moments when we were smitten by, let us say, Conrad, and these great orotund marvelous syllables kept haunting us. And so we wrote like Conrad for a while or we wrote, on the other hand, like Hemingway—this marvelously sparse lean prose. There's hardly anybody who hasn't, at one time, been influenced by it. But I think these are important transitional stages that young people should go through. If they've got it, and if they are going to be writers, they'll eventually shake loose of these influences. They are bound to in the scheme of things.

Hyman: Yeah, if they are not going to read the good ones, what are they going to read?

Blackburn: Well, I'm all for it.

Chappell: I read "Batman" comics myself.

Styron: A good example would be a friend of mine, James Jones, who was so smitten, by his own account, with Thomas Wolfe. That's the reason he chose Scribner's as a publisher, and Maxwell Perkins, the late Maxwell Perkins, for an editor. But look what happened. He wrote a marvelous book, *From Here to Eternity,* which was, so far as anyone can tell, totally free of the Wolfeian influence. The real writer is going to shake loose, on his own, from these early influences.

Price: The whole business of influence is a very interesting question, because it is the invariable thing that any reviewer says about a book. It's the first thing he can think of. "This book *sounds* like Faulkner. This book *sounds* like Conrad. *Ergo,* Mr. Blotz has been influenced by Conrad."

Blackburn: One of the worst things you can say is that it came out of a writing course, isn't that right?

Styron: The combination of the two—the "This man has obviously read all of his Faulkner in college"—is the ultimate insult.

Price: Speaking quite personally, no one ever guessed what my influences were, because they weren't the ones that sounded obvious. The obvious thing is to say that I sound like Faulkner. I think that's because Faulkner is from Mississippi and I'm from North Carolina. But I was influenced by Tolstoy because he just seemed so great that he gave me great courage and a desire to emulate anyone who calmly knew what it was like to be everyone who'd ever lived. And I think continually of Leo Tolstoy and read *Anna Karenina* about once a year.

Blackburn: You want someone who's going to stretch your imagination.

Price: It's very liberating because you realize you can never be that good. And yet it looks so easy when you read it. You feel like you could do it, if you really just tried another day.

Chappell: You *feel* that, but you *know* you can't.

Blackburn: I'm wondering about the rough-and-ready school, the hobo school, the hobo preparation for the writer. Don't go to college at all. Just experience life. I'm wondering if you gentlemen have any feeling about that—looking back?

Hyman: Tell you one thing, I think there *is* a danger in school. It's this business of analyzing a story to such an extent that if a young student gets in, starts with symbols and one thing after the other, then he kind of gets the cart before the horse. He starts out trying to write through symbols and it's not a story. A story's got to work on the surface or it doesn't work. That is one danger of too much studying and analyzing of stories.

Blackburn: Yes. You want to get inside the writer, but not be aware of his "parts" so much as the whole feeling of the man.

Styron: On the other hand, what you term the "rough-and-ready school" often betrays a total lack of reading, total lack of attention to prose. There's a nice compromise that most good writers eventually hit. Certainly it's true that some of our great predecessors, in fact most of them, didn't go to college. Faulkner had a year at Ole Miss. Hemingway, so far as I know, had no college.

Hyman: Yeah, but he had a terrific education, even leaving out college. You couldn't go to college and get Gertrude Stein.

Styron: Yes, he was lucky. So was Faulkner, for that matter, because Faulkner had Sherwood Anderson as a teacher. But the important thing here is this early exposure to the great—to your Tolstoy and to your Conrad. The college itself can be outside the walls, like Hemingway.

Chappell: How much of the immediately contemporary writer do you think a young writer should read—someone he knows, or someone next door, or someone whose book was published last week? Do you think he should spend a lot of time reading people that just came out last week or should he read the earlier stuff?

Styron: I don't think it's important to read the latest best seller because I think the works of value eventually find their own level. Good books are often damned out of hand, bad books praised out of hand. Five years pass and then all of a sudden you understand which is the good and which is the bad.

Hyman: Somerset Maugham said one time he waited a year before he read any books. That way, they were sifted out. Said it was amazing how many books he didn't have to read!

Chappell: Very discouraging to a guy who just started to write— when Maugham said that!

Blackburn: Malcolm Cowley was saying in a piece about a year ago that everyone who writes has been through a period, a rather lonely youth, and has been a *great* reader, and has been encouraged by some particular person—it may be an uncle, an aunt, a teacher, a fellow writer, or what not. I was just wondering if that sounds true to you.

Styron: Certainly it's true in my case. In spite of whatever reservation I might have already made about college, it's quite apparent to me that when I was fortunate enough to be sent to Duke in the Marine Corps and ended up in your class, it was the propitious moment for me. I found the person who, symbolic or otherwise, gave me that particular encouragement.

Blackburn: Well, that's very handsome of you and I appreciate it. I wasn't trying to make you say that, of course.

Styron: I think most all of us here would subscribe to that.

Blackburn: I was just wondering, though—to get back to this early business—if this tremendous love of reading is not the deciding factor in pushing a young man or woman towards a writing career.

Chappell: Well, that's the way you build up great patches of experience, but I remember when I was smaller, I couldn't conceive that a book was written by a man. A book was something you had between covers and it was printed. But nobody wrote it. It was just a book. It was formed like a seashell or something.

Blackburn: A work of nature.

Styron: I think that must be true because if you talk to anybody who has written, you'll always find a childhood in which, somewhere along the line, there's been a *Wizard of Oz*. Starting there and then building up to this voracious period, which probably comes between eleven and fourteen or fifteen, when your universe is made up of these fictional characters. And I am sure that Malcolm Cowley was right when he made that observation.

Price: I was made a writer by the teacher who, in the second grade, allowed me to make a book report on *Gone with the Wind*. I asked if I could, expecting to have a very shocked "No!" from the teacher, as I had already read the book anyway and there was a great deal in it I didn't quite understand but knew I had no business reading. And she said "Yes, by all means!" So I never looked back. There was no *Wizard of Oz* for me, from then on.

Blackburn: And you've been in the war ever since!

Styron: Did you say that one of Cowley's adjectives was also "lonely"?

Blackburn: Yes, loneliness, reading, and encouragement.

Styron: Does that make sense here?

Chappell: Yes.

Styron: I suppose it does.

Hyman: It's hard to admit you have had a lonely life.

All: (laughter).

Blackburn: Buried too deeply, of course!

Two Writers Talk It Over

James Jones and William Styron / 1963

From *Esquire*, 60 (July 1963), 57–59. Reprinted by permission.

James Jones's last novel was *The Thin Red Line;* William Styron's was *Set This House on Fire.* Recently, they interviewed one another on their respective novels-in-progress in Styron's New York apartment, alone with the tape recorder.

Styron: Well, James—

Jones: Who's going to interview whom first?

S: I want to interview you first. You weigh more than I do.

J: We can do it sort of in between.

S: Well, James, what are you up to now?

J: Well, I've been sort of working on a novel about professional skin divers for which, as you know, I spent about a year in the Caribbean, doing very little writing and lots of diving.

S: Have you got any of it started?

J: I've got about three, four drafts, thirty to forty pages long, of the first chapter, none of which are good enough.

S: How do you know?

J: It just doesn't smell right. How about you? You're halfway through a novel now.

S: Yes, I've got about—oh, I'd say forty thousand words, a hundred and some pages.

J: How long have you been working on this, Bill?

S: Oh, I really didn't get started until last November.

J: But you've been sort of working on it, thinking about it and working.

S: Yes.

J: That's what's happened to me in the last year. I finished *The Thin Red Line,* and then I got the idea for *this* novel, which I thought'd be pretty easy, you see, and I—all this time I've been diving and not writing and sort of feeling guilty because I haven't been working as much as I ought. Still it's been gestating, you know, which is what I guess you were doing for—

S: Yes. Do you find, like I do, that the novels that seem to be simple end up being the hardest? Because I thought this one was going to be—

J: An easy book to write.

S: A snap—

J: Yes. That's what I thought with *The Thin Red Line.* I thought I could write it in about a year. I started it in England when we first went to Europe, just to have something to do until we got settled into France long enough to start the other book I wanted to write about France. It turned out I spent four years on it.

S: This is *The Thin Red Line.*

J: Yes. Irwin Shaw once said to me that maybe we write too slowly today, you know—like Dickens used to turn it out about every week.

S: Yes.

J: For some newspaper or something? Irwin said he was wondering if we didn't all of us write too slowly. Well, I think the novel is getting more complex as a form. Whereas in the old days you could just write about any goddam thing and call it part of a novel, now you have to be more discriminating.

S: I don't know. I've never written anything yet that I didn't write so slowly that it drove me half mad.

J: Terrifies you.

S: Yes, every page was pure—you know, just as slow as molasses, but this has always been my particular cross, I guess.

J: Do you feel guilty because you write so slowly?

S: I suppose I do, a little. Yes. I don't feel guilty about writing so slowly. I often feel guilty about not writing as much as I should.

J: Yes. I took four years on *The Thin Red Line.* I can say I've spent a year on this book already, this new one, but in actual fact there's not three hundred sixty-five working *days* in any given year, you know.

S: Yes. Well, I don't know of anybody who *does* work that hard unless they're obsessed or maniacs or something.

J: Yes. So when I say it took me four years on the last book, It'll probably take me three years on this book, I'm not excluding the amount of time spent *not* working.

S: Yes. How long's this going to be?

J: I don't know. I hope it's short. I hope it's easy, because I don't want to spend too much time on it. But it's an interesting project.

S: How'd you get the idea of writing a novel about skin diving?

J: Well I fell in love with diving, you know, and then I got involved in it and I met a lot of professional divers and went diving *with* a lot of them, and I found them curiously like a certain type of guy I knew in the Army, the guys who really *like* war; you know there are a lot of guys who really *liked* it; everybody didn't want to be back home. Some of them were even draftees. When I met them, these diver types, they all seemed like the kind of guys you always envy, the guys that seem braver than you are. These guys don't seem to be really scared, they really like it. They like being in danger, like fighting, like dangerous situations.

S: What are they? Just Americans who've gone down there to get away from things?

J: Well, yes. You see I've dived some in Europe, too, and I find the European guys are pretty much the same as the American guys, most of them. They're sort of the last of the buccaneers, in a way. They're trying to get a ship, get a good ship going, get more business, get more people—anything to stay on the sea, own a boat, and dive, and they go treasure hunting sometimes, if they can get the funds. Or they'd use their boats to take people and teach them diving, or take 'em out, take amateurs out who don't feel competent enough to go out by themselves.

S: They're sort of like present-day equivalents of the hero of Hemingway's *To Have and Have Not*.

J: In a sense, yes. Like mountaineering guides in Switzerland who take people up in the mountains. Basically it's a desire to have to *live* a sort of dangerous life, where the percentages are not on your side. You're living in a dangerous element where there's a new excitement all the time rather than a man who goes to an office and works all day.

S: Which makes good sense, as a way of life.

J: Yes, sure. I'd rather do that than work in an office. I'd rather *write* than do that.

S: Yes. But of course the other side of the coin of that thing is that it can be over-romanticized.

J: Yes. Well, that's what I want to avoid in this book. As it's laid out now I've got this young fellow, a very artistic, sensitive type, who falls in love with diving because he's read Cousteau's very romantic book and a lot of other books. He goes off to start a play, but decides he wants to learn diving, so he meets these types and gets involved with them and with their *personal* lives, which are rather off and strange, along with their profession. And he finds that the great romance he had with all this diving—it isn't in fact true at all.

S: What happens?

J: Well, this group is trying to get a boat, and he's a successful playwright, fairly well off, so he loans them the money to buy the boat when they get short on funds, and it just goes on from there. But what about you? Tell me more about your book. You're further along into yours than I am into mine.

S: Well, it's something that I've been thinking about for fifteen years. Maybe there's an aspect to this book which somewhat resembles yours, in a very distant way. But it's about a slave rebellion in Virginia in 1831. I suppose I got interested in it many years ago when I was just a *boy.* The slave rebellion, you know, is known as Nat Turner's Rebellion: it took place not far from where I was born. So it was always somewhat in my background. And I don't know what significance it had for me even then, because certainly I wasn't conscious of revolution as being an important factor in human events, and if anything, as a *Southerner,* being brought up in Virginia, I couldn't have very well, as a boy, idealized a Negro slave, *consciously,* as a hero.

J: Especially when he went around killing white people.

S: Exactly. What happened was that, in Virginia in 1831, an enormous population of slaves still existed, but it was economically unfeasible to keep them and at that time the Virginia legislature was very seriously considering the abolition of slavery. You had this kind of divisive split, between the anti-slave and the pro-slave factions. But the anti-slave faction was gaining in power and it looked as if, in 1830 or '31, that Virginia would abolish slavery.

J: Until this revolt changed a lot of minds.

S: Well, the revolt came. It was a spasmodic, horrible little revolt, but it had repercussions.

J: How many people were involved, actually? How many revolted slaves, rebelling slaves, were there entirely in the whole of the Nat Turner Rebellion?

S: Well, it started with a core of eight and grew to a body of about sixty.

J: Now that's damn few people.

S: Well, it only happened in forty-eight hours. Seventy white people were killed. It had such a vast effect that the whole South was in panic. Especially Virginia. And the revolt was put down successfully, but only after a great loss of life—of white lives. And then the Virginia debates began soon after in the legislature, and it's difficult to say, but it seems that with the frequency that Nat Turner's name is brought up in those debates, the sense of horror and awfulness that he instilled in the spirits of all these men affected the debates to the degree that instead of *loosening* control over slavery and heading toward eventual abolition, this rebellion had the ironic effect of clamping down on slavery and that—

J: That may be one of the *practical* causes of the Civil War.

S: That's my complete belief, that it *was* one of the practical causes of the Civil War which very few people know.

J: Will this be in the book?

S: Well, only by indirection. I don't want to grab the reader by the throat and say, "Look, this is history you're reading." Fact is, I consider this a very modern novel.

J: Yes. It's hard. In this book of mine, this playwright feels that not only his work but everything else is being encroached upon by government, by the taking over more and more of the individual's various freedoms of point of view, and in trying to escape this, he winds up in a sort of back-in, a sort of very animalistic world, with these diving guys who are all great individualists and who are in a way like some of the buccaneers—like Morgan, who came out as a bondsman to Jamaica, you know, and escaped and went on into this very profitable but very dangerous business, and very *free* business. I mean he was about the freest of men, actually. In running into these types he finds himself in a very animalistic world where there really isn't any real government. But what he *finds* is that—without the protection of government—he finds himself really terrified. You know what I mean?

S: Yes.

J: Without all the various protections which government does give its citizens as long as the citizens don't—

S: Rock the boat?

J: Rock the boat, you know? So he winds up going back home, after his skin-diving junket, a sadder but wiser man who realizes the inevitability of this growth of government. . . .

S: Well, I think maybe these two books, the one you're writing and the one I'm writing, have a common ground in attitudes toward individual freedom. Or individual liberty.

J: Yes. My guy realizes that he has to give up his individual liberty to live in the way he wants to live.

S: Yes.

J: But he doesn't want to do it. I mean it's his only one choice. Either he does that or he becomes one of these other types, you know, who's forever running away from the encroaching arms of civilized government.

S: Yes. Well, obviously there's no *direct* relationship between these two heroes.

J: No, I didn't mean that. I was just thinking about it—how it. . . .

S: Well, there's a theological aspect which is at the center of my approach to Nat Turner. Because he was an extraordinary man. He was a man of *heroic* proportions. He was able to revolt because he was not of the plantation-slave system. The plantation slave, I do believe, all moral considerations aside, whether he was well-fed or well-clothed, that aspect aside, was brutalized spiritually in a way that the only analogy is to the victims of the Nazi concentration camps who *never revolted.* Nat, unlike the concentration-camp type plantation slaves, had a measure of freedom within which to work. He was a small-farm slave, in southern Virginia, and all the slaves in this type of subsystem of slavery had a kind of more or less personal liberty, and this bears out the dictum of the great old ex-slave Frederick Douglass, you know where he said "be they slave, treat him like a dog, terrorize him, brutalize him, and he will be your slave for life. Treat him with some decency, treat him with respect, and he will want to kill you." I'm paraphrasing Douglass, but certainly this is true.

J: I was wondering if there was any way that your theme for this book ties in with this essential problem of modern man today, that we're all being brainwashed one way or another.

S: Well, I hope so. I hope that it has reverberations. I think Nat Turner was a rebel, paradoxically, *because* of a certain latitude of freedom.

J: He was treated more decently.

S: He might never have revolted otherwise, and I certainly do think that this has large implications today. Who actually revolts from IBM or the big-corporation complex, which is a form of slavery?

J: You see in this book of mine, which I haven't yet found a title for, these diving fellows essentially want to be out on the sea away from society, away from being caught this way, but in the end each one of them, for reasons which come out in the book—for personality flaws in himself—destroys his own ability to *remain* free on the sea. And in the end they all lose the boat that the guy loans them money for, and everything else, and one of the greatest guys winds up working in the parking lot as a parking attendant. It turns out that these guys were not *capable* of remaining outside, and in the end the playwright, who might well have become *one* of them, is forced to go back to writing plays, which don't say really what he wants to say, anyway.

S: Yes. Well, I think that's what both of these books perhaps are really involved in, the question of freedom.

J: I'm not at all sure that our whole American heritage is not in fact a sort of backwater in the stream of history.

S: In what way?

J: If we take the image of history as a stream moving in a certain direction, I think the whole American experiment corresponds to a backwater, sort of hidden behind a small promontory or peninsula so that the water of the current of the stream of history never touched it. We were separated from the rest of the world geographically, during our emergence, the beginning of our American beliefs in individual freedom and so on and so forth. I mean what happened in America couldn't have happened in Europe or in Asia, and we had this whole damn continent to futz around with, but it was outside the stream of history because we were so far separated geographically. But now we've become a great power, it's as though the stream of history itself, with its own force, gradually ate away the promontory which separated us; and now with that gone, the backwater becomes part of the current again, and all our cherished American ideals are being swept up into the future of history. Think of our ideals as the plankton, the algae that grew in the backwater. Now this algae can't grow in the stream of history. The stream is moving too strongly.

S: Well, we have never recognized until recently that the obvious stream of history could be in a great measure the story of what happens when X million Africans rise up and assert themselves. The story of Nat Turner is a little microcosmic—a thing which took place *here,* but which represents to me the whole continent of Africa. Though I don't want to strain the analogy.

J: Well, it seems to me so far from what I've read about it that the continent of Africa is taking up all the bad things which our society has created, and damn little of the good things. The way it looks, political leaders and demagogues are rising up all over the place. They all want power for their own personal reasons—whatever they may be.

S: Well, the late Professor Melville Herskovits, the anthropologist, had the theory that the new African nations should base their emergent structure on tribal traditions rather than emulate us.

J: Romain deals with that in *The Roots of Heaven.* He has a character in there who is a leader of an African revolt in a fictitious country. He has sound reasons for hating the white masters, but is emulating them in everything. And he wants to industrialize his country. He doesn't want to leave it free, he wants factories growing on the veld. And of course he has no idea of the problems he'll have to face, problems we're facing now or problems that Russia's facing now, problems that the Chinese have not yet had to face.

S: Well, it seems quite apparent the coming conflict's going to be one of color, to my mind. I think this is the tragedy of the era.

J: I don't think it makes any difference.

S: Well, perhaps it makes no difference but it's going to happen.

J: Do you include the Chinese as being colored?

S: Well, I think the Chinese *are* going to be colored, yellow, plus black, plus brown, against what we call white.

J: Then I don't think that's a good comparison. There'll probably

be a conflict of that sort, but what's to keep the Chinese from thinking black is colored, and yellow isn't? There'll *be* a conflict of that
kind probably, if the world lasts long enough for it to happen.

S: Well, tell me—getting back to your book—when do you expect
to have it done?

J: Oh, Christ, I don't know. A year, maybe—if I'm lucky. I figure
probably that means two years.

S: Do you ever have the feeling that contemporary events are
outstripping your own insights?

J: No, but they can outstrip your material.

S: Well, maybe that's what I mean.

J: Not the insights, I don't think, in my own case. But it's so hard
to try and do this. . . . Everybody is getting very set in his ideas. I find
all the time in conversations that it's next to impossible to explain to
anyone what I *see* or feel about what's happening to the world. I
suppose I do the same thing when other people say it to me. I suppose maybe it's always been that way but it's so much more important not to do it today, you know. It's so much more important today
because there's not all that much time left—to be able to look at
another man's viewpoint without transposing it or working it around
so that it comes out with *your* viewpoint or as a corollary viewpoint.

S: Yes.

J: And we don't do it.

S: Well, I think that maybe we all talk too much, you know.

J: Like right now.

S: Yes.

J: When do you think you'll have your book done?

S: I hope the end of the year.

J: How far along are you? Halfway done?

S: One third. Maybe more. Maybe less. I like to think it's a third.
How the hell can you ever tell?

J: Ayah. It's kind of like—every time I start a book it's like having
to learn to write all over again.

A Conversation with William Styron
Jack Griffin, Jerry Homsy, Gene Stelzig / 14 January 1965

From *The Handle* (undergraduate magazine, University of Pennsylvania), 2 (Spring 1965), 16–29. Republished in *Pennsylvania Review*, 1 (Spring 1967), 20–32. Reprinted by permission.

Q: We understand that what led to your definite decision to become a serious writer was William Blackburn's course in creative writing at Duke.

A: That's more or less the official beginning. He happened to be a very good teacher and a man who had that kind of natural passion for good writing; and I guess it was Blackburn who got me started initially, if a writer can say any particular person did.

Q: Did you write any short stories or poems before *Lie Down in Darkness,* or was this your first substantial work?

A: I wrote some rather bad short stories which were published mainly in a college magazine at Duke, and then afterwards I continued to write short stories, but for some reason I could never get them off the ground. They weren't terribly good. Along about this time I was in New York, and I'd gotten to know Hiram Haydn, who later became my editor. At that time he was teaching a course at the New School for Social Research. I don't think he was insanely enthusiastic about my short stories, though he did like the quality of the writing, and he encouraged me to cut out the nonsense and start a novel. I did, and it happened to end up as *Lie Down in Darkness.* So, technically speaking, I had nothing really published of a professional nature before *Lie Down in Darkness.*

Q: Do you ever write poetry now? We ask this especially because you have many poetic passages in your novels.

A: I've never written poetry seriously, except at several moments when I was quite young during the war, and I was filled with a sort of a Weltschmerz, you know about life and war and that sort of thing. I wrote some very bad poetry along about that time which fortunately was destroyed. But that's the only poetry I've ever written, though I would like to conceive of some day, à la Thomas Hardy, writing poetry in the future.

Q: About how long did it take you to write *Lie Down in Darkness?*

A: I began it in New York, and I suppose I wrote, oh, perhaps fifty pages and bogged down as I often do in the books that I write, and I just couldn't go any further. This would have been around 1948 or 1949, I guess. I went back down to North Carolina, to Duke, and lived down there for the year, doing no writing, but trying. Being stumped. It's that agony that every writer has more often than he should, which is, you know, the writer's block. I think that Hiram Haydn sensed that I wasn't doing anything down there, so he wrote me a letter and asked why didn't I come back up North where he felt I could get the thing done. Well, I happened to find at that time some very sympathetic, friendly people who had a house in Rockland County, and they encouraged me, too. I lived with them for the next year, writing. I suddenly saw pretty clearly how I had to go about beating this book. So I lived out there and wrote pretty steadily on it, and I got, I suppose, well over half of it done in more or less the same shape that it is now printed. I moved back to New York for various reasons. I just moved out of that place and back to New York, and finished the book the next spring. So, if you can make any sense out of that chronology, it would be the first fifty pages in a very brief length of time, followed by a gap of a year when I did nothing. Then the rest of it was written in, I would say, approximately a year and eight months.

Q: Do you write from the beginning to the end of a novel, or different sections at a time?

A: I have struggled over that problem. I have a need to write from the beginning, perfecting as I go, and making each bit as good as I can. What I have written is, in effect, a final draft. I don't write many drafts as certain writers do. At least it's been my impression that most writers write several drafts. I don't simply because I just don't. As I say, I have this compulsion to perfect each page, so that it mounts up, it ends up being a completed work. I do some revision, but by and large not much. I've always had a feeling that stuff that came— not fast, but stuff that came with a sense of ease and speed in writing, was the best. Stuff that is labored over, sweated over, is often all right. But, for instance that monologue, that last interior monologue, I wrote in about six or seven days, because I was under pressure at that time. Everything that I have felt succeeded pretty well was written at a fairly rapid pace. Right now I've had success with getting a lot of it down. The awful thing is when you just reach a point where you don't want to go on because it's such a sweat and struggle to just start thinking. What was that famous line of Paul Valery, who said, and I'm paraphrasing him badly, that he'd never write a novel because he could not possibly write a line saying, "The Duchess got out of the carriage and went up to the front porch," which you have to have, you know. So much of writing is filled with pushing people around, getting them in and out of doors. That's the tedious part but you've got to do it. You know that certain parts of the book are sort of stage directions. Nonetheless, I think even those things give a kind of texture to it. You can describe people going out of doors in a certain way which is really fresh. The wonderful thing about a writer like Scott Fitzgerald is his ability to give a sense of poetry to very commonplace gestures, which is what makes good writing—when you transfer the reality of the thing even when it's a very commonplace situation. There's a passage in *The Great Gatsby*, often quoted, but which I cannot quote unfortunately, where the narrator goes into a room and sees Daisy and Jordan Baker, the two girls, on a couch, and the wind somehow balloons their skirts up so that they seem like they are flying, sort of half-suspended in the air. It's just that Fitzgerald's eye caught this unique thing which most of us don't see and gave it a magnificent sense of life.

Q: Do you find that your characters seem almost to assume personalities which shape themselves?

A: That's almost a metaphysical question, because it's a mystery to me how a character does develop. Certainly though, the character's either there alive and kicking, or he doesn't exist at all. I've often had to throw out of certain works characters who were so unbelievable to me that I just couldn't buy them. They are usually minor characters who don't ring true, so I exterminate them. I think, though, that as you write and as you get more experienced at it, you suddenly become aware of whether a character is really convincing. As they do develop in a kind of organic way, they either live, are real, or else they're wooden.

Q: How about Peyton in *Lie Down in Darkness*—was she alive and kicking from the very start?

A: I had funny ideas about her. I had resolved when I wrote the book to make the climactic thing the ending where she commits suicide, that interior monologue, which of course is an intense kind of meditation from her point of view. I didn't end the book this way, but I do know that I said to myself that you would never, in the course of the early part of the book, ever have any of her thoughts. For, up to her interior monologue, you see her from every angle, from the point of view of every other character, but she herself is never seen in an interior sense. You never get any of her reflections or thoughts. Now, it seems that most readers find her very real and convincing. Whether that technique of inserting the first person section is responsible I don't know. I do believe, though, that certainly by the time she has committed suicide, you do get a sense of a living, flesh and blood person. If I've captured the reader in the early part of the book, there's set up in his mind a desire to know this girl, so that, when she does embark on this long interior monologue, I think it's perhaps more powerful because she has been seen before from objective vantage points rather than from inside.

Q: You served in the U.S. Marine Corps for three and a half years. Was this during the second World War? Was this experience in any way germinal to your becoming a writer?

A: About two and a half years during the second World War, and then another nine months during the Korean War. I was called back. For some idiotic reason I stayed in the Reserves after World War II, and it was something which I came to regret because I was called up in 1951 at the very height of the Korean War. I was just finishing *Lie Down in Darkness,* and I was working against time because I wanted to get the thing done before I went back into the Marines. So if that final monologue of Peyton has any intensity, it might be due to the fact that I was monstrously oppressed by what I was certain to be another, you know, bad time—in Korea this time. So I wrote it very fast.

Q: Out of this experience came *The Long March?*

A: Yes. *The Long March* is to a large degree autobiographical. The march that took place in the book actually happened to me. I wrote it all in Paris, the following year after I got out of the war.

Q: What would you say is the most difficult problem for a writer, at least your most difficult problem?

A: I would say it's that classical old problem of reconciling truth and imagination, producing an effect which is poetic and exact, and which gives the effect of life, the function and the real substance of a novel. A novel involves an enormous amount of self-examination, and, unless you can make truth and imagination come together, you're not writing anything which is going to live, which is going to have value. The story telling itself is, for me at least, rather easy—that is, to conceive of an event and to take that event from point to point is a very readily visible sort of task. But to put clothes on this sort of vision, to garb it with a sense of reality, to make the words meaningful, to make them sing and to make the reader see is the daily, difficult task. To put it down so that when the reader reads it he says, this is the way it is. It's the difference between slick writing and fine writing. I don't mean fine writing with quotes around it, but what we all consider good writing. Slick writing comes about when the writer has really not tormented himself enough over the actual implications of every word he's saying, and it shows. You can see it sometimes even with the best writers, where you feel that they got tired and just wrote without that passion which you know is in all good writing. I'm just free associating, I'm not trying to give a programmatic description of what the major problems of a writer are. What I'm trying to get at is this absolute demand that you impose upon yourself, that everything you write must somehow be touched with passion and reality. That's the thing that I have struggled with daily. Since I am basically rather lazy, it doubles the misery.

Q: Your style seems to be in a state of transition. From *Lie Down in Darkness* to *Set This House on Fire* you seem to be pressing toward a more narrative style.

A: They say your signature changes throughout your life. In the letters that any person writes living from the age of twenty, let us say, to the age of eighty, the signature is always similar, but any casual observer can detect change. I think that it's true for a writer's style. I don't think that any style remains constant. Because the person is developing, he should be enlarging the capacity for his imagination. As a result, I think that this is going to absolutely dominate his style. In most writers, I'm thinking here of Faulkner, you can detect a complete change of style. The end of the Snopes trilogy is written, for Faulkner, in a very simple and direct way, not of course ever simple in the strict sense of the term, but, as I say, by Faulkner's own standards, far less tormented and intricate. Less complicated than, let us say, the style of *Absalom, Absalom!* or *The Sound and the Fury*. As for myself, I think this is true. In the book I'm writing at the moment, I'm certain that it's more direct and less self conscious, perhaps, and less ornate and complicated than *Lie Down in Darkness*. I feel that every writer tends to think that, if he's honest, the work he is working on at the moment is his best. So perhaps that prejudices me in favor of this book. But I do think that the style is similar to what you just pointed out, that I am getting more toward a direct, narrative style.

Q: Malcolm Cowley, like many good reviewers, suggests that you lean heavily on Faulkner as a literary model. He also states that authors who stay with their literary models have no value of their own. But in your case, he added, Faulkner's model is actually liberating. With all this talk of influence and models, to what extent do you consciously use models? To what degree was your style consciously worked out?

A: Well, I would not be honest if I didn't say that when I was beginning to write I was very much under the influence of Faulkner. I don't consider it a handicap or a defect for a young writer to be influenced by another writer. It would be impossible to conceive of a writer who is not deeply influenced by some other writer or writers. Where would Faulkner have been without Joyce? Where would he have been without Hemingway? Read a marvelous story of Faulkner's called "Red Leaves" which is about the Indians in Mississippi back in the early part of the nineteenth century. It's a wonderful story, and it's curiously influenced by none other than Ernest Hemingway; it even has a phrase in it that says "Olé, grandfather." Now this is right out of Hemingway. And yet it is a wonderful story. A fellow I know who knew Faulkner quite well toward the end of his life, asked him about this, and Faulkner said, "Of course, I was influenced by Hemingway." In other words, even if you're someone like Burroughs, you don't spring full blown from the brow of God. You have your predecessors, and your influences. I was very much influenced by Faulkner. However, I was aware that, unless I could shake off the obvious in the surface influence, I would be writing more or less imitation Faulkner. I struggled, and I think I've succeeded. I think that, whereas almost any fool could detect an influence of Faulkner in *Lie Down in Darkness*, I shook the more obvious qualities of Faulkner, and was left with a book which had its own distinctive and original stance. I don't think that the book would have succeeded had it remained heavily under the influence of Faulkner, though I'm more than happy to acknowledge his influence.

Q: What do you feel is the role of critics in literature?

A: Well, I think that there are very few critics. There are book reviewers, who don't count, and a tiny handful of critics who are very valuable to literature. I used to be very disturbed by criticism about me, especially by book reviewers who would attack me. But I've gotten quite used to it now, and I ignore them. I do read criticism of a high order. I think Edmund Wilson a very fine critic. Almost anything he writes can be read with profit. I think that criticism of the order of John Crowe Ransom, and Allen Tate is all very good stuff indeed. I wouldn't knock it. But I don't think writers should pay any attention to what is said about their works by critics. It's nice if a critic whom you happen to respect does say something nice about your work, but I don't think any of it should be taken too seriously, whether it's pro or con, simply because you have other things to do.

Q: Why do you prefer the particular time sequence that you use in your novels?

A: I've always thought that time was a challenge. I have a feeling that the good writer will set up obstacles for himself. He will try to make his story as difficult to write as possible, to see if he can leap over these obstacles with grace. I've always felt that I had to do this with everything I've written to give the work a sort of tension. If I'd ever written anything in a simple straightforward way, it would have lacked that tension. The use of time is often the most convenient way to set up these obstacles. Another thing is that the use of time is a way to order a book. The book I'm writing at the moment is, briefly, the story of a slave revolt in Virginia, the only American slave revolt. It's something I've been interested in for years. I could have told it in a dozen different ways. The standard way would be to involve a whole lot of characters, white and black, from the omnipotent point of view, starting way back with background and working up to the rebellion. But that would have been the easy way to do it. What I've done is to severely order time by imposing a limited vision of time on the book, in that the story starts on the day the Negro who was the leader of the revolt, Nat Turner is his name, is being sentenced to death for leading the revolt; and it ends five days later when he is actually executed—all of this present time taking place in a jail cell. But within these confines I have woven a sense of the past, so that it finally does include all the things I said before that I could have done had I taken this other tack. This use of time, for me at least, imposes on the whole thing a sense of order.

Q: In an interview with the *Paris Review,* Spring 1954, you state that a writer should be somewhat independent of his themes; they should not be totally immediate. Do you think this can or should be applied as a criticism against such people as Baldwin, Ginsberg, or LeRoi Jones?

A: No. I think it's perfectly all right for a writer to be involved. I think that a good writer will be involved in a good way. The writer who is an artist is almost always going to be aware when he is slipping off into selling messages or preachments. I think one of the advantages of living in a society like ours which allows the writer great leeway in every regard, is that it permits him to write an article, to write a review, to get things off his chest, that which might otherwise hamper his work. He can use these means to be engaged and apply himself to his work in the way to which he is accustomed, mainly to create a work of art; a different thing entirely. In other words, he can do both.

Q: You have often mentioned the word "Truth." Would you agree that truth is beauty and beauty, truth?

A: I don't mean that truth is beauty and beauty is truth but I believe that there is such a thing as truth, and the successful work of art, let us say, a novel, is the one in which imagination is made to serve the writer's vision of truth and the two blending through the writer's own passion or commitment to art, produce that ineffable thing we call a fine novel. What truth is, is much too insubstantial to even talk about. I can't define it. But I do know that, when we are in the presence of a work which we admire, it usually involves a beautiful merging of the two: truth and imagination.

Q: What part does early environment play upon the development of the characters of your work?

A: I'm rather occupied with the question of environment at the moment in my book. Why did Nat revolt and nobody else? Well, the little research you can do on this guy indicates he was in that tiny minority of slaves who were taught to read and write. He was an intelligent guy, but why should he revolt? Well, as I brooded over this, it became fairly clear to me that this is the secret of revolution. If people are kept in total oppression, if they are made to suffer a total kind of dogged, day in and day out oppressiveness of spirit, they are so emasculated that they are slaves by definition. On the other hand, when a master gives a boy a vision of what life might be and, then, through the force of pure economics, is forced to sell him and make him revert to a former state, the state of all the black, oppressed people around him, there is going to be revolt. It would be the most natural reaction. The uniqueness of being taught to read and write made Nat in the end this extraordinary visionary firebrand.

Q: Do you attempt to teach the reader as distinguished from preach?

A: Well, I think that writing is by definition a form of teaching. It's easy like medicine with syrup. You must leave a work which is good with a sense of enlargement, with a kind of enrichment of your life and your horizons. And to that extent I think it is a form of teaching. On the other hand, there's something very disagreeable about books which are didactic in a graceless way.

Q: What is your conception of free will? Your major characters are in a sense determined. Cass feels that he is mysteriously drawn to Sambuco and to involvement in the subsequent chain of tragic events; Peyton enters a hellish labyrinth that must have self-destruction as its only exit. Is man determined solely by his own nature, or are there rhythms larger than man that control his actions?

A: That's the old question, isn't it? Hopefully not unanswerable. People have been struggling with that for about ten thousand years. It's a very good question, though. Yes, I think everybody has free will. I think that events tend to alter our free will; certain tragic events or certain aspects of a man's nature can tend to sort of warp and twist his will, so that it becomes a conditional free will. Luck is simply too enormous a factor in life to deny that. I think it's certainly one of the great moral dilemmas. One of the things about this Negro, Nat Turner, is that he took it upon himself to do this incredible thing, to slaughter a lot of white people, which for an American Negro was probably the most prodigious and decisive act of free will ever taken. And he thought, you see, that God was ordaining him to do this. I mean all you have to do is read any of the prophets, bloody prophets; they're filled with admonitions, orders, to go and kill everybody. A religious fanatic like Nat could easily interpret these to his deity, and he did it, only to find in the last days of his life, as he was being tried, that what he had done was so futile that it called into question his relationship with God, because everything he had done worked out not only against him, but against everything he was fighting for. What this really did, for instance, was to cause enormous restrictions on the slave—several hundred slaves were killed in reprisals.

Q: It seems tragically ironic . . .

A: It does; one of the most horrible ironies imaginable is that Virginia was on the verge of freeing slaves. They had been having arguments on emancipation for a long time. And there is enough evidence in the debates that followed this insurrection, I think, to indicate that Nat and this rebellion caused such irrational fear among the legislators as to make him the single factor which caused Virginia not to emancipate her slaves, but retain slavery. Had Virginia emancipated her slaves, most of the upper South certainly would have emancipated slaves, because Virginia was always the leader among these states. And can you imagine what the effect would have been on the Civil War? In other words, there's the dilemma of free will if ever there was one. The picture of this guy, who was finding himself faced with a truth, which was that everything he had labored for had been reversed. So this is one of the things that I'm trying to get after: what is the relationship between man and God, God being anything you want to define. In Nat's case, because this is a Negro slave, God is simply a guy with a beard up there in the clouds.

Q: The critics, in discussing *Set This House on Fire,* state that Mason Flagg is the embodiment of human evil. Yet, in death, Flagg does not have the face of a murderer, but rather that of a puzzled boy. It seems then that your "evil" characters, Helen and Mason, are not conscious evil doers. Would you say that the evil in the world is not a sin of commission and intent, but instead one of omission, confusion, and lack of understanding.

A: Well, first, I would have reservations about what the critics say about him being the embodiment of evil: I don't think he is. I think they have misconstrued that. He wasn't a very nice guy—that's quite apparent. But, I honestly don't know. The older I get, the less I know about what evil is. I know it exists, and I know there are evil things in the world. But I tend, however, to interpret certain evils in a certain way, in a different way than I did ten, twelve, fifteen years ago. I think one of the slightly more important things about a person's life is that he is able to alter his notions about right and wrong, good and evil, as he goes along. If indeed Mason was evil, I don't think he was in the classical sense of the word. I was trying to draw a picture of a neurotic young man, who has a mother obsessed background, too much money, as representing a kind of ugly personality in American life. I've seen too many of them to deny they don't exist. They do. They are an abstract of our American personna of being.

This is to me still a somewhat Puritanical country. I think, for instance, that we have for a long time equated evil with sexual wrongdoing—which has been rather too bad. But it is our heritage and it has tended to color our relationships with one another to a rather large degree. I think I'm able, at least, to see this flaw in our culture: equating of sexual misbehavior with evil. This is one of our unfortunate qualities. Evil for me is often the result of neurosis. I think there is an evil which emanates from a person which is totally beyond his own capacity for control. In this case I use neurosis as a kind of loose definition of a slightly unbalanced thing that a lot of us have, it doesn't necessarily mean a candidate for a nut-house. But we are all deeply imperfect. And when you use the word "misunderstanding," I think that's a very good definition of one of the major factors in certain evil by-products of human relationships: the misunderstanding arising from one person's natural and understandable inability to excuse or to comprehend the other person's neurotic behavior, leading to all sorts of terrible situations. This is what causes us to edge up on evil. I think there are all sorts of subdivisions of evil. Certainly the Nazi-madness was a sort of mass evil beyond anyone's comprehension. That's the sort of super-evil we still have difficulty in understanding. That sort of evil has to do with the evil of crowds, with crowd behavior, where people lose their identity as morally responsible individuals, when the concept of the Mass overtakes that of the Moral. I think all human beings are capable of this. That's why, though you can condemn the Germans, I don't think you can say that Americans under the same conditions wouldn't have done the same things.

But, as I say, I don't think you can really define what evil is. Your use of the word "misunderstanding" is interesting, because somehow the idea of misunderstanding is at the center of all human relationships which go awry. If we understood each other perfectly, it might be more than any of us could bear. But it would likely avoid some of these tragic misunderstandings. What do you think about evil?

Q: I really don't know. On the one hand, psychology teaches us and from my limited experience I can see that some of this seems true, that it's involved with neuroses. But then, of course, there is the almost supernatural force like pure evil; people can be 'naturally' evil. But I really don't know where you can start assigning the responsibilities.

A: Yes, I think certain people are capable of absolute evil. It's a thorny question now, especially since we tend to start justifying certain aspects of evil as the result of sickness in the head. That however does not minimize the very fact of evil. I would say that anything that aggressively tends to hurt someone else is an evil act. One is in this sense always capable, or not always, but should strive to be capable of the use of his own free will to avoid hurting other people. For instance, I was talking about sexual misbehavior; I don't think the worst thing on earth is to commit adultery, by any means. On the other hand, I do think that it is evil when, as is so often the case—or quite often the case—when one of the guilty parties flaunts this in the eyes of the innocent person, wife or husband. Whether or not "evil" is too strong, I don't know, but this is universally a very aggressive, "bad" act. The act of adultery itself is of relative unimportance. It's the upshot of it, for instance when you read in the *Daily News* about these messy divorce cases—you know, the ones that involve detectives and photographers going over the tops of doors, and so on. It is almost always the result of one of the members of the offending couple blabbing, making a noise about it, hurting the innocent person. Otherwise the innocent person wouldn't know about it. But this is what I mean about the difference between the morality of the act itself and the evil, if you want to use that word, attenuations, the enlargement of the act, the making of a relatively harmless thing into something evil.

Q: I'd like to get back to your book, *Lie Down in Darkness*. To me, Helen, the mother, seems to be an almost totally evil woman.

A: You're right. I think I was trying to portray a woman who was irredeemably ugly, by nature. They exist. And maybe it's an unanswerable question whether it's the product of the wicked series of events; it's too infinitely complex to claim that there's an answer to it. She's a good example of it. I don't intentionally try to create representative characters who are "evil," "good," and so on; but if she developed in the way she did and one, as you say, feels she is evil, then that's the way she is, and there's nothing to be done about it. The morality is so complex that it's almost unamenable to discussion. But I think one of the touchstones you can use is the concept of evil as an act. If we could slit open the skull of any human being alive and look at what goes on in that brain, the evil that exists there would be unspeakable. That's why I tend to regard evil in a totally abstract way, simply because I believe that every human being is capable of it. I think, as I say, in this sort of oversimplified horror, that evil is evil when it is transmitted from thought to act to harm another person, and people who habitually do this correspond to our definition of evil people. Though, again, at least if I had to insist on my own definition, I would have to say that the central fact is the hurting of others.

Q: In *From Shakespeare to Existentialism,* Walter Kaufmann at one point advances the theory that our age is one of general anxiety and insecurity, because so many of the people are confronted with so much diverse knowledge which they are incapable of synthesizing or coming to terms with. You mention somewhere that anyone today can go to a public library and read the best in modern and ancient thought. Would you agree with Kaufmann that the mass of modern men, lacking the intellectual strength to achieve a focus in this diversity, is caught in a vacuum of insecurity?

A: No. I don't feel that particularly, but there are far too many things to read, there's no doubt about that. I tend to suspect this notion about our's being an age of anxiety to a degree that other ages were free of it. I read what I thought was a very ridiculous book review, I think it was in the *New Yorker*, by a guy who pains me very badly anyway. He was talking about the inability of the historical novel to make any sense, which struck pretty close to home because I was writing one myself. And there is some validity to part of what he was trying to say, because the historical novel, by tradition, is a boring thing. But one of his points was the extraordinary, arbitrary one that you cannot treat anything that happened more than fifty years ago. One of the best novels I've read was *Hadrian's Memoirs*, which was about Hadrian—written somewhat more than fifty years after the action took place. One of the stupid things in the reviewer's catalog of stupidities was that another thing that prevents the writing of a historical novel in our times, and I'm paraphrasing him of course, is that the people who existed, let us say anytime before 1900, about whom people would be writing now, lack the garden variety of anxiety that we have today. Therefore, the writer of today could not feel any empathy with these people, because presumably the writer of today is instilled with anxieties that people of that time did not have. There was no correspondence between them. Well, I pondered this, and I'm glad he wrote it, because it's something I hadn't thought of. The more I think of it, the more I become convinced that it's absolutely untrue. It's to be fairly condescending to your ancestors to feel that they lack the same humanity that we have, including the same anxieties, nervous spasms, or anything you can name. Anxiety is part of the human condition, and probably a valuable part, too, because it serves a function: it can get neurotic, it can get sick. But anxiety is a very valuable protection against the menaces of life, in the form of fear. That's the way we guard ourselves. What I wanted to get was that Kaufmann is not accurate in this case, in describing a peculiarly modern anxiety, because I don't think human beings have ever been without it. We're constituted just like everyone else. The menace of the hydrogen bomb doesn't make us any more anxious than the fact that everyone in 1831 feared they might die of smallpox. I can recollect the fear everyone had, when I was a boy in the early forties, about getting tuberculosis. Everytime you coughed, you thought this is it. This was before they discovered streptomycin, which is almost a complete cure for it. I have been getting better and better, but I have been sort of a hypochondriac in my day. I can remember the kind of anxiety I had over getting tuberculosis, or even earlier over getting a

boil—you could die in those days from a boil. And we don't have
that anxiety anymore. We have cancer but, you know, so what? We
get cancer. Well, I quit cigarettes a couple of years ago. But what I'm
getting at is that the fear of the disease must have been an overwhelming anxiety for these people, especially when there were so
many diseases and they were so incurable. Somebody like that *New
Yorker* reviewer cannot tell me that these people were not filled with
what might be called a garden variety anxiety, just like we are today
over other things. Though I have been guilty of it myself, occasionally
trying to find a definition for our way of life, I tend more and more to
think that we are the same people our ancestors were, only with
different clothes and furniture.

Q: Who in your opinion, beside yourself, are the best among contemporary American authors?

A: I've gotten to the point where that's the kind of question I don't
like to answer. I've been asked it, and I've answered; but I find I'm
always giving different people each time. I think that you have to wait
a good long time before you can tell a person's quality. I think that
one can now say that Faulkner was a great writer. Some people were
saying it about him when he was still a youngish writer. A lot of
people were ignoring him, too. I find certain writers vastly over-
praised or, on the other hand, neglected. I find, for instance, that
there is a very bad thing going on which is to ridiculously over-praise
a book like *Ship of Fools.* A book like that, oddly enough, becomes a
commodity. Now I find that when I see a book like *Herzog,* I want to
wait three years to read it. If it's a good book, it's still going to be
there, and I'm going to enjoy it—maybe even more, if it is all that
good three years from now, than I will now. But I don't want to be
taken in too soon. This has been true for many books. We just mentioned *Ship of Fools,* which exploded in all directions. It was unbelievable. Do you recall all the commotion about *By Love Possessed?*
Front page reviews. That piece by Dwight Macdonald in *Commen-
tary* on the reception of the reviews was quite funny. He quoted people like Brendan Gill in the *New Yorker* saying "masterpiece" about
five times in one paragraph. And this was "universal." The point is
that the book was unreadable, a great, big, hulking monstrosity of a
book written in the most atrocious style of any book ever seen. I find
this very disturbing, and this is why I like to be considerably more

certain about my contemporaries: I think I'm relatively free of com-
petitiveness and envy, but I do just like to wait.

Q: Do you think that the devoted and serious artist in America is a
social outcast?

A: Very good question. I don't know if he is or not. A guy wrote an
article recently on Norman Mailer and me, which I haven't read, in
the *Hudson Review,* taking us to task because we had been invited to
the White House. I'm only repeating this because it expresses basically a very self-conscious attitude about writers. Norman Podhoretz
read it and told me about it—that it was done with fine judgment and
high anger and a great deal of concealed jealousy. It shouldn't matter
to this guy so much what a writer does with his time so long as his
work is good. For instance, a guy like Capote, who is a very good
writer, extremely sensitive, keen mind, great gift for words, all the
things that make a guy a good writer. I know Truman pretty well,
don't see too much of him—but his idea of heaven is talking to the
Queen of England, literally. And he does, you know; it's his entire
obsession to be seen with café society, to eat at the Colony or at
Twenty-One, but I couldn't care less, you know, so long as he keeps
turning out good work. And I have read part of his new thing, and it's
a wonderful, or maybe wondrous would be a better word, kind of
book. Somebody on the other hand—well, I guess the opposite pole
would be somebody like Salinger, who lives in a cave or a mailbox or
something like that, but—Someone thought he was really Norman
Mailer. It was Nelson Algren, in fact, who said he thought Salinger
was Norman Mailer. I asked him why, and he said that he had never
seen them together. He's usually in disguise. So Salinger's the opposite end: a very self-conscious recluse or social outcast, though God
knows, he's certainly had enough acceptance as a writer. And, then,
somewhere in between, you have a writer like Kerouac, who is very
much the poser, "the social outcast." In other words, I think that in
this big, free, society a writer can be anything as long as his work is
good. I just happen to like to live without too much emotional strain.
I live up here and I go to New York occasionally, and I don't know
whether I'm an out-cast or whatever the opposite is, you know, in-
group.

Q: Jet-set . . .

A: That's right. In other words, in this day and age it should be of no particular concern to anyone what a writer is or does, because it's the work that counts. I have a kind of naive belief in what Hemingway once said, which was that a writer wrote on the basis of the experience of his first twenty or so years, that what you are, what you register, what you store, in your first twenty-five years you live off of for the rest of your life. I more or less believe this. We are here on earth, we can't seek too many wild adventures or exotic themes, we have to be more or less what we feel ourselves to be. And it seems to me absurd to castigate somebody for going to the White House, or for liking to eat at Twenty-One, or for doing anything, so long as they keep up a high quality of work. Now, I presume that this guy who was writing in the *Hudson Review* thought Mailer and I were already totalled out as writers, that our work reflected this. Well, you know, he has a right to his opinion. I don't think this is true myself. But in any case, because I have spent an evening with the Kennedys, that has nothing to do with what I am as a person, nothing to do with what I am as a writer.

An Interview with William Styron

Robert Canzoneri and Page Stegner / September 1965

From *Per/Se*, 1 (Summer 1966), 37–44. Reprinted by permission.

In April 1965, *Harper's Magazine* issued a special supplement on the South (now available as the book, *The South Today*, edited by Willie Morris) which contained an article called *"This Quiet Dust"* by William Styron. In the piece, Styron is concerned primarily with the Southerner's experience of "Southern experience," but he uses as a platform for his observations the novel that he has been working on for the past three years, *The Confessions of Nat Turner.*

The conversation that follows took place at the Styrons' home in Roxbury, Connecticut, in September of 1965. Styron concerns himself here with the psychological implications of Nat's revolt and the novelist's problems in dealing with an historical Negro character about whom little is factually known.

Canzoneri: You have written in *Harper's* about your interest in Nat Turner as it is related to present circumstances in the South. I wonder if you would talk about it now as it is related to the novel you are writing.

Styron: I have given, I think, only two very brief readings from this novel, one at Wesleyan in Middletown, and one to a very little audience at NYU during a snowstorm about two years ago, about 1963. After I read a part of it at NYU, a fellow got up and said, not in a sarcastic manner, "Do you feel that there's anything opportunistic about this book in that it is about something quite clearly related to our contemporary problems?" I said that that's the least thing that concerns me. Anybody who wished to have an *a priori* disapproval of the book and its themes might possibly say that, but it wouldn't be worth the time it would take to convince them that I've been interested in this ever since I was fifteen years old, before the last war.

Stegner: As a matter of fact, anything you wrote about the area in which you grew up could be considered opportunistic at this time.

Styron: Of course. Yes. And the theme of a slave revolt certainly does, I think, on the surface smack of grabbing a bandwagon and climbing on, but this book has been a long time germinating and was on my mind far in advance of what we call the present Negro civil rights movement.

Canzoneri: Was it the revolt itself, or was it the particular character, Nat Turner, that had captured your interest? Or was it a combination?

Styron: It was the combination. In that *Harper's* piece I stated, I think with some accuracy, that when I was in grammar school I read a history of Virginia (in Virginia you have to study Virginia history as well as American history), and it had a glancing remark about Nat Turner, just sort of saying that in 1831 a fanatical Negro slave named Nat Turner led a terrible revolt in Southampton County, which happened to be very close to a part of Virginia I lived in; of course I had heard of Southampton all of my life. It went on to say, very briefly, that a number of white people were killed and Nat and his followers were caught and hanged for their cruel and disgusting deeds. This history was still very much under the influence of the Jim Crow philosophy of the South, but I think that was the moment I got the tiny germ. It brewed away in the back of my mind for many years. I've always been interested in the period of American history which I call slave times, which for me means roughly 1820 to the Civil War, although, of course, there was slavery far in advance of that. Somehow I've kept this kind of amateur interest in slavery, and along about 1949, I began to gravitate back toward the idea of Nat Turner, who fascinated me partly because I knew so little about him. I began to collect whatever information I could and found to my great surprise that there wasn't anything to speak of. There was a contemporary document called the *Confessions of Nat Turner* which was taken down, transcribed from Nat's lips so to speak, by a man named Gray while Nat was awaiting trial and just before his execution—a very brief pamphlet, about five or six thousand words told in the first person. In addition to this there were a few little newspaper clippings of the time, all of them seemingly sort of halfway informed and hysterical and probably not very reliable. And then added to that there was a single book which was published in 1900, seventy years after the event, called *The Southampton Insurrection,* which again, as I pointed out in that *Harper's* article, was written by a very proslavery, postbellum, unreconstructed Virginian named William S. Drewry. It is a biased book, but at the same time a book of considerable information and detail, and valuable to that degree. Basically, these few are the only documents on the insurrection.

Stegner: Do you plan in writing this to stick to the documents fairly closely and fill in what you don't know, or are you taking liberties with the documents themselves?

Styron: Well, I'll put it this way: The beauty of the story to me—of the subject as a takeoff point of history—is the fact that so little really is known about this event. The outlines are there. We know that on such-and-such a day in August 1831, Nat, accompanied by five or six Negro slaves (a group which later became augmented by maybe forty more), went through the countryside and for three days ruthlessly annihilated sixty white people before being tracked down. It was the first insurrection of its kind, and the only full-fledged slave rebellion in the history of American slavery. We know more or less the nature of the families and the people who were slaughtered, but we know almost nothing about Nat and his background. We know he was a Baptist preacher, that he was a religious fanatic, but of his whole early career and life there's almost nothing known. We know the names of a few of his owners, but that's all.

Canzoneri: He did change owners?

Styron: He changed owners mainly because it was very rough economically in Virginia at that time; people were selling their slaves right and left. Depression times. The economy was on the upswing later, but from 1820 to 1830 was a slump period and therefore there was a lot of selling—especially around 1820 when there was deep depression in the slave market. The fact that so little is known about this event seems to me to make it a wonderful ground for exploration imaginatively, whereas so many historical events are not. It seems to me that when you have a historical event which is documented almost to the point of boredom its validity as a subject for fiction is reduced. And, as I say, the beauty for me of Nat as a subject is the fact that I can use whatever responsible imagination I have trying to create my own myth.

Stegner: Is your principal focus in the book on the psychology of Nat Turner himself, or on the whole insurrection?

Styron: The book is, as I think most books should be, a lot of things, not just a story about a revolt. I hope that it deals more or less responsibly with the problem of responsibility itself, or moral choice, use of violence. It is also a religious allegory in its own way, and all these things are essential to the theme of the book. It's not just a novel about a violent, Gothic upheaval in the South; if anything, I think (though I haven't completed it) it successfully shies away from violence. Nat himself murders only one person, and the revolt sort of collapses internally once he has killed. That's what my reading of the *Confessions* tells me. You have to dig it out yourself. No one else among the few commentators on the revolt seems to have noticed this. To my mind it was his dealing with violence that led him into a hopeless trap. He found out that he couldn't deal with the violence that he himself had ordained, so to speak, and this is part of my story. I think it's very central to the book—the idea of what happens when a man boldly proposes a course of total annihilation and starts to carry it out and finds to his dismay it's not working for him. I think it's unavoidable in an honest reading of Nat Turner's confessions that he himself was almost unable to grapple with violence, to carry it out successfully.

Canzoneri: In exploring Nat Turner, do you discover things about yourself as well as your character?

Styron: Yes, I think you do. This is sort of a problem with fiction in general. For years, when I was considering writing this novel, I had no idea how I was going to tackle the thing. I had the idea of telling it from an omniscient point of view, from many reactive standpoints, such as that of one of the white victims, one of the farmer types. It just didn't seem right to me, and I don't know how these things evolve, but when I began finally to tackle the book itself, I realized that the only way to do it was to do it from Nat's point of view. I have a feeling that writers set up barriers for themselves. If they don't, they should. And I know I do. I think that one of the central mystiques of the writer of novels is that you don't take the easy way, you take the hardest way in order to see if you can surmount the problems. And I know that imposing upon myself this kind of tension has, to my mind, produced whatever good stuff I've ever produced. It has always involved taking the most difficult path from point A to point Z, and in this case I realized that inevitably one of the profoundly difficult things I would have to set up for myself would be the telling of this story from the point of view of Nat himself—a first person narrative which would somehow allow you to enter the consciousness of a Negro of the early decades of the 19th century. It seemed to be the only way out, so I did it. More than any other, I think this way of telling the story comes to grips with the problems you just mentioned. If you start finding out about Nat, discovering things about Nat, well, of course, every passage, every chapter, every section is kind of a revelation both for yourself and for Nat. To this degree the book is also, I think, a psychological novel. I don't like to call it a historical novel, because in the banal, classic American sense of the word it's not.

Stegner: You're writing from Nat Turner's point of view. Are you attempting at all to use Nat Turner's language—a dialect or restricted vocabulary, for instance?

Styron: I'm telling it in what I would like to believe without shame is my own literary style: that is, the way I would be writing in the first person if I were writing about Joe Blow who lived in 1965 in New York. I do, however, have certain obvious limitations that I impose on myself. Obviously I don't use anachronisms. I try to avoid any suggestion of 20th century vernacular. On the other hand, I don't strain to achieve a literary style of the early 19th century. And when I write a dialogue I have to obey the rules of dialogue of the 19th century. I don't think this at all turned out to be difficult, because I know recent backwoods speech, and it is quite similar to backwoods speech of 130 years ago. So, what looked to me as if it were going to be one of the most difficult problems in the book I have, at least to my own satisfaction, solved. I read part of this book, as I said, up at Wesleyan; and after I'd finished, one of the boys got up and said, "Well, this is a literary style. Would a Negro like that think in these terms?" I had to tell him—I'm afraid it embarrassed him—that I found that question very condescending to Negroes. It implied that Negroes didn't think like the rest of us folks. I think it is true that the boy was buffaloed at first by the fact that this is a literary style, when in reality it is a form of translation. That is, given the fact that Nat was an educated Negro, it seems to me perfectly plausible that if you were going to read this

novel anyway you would accept the fact that he thought in the way
that I'm describing things—that is, in a regular literary fashion. And I
can only say that I've tried this out on enough people to feel that I'm
right. No one has yet really had any major reservations about this
form of narrative.

Canzoneri: Actually, that form has been used quite a bit, hasn't
it? In Faulkner's dealing with Benjy, in *The Sound and the Fury,* you
have a similar kind of thing and it has been accepted. It's interesting
that when you're talking about a Negro in the 19th century the question does arise.

Styron: That's right. I think *The Sound and the Fury* is a good
example. You have the three first-person sections of Benjy and
Quentin and Jason. Quentin is a college student, and Jason is a mer-
chant, and Benjy is an idiot. You accept their varied modes of expression as being the gospel truth. At least it didn't upset me when I
reread it several times. I'm not flustered by this approach, and I'm
fully convinced that what's on the page is what's going on in their
minds, even though I know in reality that they wouldn't be express-
ing themselves this way. It's a matter of willing suspension of disbe-
lief. If I haven't solved that problem, the book is a failure from the
start; but I don't think I have too many worries on that account. The
question of the boy at Wesleyan was in a way very condescending
because it smacked of a kind of Northern racism, you know. One of
the enormously fascinating things about Nat is that he was a very
complicated man. He was no primitive sort of psychotic killer from
the jungle. He was educated—not highly educated, but a man, I
think, of some genius—and therefore one has to allow him a mode
of expression which will take in these complexities.

Canzoneri: In at least two of your novels you have more or less
begun with the final action and then looked back to see what led to
it. Is the structure of this novel on that order?

Styron: Yes, it is. The novel fell into a very easy architecture after I
pondered it long enough. It seemed inevitable to me that I would
have to start the book (as I have done) while he is sitting in his cell
awaiting trial—on the day of his trial. I did this for several reasons.
For one, it allowed me to introduce Mr. Gray, who took down the
original confessions, and to have a kind of ironic counterpoint between these confessions—which had a lot of white man's hokum in

them—and Nat's own story. The major reason, however, was that I wanted to get Nat after the insurrection, when he was questioning the entire relationship he had with God, with the God who had been his guide and mentor and light throughout his life as a preacher. I wanted to discover what was going on in his mind, now that he had instigated and committed murder, and now that he is bereft of God. The relationship with God seemed to be the central thing in my own conception of the man. The book ends on the day of his execution, and part of it is the story of his redemption. How does he achieve redemption before he is executed, before he goes to his maker, so to speak? So the plot divides itself into roughly four parts. The first day is the day of his trial, in the jail cell: his conversation with Gray, who is both his prosecutor and defender, a kind of nemesis figure who is Nat's enemy but also his confessor and even a friend, in a vague way. And through all this first part I have flashbacks—not real flashbacks, but kind of interwoven recollections and realizations about certain areas of his past life as a slave. There's a section within that section, of the trial itself. It's a very complex time scheme, a fluid time scheme, but I think it's rather rich. Part one ends with Nat after the trial that same day in total despair and totally adrift from this godhead, who has been the guide and light throughout his life. He feels God has abandoned him and he has abandoned God. The universe is very cold indeed. And that's how we leave Nat at the end of part one. We know he will be executed in five days. The second part is called Old Times Past, which is a direct, first person recital, of his life as a slave, his life as a little boy. There's a bit about his grandmother, who was brought over on a slave ship—just little reminiscent pieces, fragments, stuff out of his memory. There's the account of how, because of his grandmother's early death, his mother was brought into the plantation house and became a house nigger, and therefore he became a house nigger, too, and was adopted, was taken under the wing of these people, the Turners, who were enlightened masters like so many Virginia planters of the time, opposed to slavery but trying to find a way out—all this because it seemed to me that there could be only one way to justify the fact that Nat *had* been educated, *could* read the Bible and knew it by heart. This seems to me incontrovertible historical fact: he would have had to be taught somewhere along the line, taught well, and taught with some sense of guidance. This is my speculation (I have to confess that this is the part that makes it fiction), but I'm trying to describe a kind of slave life in which—as a child, as a boy, as a young man and so on—he once was happy by anybody's standards. In fact, here's one of the central ironies of the book, because something happened. At some point all this was swept right out from beneath him. Nat was born in 1800 and the first great depression of that century was in 1821, when quite creepily and spookily the land of that Virginia tidewater was being devoured by the overcultivation of tobacco. Two-thirds of the big planters, who in 1800 were men of wealth and means, had to sell out by 1821. There was nothing left. They were men who had to go to Alabama, as so many of them did, and to Mississippi, and develop new land—or go bankrupt, or become something else. But at that point, in 1821, came the first large-scale selling of slaves, the breakup of families, the cause of many moral pressures in Virginia. And it seems to me quite inevitable that if Nat was brought up under these happy auspices by a man of wealth and means—if history was working for this man as it was working for so many others of that time—there would come a time of sudden, extreme change. He would have been told as a youth, "Look here, young Nat, when you're twenty-one, I'm going to set you free in Richmond and you're going to be a wonderful carpenter. You're going to be educated in Richmond. There are a lot of free Negroes, and you'll get a wife and be married, and you'll have a fine family, and you'll be as well off as any Negro can possibly be." Instead when he reached twenty-one, the man who had told him this suddenly had to say, "All my dreams are gone, Nat," and in effect to add, "I hate to say it but you're worth $1000. I hate to sell you, but I'm going to sell you to a good man, and after I've gone down to Alabama and made a new fortune— which of course I will, partially from the capital that you represent— I'm going to send for you and you're coming down there, and so on and so on." The point is that this is the most incredible, crucial psychological betrayal that could ever happen to a young man. After having been taught that you were a young man—a *man*—to have in your twenty-first year your manhood destroyed, and to be sold, and to have none of your dreams come true; to be sold, and again to be sold after that; to have the master of your childhood fade off into oblivion, and to find yourself at the age of twenty-five the property of some illiterate woodcutter who couldn't read or write, and who abused you, the black man. If you had a measure of madness in your head, anyway, I think it would be a perfect setup: you would be in a perfect position to start a revolt of some kind, because this, I think, fits the pattern of revolt. It's not oppression I mean. If you oppress people, you've got them under your heel. It's when you've given them a smell of something grand. I have a line somewhere in the book, which I think I can quote, when Nat is ruefully reflecting on the way in which these circumstances came about; he says, "Better I say to rot and wither on the dead vine of life a toothless old coon, gumming his spoon bread and gravy on the back stoop, than as a young man to have briefly savored the glories of the banquet only to be hurled out the front door." The seeds of revolt are in the *promise*. This—of course without belaboring the thing—is what's going on right now: it's the smell of grandeur that causes the hatred and the apocalyptic acts. This is the way I've conceived of the whole central part of the book, describing Nat's relationship with this naive, well-meaning father-figure, and the closeness of the bond between them, and how it turns into something sour and awful. Instead of becoming a man at the age of twenty-one, he became a piece of property. It's hard to believe that almost within our grandfathers' lifetime this could happen to Americans, but it has.

Stegner: Did Nat ever say specifically why he instigated this revolt?

Styron: No. That's a good question, because that's one of the things that is not clear in the confessions. You get a lot of those hypnotic religious visions, which I think are accurately recorded, but obviously the religious fanaticism must have disguised a profounder reason. Basically, the confessions themselves don't reveal anything about the actual cause. Over and over in the confessions you have Mr. Gray saying, "Isn't it true that your master was a kindly man?" That is, Travis, his master at the time of the revolt. And there's Nat, over and over again replying, "Yes, he was a good man." One of the beautiful paradoxes of the actual thing is the fact that the Southerners of the time couldn't understand why in Virginia, of all places?—not Mississippi or Alabama but in Virginia, where the slaves were by comparison usually much better treated than in other parts of the South—why *here* a revolt would take place, among all these kindly, educated people influenced by the University of Virginia and Thomas Jefferson?—when of course in reality that's just the sort of place it *would* take place.

Canzoneri: Where else but in a Jeffersonian environment?

Styron: Yes, where else could you get the smell of success, the sweet smell of success. Down in Mississippi you were under the swine all the time. You wouldn't have a chance to smell anything.

Canzoneri: You've talked about the first two sections. I'd like to hear you go on, if you don't mind.

Styron: Like most novels I suppose it leads from climax to climax. But one of the most crucial moments in the second section comes when Turner, the old man (well, he's not old, he's in his forties), tells Nat after these years of promise that he has to sell him, and of course this is a traumatic, terrible moment. There are letters from Alabama from the old man. They're very kind letters, but they peter out; and Nat realizes that he is saddled with a life of slavery in the service of these very low-grade, illiterate yeoman farmers who are the only ones left to take up the slave population. Part two ends there—ends with a sense of suspension and of despair—and in the third part I jump ahead to the time preceding the revolt; and here I go into relationships. This is another theme which I haven't even touched on yet: Nat's relationship with the one person he himself killed in the insurrection—a young girl of eighteen named Margaret Whitehead, whom Drewry in that book of 1900 describes as the belle of the county, and I think there's good reason to believe that she was a fascinating young creature. One of the really deeply stirring scenes of the whole book, in terms of my quest for answers, is this relationship. There must have been—I say *must* have been because I have no proof, but I'm convinced—some kind of relationship between the two, and I think it was a very guarded sexual relationship. I don't think that there was anything overt. I think that at one time Nat must have been—as so many Negroes were in those days—hired out by his owner, Travis, who was a man of more or less modest means, a wheelwright, and was hired out for some time in the employ of the mother of this girl. The major portion of this last part of the book has to do with the conflict between the incredibly puritanical religious feelings he had about life in general, and his strong physical desires. I see him as being thrown into very close contact with this girl, in the

rather easy-going sort of racial relationships of the time. He was enormously unusual. He was an educated slave, and a man even of some
refinement in a curious way. A man of that sort I think in a deep part
of his heart would scorn the average, illiterate, pathetic colored
woman—slave woman—and gravitate especially toward an eighteen-
year-old nubile, religious nut very similar to himself. A reciter of the
Psalms, a reciter of the Sermon on the Mount. Without overly ro-
manticizing it, one could say that they sat under tulip poplars among
the buttercups, with the bees buzzing around them, reading the Bible
together. She's quite unconsciously flirtatious, and she's a little dish—
a little sweetheart, you know—and although Nat is a puritan of the
finest stripe, he's a virile young man of thirty, and he's obviously
going to go right out of his mind. The barrier is incredible, but it's
tissue paper thin, and for just that reason it's all the more imperme-
able. And so the way that you break it down is in the most apocalyptic way that is possible to a human being. You break through it by
killing. And it seems to me that this is symbolic of the human condition as we've experienced it in this country with the black and white
races so incredibly on edge and so incredibly bound to each other. I
don't want to set up a cliche. I don't want the usual black-man-white-
man miscegenation nonsense. But I do think that there must have
been a powerful thing at work here. I can't explain otherwise the fact
that of all the people killed in the insurrection—all the white people;
and there were sixty—that he should kill only one after trying, as he
says himself in the confessions, to kill several and failing . . . why he
should succeed with this one girl, an eighteen-year-old girl who's the
only nubile girl, so far as I can find out, killed during the insurrection.
So I think that this is a classic example of some sort of love-hate
relationship. I think she's a sort of religious fanatic herself, of that
dewy-eyed, early 19th century, more-or-less-primitive Methodist or
Baptist background. The first part of part three has to do with that,
and of course the last part is a fairly compressed description of the
revolt, the inception. Nat knew exactly where he was going. He was
going ten to fifteen miles from his master's house up a general route
toward the county seat of Jerusalem, there to break into the armory—there was a small armory there—and to get all the weapons
and ammunition he could, then march across the neighboring county

(Nansemond County) and into the Dismal Swamp, there to set up an empire.

Canzoneri: Jerusalem is the name of the town?

Styron: Yes, it's a marvelous name, isn't it? He had a few hard core followers: one, a young Negro named Hark, who worked at Travis's, too—who was convinced by sheer passion that this was the only way out. None of his hard core followers (and there were several) was religious, with the exception of one. This is my own gloss on the thing. I don't know whether this is true or not; I *smell* it to be true. Most of them were desperate Negroes, who for one reason or another were just fed up and were set afire by Nat's conviction. Altogether at least thirty Negroes were involved. So what you've got is a hard core of true believers that Nat has inspired and enflamed, as many as seven but with an inner-inner core of just four besides Nat, Hark and two others, plus Will, the really wild fanatic. And beyond that I think in the course of the rebellion just a kind of rabble of young kids who were just excited by the adventure. And here we have the conflict between Nat, who can't kill, and the Negro he has been afraid of throughout the whole book: the Negro named Will, who is a contemporary and a killer, and who, when Nat fails, is the man who goes in with the ax and swiftly decapitates every white head in sight. Nat fears and hates this demonic man who is so vividly—too vividly, to Nat's horror—a personification of the retribution he thought was his own but wasn't. Will is also a threat to his leadership: a man who is possibly saying, "Man, you better kill, or else you're not in charge here no more." This is what I'm dealing with in this part. They're at the Whiteheads' house, and of course Nat doesn't realize that he hates—loves—hates—loves Margaret Whitehead, and the combination of things causes him to sicken. Anyway, that's the climactic point of the book when he kills this girl, the only person he does kill. Then there's a swift diminuendo and we cut off and go to the last part, which is again back in the jail cell.

Stegner: You say the revolt lasted three days?

Styron: Yes. About three days. Of course, there's another thing I haven't mentioned that I think is interesting. Aside from Nat's terrible traumatic experience of killing this girl, which I think doesn't bring the revolt to a halt but breaks its back, there is the fact that toward the

end of the revolt—andthis is historically true—many of the houses
were seen by Nat, as he approached, to be defended by Negroes.
That is, the slaves in many of these houses—and not at gunpoint
either, but quite voluntarily—were rallying to their masters' defense
against this incredible invasion. I'm sure the cliche liberal of our time
would ask for proof that this is true, but there were a lot of motives,
quite real ones, that would cause a Negro to defend his white master
against other Negroes of that day and age. One was to preserve his
own skin. He was shrewd, and he figured that if he played his cards
right he'd get off better. And also I think that there was quite frankly
often a very profound loyalty in those days. The fashionable historians can't convince me otherwise, because there's too much evidence. This adds an interesting complexity to the thing. I think it was
Nat's ultimate, final disappointment—the thing that really crushed
him—when, instead of gathering all the troops that he *thought* he
was going to gather to him, he found that these places were being
barricaded by none other than Negroes. I think, too, that this made
him even more convinced of the horror of his failure. As I said, in the
last part of the book he is in his jail cell, and he's on the verge of his
execution. He's trying to find an answer to what he's done. He
knows by now that what he's done is pretty terrible, because nothing's happened; it has all worked out wrong. All of his Negroes have
been executed, and he has accomplished nothing in terms of his
early goal to capture the county seat and flee to the Dismal Swamp
and set up an empire there. In addition, there's been a violent retribution on the part of the whites, who killed about two hundred
innocent Negroes in vengeance, and he's aware of this. He realizes
that he's been working on rather one note, that he's been getting
these messages from God through the prophets to go kill, to annihi-
late, to slaughter ruthlessly men, women, and children; but somehow,
during all the period that we see him in the jail cell after the insurrection, he's getting the message that maybe this wasn't the real message at all, that his book which guides his entire life, the Bible, maybe
wasn't the answer; the answer is somewhere else. The way I'm going
to see this man's redemption is that just before he dies he recalls that
the moment that he killed this girl—she of the religious chatter, and
the childish palaver of Christian love and fellowship to all, and all
that—at the moment of her death at his hands she regards him with

a look of compassion and love, and this is his revelation. This is, of course, the final message of the Bible. Not all of that old, you know, let-us-slay-women-and-children; but it's this, it's this other message, and this is his redemption. Of course, it's too late for his mortal salvation, but it's the answer for him, and it's the answer for the book.

Canzoneri: Do you have anything in the book that follows Nat Turner's death, like an epilogue?

Styron: I have a sort of thing you might call a postscript, which is about what happened to the remains of the people. Drewry recounts this in his book, saying that the bodies of those executed with one exception were buried in a decent and becoming manner; that of Nat Turner was delivered to the doctors, who skinned it and made grease of the flesh.

Stegner: What did they do with the skin?

Styron: Well, it might be explained in the sentence that comes after that: Mr. R. S. Barham's father owned a money purse made of his hide. It says then that his skeleton was for many years in possession of Dr. Massenburg but has since been misplaced. That's the epilogue, or the postscript, and then the final postscript is the great line from Revelations which is, "And he said unto me, 'It is done. I'm Alpha and Omega, the beginning and the end. I will give unto him that is athirst of the fountain of the water of life freely. He that overcometh shall inherit all things and I will be his God and he shall be my son.' " So that's it.

William Styron

Alice Rewald / 1967

From *La Quinzaine littéraire*, 15–31 October 1967, pp. 12–13.
Reprinted by permission.

AR: Do you enjoy writing?

WS: No. I experience a certain degree of satisfaction when things go well, but it is a pleasure nearly obliterated by the constantly renewed agony of having to start again.

AR: On the average, how many pages do you write on any one day?

WS: When I work regularly on a project which interests me, that is to say on one of those stories whose end can be anticipated, I write two-and-one-half, three pages a day.

. . . .

WS: It was while studying the history of Virginia, the state in which I was born, that I first encountered the name of Nat Turner. I must have been ten. The reference was brief, almost hasty. It may have been this very hastiness which aroused my curiosity: "In 1831 a fanatic slave named Nat Turner fomented a terrible rebellion in Southampton County, Virginia, killing several white people. The revolt was quickly repressed and most blacks who participated were hanged." That's very nearly what the obscure author wrote. He was in a hurry to move on.

These lines depicted vivid and bloody facts, one of those astonishing dramas that form the past of the South. This Nat Turner was a self-taught slave, about thirty years old, who believed himself chosen by divine will to exterminate all the whites in the area. His ultimate goal was to liberate his people and, with his companions, to establish a black empire in the Dismal Swamp, a marshy, snake-infested area where, as legend had it, only blacks could survive. On 21 August, going toward the town of Jerusalem, the county seat, Nat Turner, with a half-dozen of his disciples, broke into the houses of isolated plantation owners and killed all the inhabitants. The rebellion lasted three days; seventy blacks participated. Nat Turner was captured after a two-month chase. He pleaded not guilty, saying he felt no guilt. His body was turned over to a group of doctors. Fat was made from it and change purses were carved from his skin.

AR: Did the fact that your hero is a historical character give you any particular difficulties?

WS: No. Each book brings its own special problems. I have not been limited by history because very few precise facts are known about the life of Nat Turner, about his early years and his true motives. I found scanty information about him in a thin volume which bears the same title as my novel and contains a few remarks made by the accused shortly before his execution. They were written down by a lawyer.

AR: Was it hard to identify yourself with a black man?

WS: Yes, but I believe I succeeded. [*Ironically:*] One ounce of imagination can work wonders. Besides, my book is less a historical novel than a meditation on history.

AR: How did your curiosity, unconsciously awakened at first, lead you to come back to and meditate on this particular event?

WS: Because it is impossible to live in America these days without giving the racial problem a great deal of thought. And I suspect that the efforts I made to recreate Nat Turner, to bring him back to life, represented at least partially the accomplishment of an imperious moral duty: to get to know the blacks. Most southern whites can neither know nor go near blacks out of moral fear. You feel it everywhere, even in the works of a writer as exceptionally well informed on the black mentality as William Faulkner, who admits to being hesitant about "thinking Negro." His marvellously drawn black characters seem more "observed" than "lived." Thus in *The Sound and the Fury,* the Negro Dilsey is the only one who, unlike all the other main characters, is not telling the facts in an interior monologue but whose perspective is given in a narrative, from the outside.

AR: Then you share the point of view of Ralph Ellison, the black writer who affirms that, in America, the black man is the invisible man?

WS: Certainly. Contrary to what they believe, southern whites live in complete ignorance of the soul and character of the blacks, although blacks are always and everywhere present, even more so than in the northern states. Ignored, negated, they weigh down, often paradoxically, on the collective subconscious mind of the white population.

AR: Were revolts such as the one you describe in your novel frequent during the age of slavery?

WS: No. On the contrary, there were very few organized rebellions during the two hundred and fifty years of slavery. Historians mention only three; Nat Turner's was the last and the only one that met with a semblance of success.

AR: What is your position with regard to today's black problem?

WS: That's a difficult question, hard to answer in a clear-cut way. Of course I am sympathetic to equality for blacks, to the civil rights movement.

AR: Are you actively engaged in the struggle?

WS: No. I have a certain amount of energy at my disposal, not more. I use it to write. This book is my contribution.

AR: Do you think that your novel will be well received by blacks?

WS: It depends. I asked James Baldwin to read it and he liked it. But I imagine that the Black Power radicals will hate it.

AR: Perhaps. Yet the portrait of Nat Turner—a Negro of superior intelligence, leader of a rebellion, exterminating angel of about sixty whites—corresponds rather well to the image some contemporary black youths strive to project. But Styron's Nat Turner (after all a character brought to life by a southern white) cannot personally kill the hated white man. He is moved by the pale complexion and compassionate soul of a young white woman. He spares a family of poor whites. He is a fanatic inspired by the Bible. He will not please.

WS: Some whites will not like this novel. Generally speaking, America refuses to remember this dark era. There are numerous Americans who prefer to maintain the comforting illusion that slavery, though morally reprehensible, was justified by the generosity and superiority of the masters. Textbooks carefully avoid mentioning individuals in whom blacks could take pride. They avoid digging up the dirt in which this infernal misunderstanding is rooted, a misunderstanding which, still today, polarizes two segments of the population.

The Confessions of William Styron

C. Van Woodward and R. W. B. Lewis / 1967

Transcription of a radio program originally broadcast 5 November 1967. A cut and condensed version appeared in *Yale Alumni Magazine*, 31 (November 1967), 33–39; the text below is a transcription of the original broadcast. Copyright by Yale Alumni Publications, Inc. Reprinted by permission.

Announcer: This is YALE REPORTS, a weekly broadcast review presented by Yale University and WTIC.

With burning and bloodshed, in a remote part of southeastern Virginia in August of 1831, occurred the only sustained revolt in the history of Negro slavery in America. Its leader was an educated slave, Nat Turner.

William Styron has written a novel in which Nat Turner, facing death, tells his story. Mr. Styron calls the book "a meditation on history." He discusses it now, as history and as literature, with C. Vann Woodward, Sterling Professor of History at Yale, and Richard W. B. Lewis, Professor of English and American Studies. Mr. Styron:

Styron: I was fascinated by this story long before the civil rights movement became an overwhelming aspect of our life. Obviously, there are parallels; I would be the first to admit them. However, for me to have twisted anything in the book to heighten the relationship of its events to events today would have been some sort of betrayal of my own vision of Nat Turner and his story.

Woodward: I am very glad you refrained.

Lewis: It puts the reader in mind, of course, of the uprisings, of the riots, of the rhetoric of black power and the instant white reaction that we must have tougher, more stringent laws. However, I would take it that one of the meanings of the phrase "a meditation on history," is that while never alluding to the present situation in the so-called Negro revolution, this novel probes to the sources of what we are undergoing now, and in that sense, deals with a generality of history.

Styron: Right.

Lewis: That's why I think the book has one of its great distinctions.

Styron: Well, I am glad that you feel that, because a book like this certainly runs into danger, and I am afraid already the danger has begun, of being heralded as a kind of paradigm of current events; that one must draw strict parallels from Nat Turner in order to explicate current events. I would be appalled if some person lacking the proper insight would do this in a dogged and deterministic way. I don't intend that in the slightest.

Woodward: In discussing the revolt, we are confronted with an historical event. It recalls to my mind a comparable historical event which took place later in the nineteenth century . . . John Brown's rebellion. I suppose that of all the figures who have appeared as rebels in the history of slavery, John Brown and Nat Turner stand out. And yet I am struck by the remarkable difference in the historical and literary attention given these two men. There are forty biographies, perhaps, of John Brown, and yet very little until now, written about Nat Turner. I have a theory that this is because there is so much available from contemporary sources about Brown and the places and time he lived in. Do you agree?

Styron: Well, I think the major reason that so little is known about Nat, compared to John Brown, is the simple fact that Nat Turner's insurrection occurred at a time when communications in this country were primitive. It came before the invention of the telegraph, before the railroad. In other words, I think that had this revolt occurred, let us say in 1941 or '42 instead of 1831, you might have had an entirely different situation. By that time, railroads had invaded that part of Virginia and I think we would know a lot more about Nat Turner. However, 1831 was too early for these technological developments; that is, I think, one of the central reasons that the rebellion was so little documented.

Lewis: Was the rebellion nationally known? Did it become nationally known?

Styron: It did become nationally known, especially in the South. It caused a wave of terror in the South, as a matter of fact. But it was an isolated incident. I think about a year later it was forgotten all over the country.

Woodward: I think that Nat Turner's rebellion was far more of a threat to slavery. John Brown's raid really never had a chance. Turner's revolt was a terribly frightening thing to the slave society, the slave economy in which it took place.

Styron: Yes, there is no doubt that it caused absolute, insane panic. I remember you, Vann, sent me once an account from some upcountry Virginia resident describing the near frenzy that had taken possession of a part of Virginia which was far removed from Southampton County where the revolt occurred. One hundred and twenty miles away people were packing up, looking over their shoulders, just in a frenzy.

Woodward: Another notable characteristic of this rebellion was that Nat Turner did not know or have sympathetic white supporters. For example, John Brown knew men of consequence, writers and others who were in some sense involved in the conspiracy and who left their own accounts of it. Nat was in quite a different position; he was isolated from this sort of influence.

Styron: Oh sure, and by that time the sophistication of communications was apparent, compared to 1831. I mean, there was considerable newspaper coverage. There were telegraph reports of the raids going to Washington almost on the hour.

Lewis: Well, in the case of Turner's rebellion, his confession in jail is your basic document, isn't it?

Styron: That's the single document that means anything. There are newspaper reports from the *Richmond Enquirer* which, of course, gave it a very heavy play, but one feels that the accuracy is always in question. They seemed to be bewildered by the revolt, so that newspaper accounts of the time (there are more than one) nonetheless seem to me to be somewhat sketchy and unauthenticated.

Woodward: We are discussing, really, questions of accuracy: questions about the fictional treatment of historical events. I'd like to say a word about that. I've read this novel carefully; twice, as a matter of fact. Though there may be differences among historians about such fictional treatments, I find that this work is not inconsistent with anything historians know about this event, or about the period. It doesn't pretend to be history, but it seems to me a very valid and authentic use of history for the purposes of fiction. It seems to me to be faithful in its respect for history, not only in its consideration of events—facts—but in the way it views the time and the place in which these events happened. In that respect, I think it is above criticism.

Lewis: That's pretty good testimony.

Styron: That's the best you can get.

Lewis: I should think so.

Styron: I am grateful you do feel that way because I realize that in a book like this there is a basic responsibility involved. It's a tightrope walk: you want to use the art of fiction as much as you can, and at the same time you want to be faithful to the time and place, so to be ratified in this manner is gratifying.

Lewis: You say in your author's note that this was not intended to be an historical novel, but rather a "meditation" on history. That is, I take it, a meditation on the mysterious processes of history in general. However, are you meditating, or is Nat meditating?

Styron: I think that's a good question. I intended that statement to do two things: first, to take the curse of the label "historical novel" off the book, because it has regrettably acquired a pejorative connotation, especially in the United States; secondly, it is a meditation on history, because I hoped that I would encompass a meditative quality as I wrote.

Lewis: I wanted to ask about the meditational quality. What is interesting is that although the actual rebellion is the climax of the story, the way in which the rebellion turned out is known by about page forty. We know pretty much who was killed: we know that Nat only killed one person; we know how his owner was killed; we know how several other people were killed. There are no facts held back, which means, I take it, Bill, that what you wanted to do was not center so much on the melodrama, but on Nat Turner brooding about the entire adventure as he was about to be hanged, is that right?

Styron: Right. I feel that it would have been too easy to write this story from the point of view of melodrama. I think had I written it fifteen or twenty years ago when I first conceived the notion, it would have had a melodramatic overlay. Obviously, bloodshed and violence had to be there, however. It would have been shirking my responsibility not to describe it. On the other hand, that was not the sole reason that I had for writing this book. I wanted also to explore in some kind of depth this whole area of American life and history, to take on the lineaments (as well as I could) of a slave, and using that persona, to walk myself through a time and place, in a manner of self-discovery. I was learning all along, as I wrote about Nat from his point of view, what it was and what it must have been to have been a slave.

Woodward: I think that is perhaps the most important and, certainly, the boldest decision that you made: to tell this story as Nat Turner himself. We know that historians can tell what it was like to have slaves, but not very much about how it was to be a slave. That, I think, is what you tried to do, without, of course, being either a slave or Negro yourself.

Styron: Yes, I think there was a wonderful combination of lucky shots there for me. Obviously, I was fascinated, as other people are, with the time, but to have taken on the garb of any old slave would not, to me, have been a very interesting adventure. Just by the sheerest fortune, of course, I hit upon an actual slave. After all, when one considers the total anonymity of slavery, one would find oneself hard put, I think, to become any slave: I happened to be able to turn myself into this almost unique slave, one of the few slaves in history who achieved an identity. That was for me a very important factor in writing this book. Of course, when I make that statement, I am talking about American history. That is, the number of slaves whom we can remember can be counted on the fingers of one hand, and Nat Turner happens to be one of them.

Lewis: I'd like to return to this process of meditation, of self-inquiry, by Nat Turner in which you participate. The very structure of the book fascinates me because of this: it reminds me of what Joseph Heller said about Faulkner's *Absalom, Absalom!* (with which I think this book has something in common). He said it had a haunting structure, and I think this book does too, since it begins in and always returns to the jail, to Nat at that moment before death, meditating on the development of his plan, his hatred, and also on the failure of the rebellion. He is meditating a failure, isn't he?

Styron: Yes, I think he is. This is part of his anguish. That anguish over his failure to have achieved anything in the rebellion is more or less connected to his failure to make contact with God, who ordered his life and with whom he carried on a very close relationship.

Lewis: The religious element is consistently strong as well as the biblical element.

Styron: Well, it had to be. The few people who have ever mentioned Nat Turner in the past (there was a play made of Nat Turner's life back in the '40's or early '50's; there have been other accounts, such as Herbert Aptheker's) tend to view Nat Turner as a sort of proto-Marxist.

Lewis: That is another view of history.

Styron: Another view of history, of course. I believe that he had a very strong sense of social betrayal, but that far more predominating in his personality was a deep, abiding sense of religious fanaticism. His motivation came straight out of the Old Testament.

Woodward: I am interested that you say that about the Old Testament. On the surface of the story, he conforms to a kind of Christ-figure. Consider his age, his trade as a carpenter, his march on Jerusalem, his martyrdom. And yet, rightly, I think, you did not make anything of that: he is not a Christ-figure. He is rightly an Old Testament figure.

Styron: He was an avenging Old Testament angel, and naturally, as I wrote, the parallels that you speak of became quite clear to me. I intentionally avoided mention of Christ as much as I could throughout the book. He is almost never mentioned. That is because, if the book does have a redemptive quality, it appears only at the very end, and there can be interpreted in several ways. I really saw Nat as a man profoundly motivated by the empathy he feels with the old prophets, Ezekiel, Jeremiah, Isaiah.

Lewis: To some extent, I take it, the Book of Revelation too. There is a good deal of Apocalyptic imagery, isn't there?

Styron: Yes. This is my own invention, of course, but I think it would have appealed to Nat's mind, this kind of crazy, entangled mind, because I think that certainly the author of the Book of Revelation was a man similarly tormented, perhaps even insane.

Lewis: Well, perhaps that is true, as the totality of the mission to exterminate all the white people in the country (and perhaps everywhere) became evident.

Styron: I think that he did intend certainly to kill everybody on the way. There is a book I might mention as the only other reference. It is by a man named William S. Drewry: *The Southampton Insurrection*.

It was published seventy years after the event, in 1900. Drewry has all sorts of interesting theories. They *are* theories, however, and one sometimes takes them with a grain of salt. He theorized that Nat, once he had captured Jerusalem, might then have lessened the totality of his fury and become more civilized in his approach toward warfare. My own theory is that a man who was as gifted and intelligent as Nat, would have realized that this scorched-earth policy, this total war, total destruction, total annihilation, would have been the only effective way to seize a prize and to gain momentum. To a slave, so ill-equipped, total death, total murder, would have been the only logical course.

Woodward: I think he steeled himself to this act with adamant hatred. However, as you picture him, when he came down to the act, he could not go through with it. He killed only once, and that came late in the course of events. I have wondered about your theory of his motivation there, toward the people he thought he had to kill. You quote him as saying his greatest resentment was for those whites who had victimized him by their friendliness or their beneficence or their good will. Yet, his reaction was to kill them.

Styron: That is right. I do not know if this was true. This was part of my insight as a novelist rather than anything in the facts of the matter, because the original confessions of Nat are sketchy and one has to read between the lines constantly. I do feel, for instance, that it was quite clear to me that he was unable to kill. In his confession, he says more than once, that the sword glanced off his head or that the sword was dull and he could not kill. Now, this seems to me to be patently an evasion. He does eventually kill one person, an eighteen-year-old girl, named Margaret Whitehead.

I had to plunge into some sort of psychological state in order to achieve the kind of insight I did. I hope it has some accuracy.

Lewis: Well, is it a fact that he killed only one person?

Styron: It is a fact that Margaret Whitehead was the only person. The Whiteheads, it is clear from Drewry's book, were prosperous people; they lived very close to the farm where Nat was a slave. They were among the more prosperous and better educated people in that region. All these things began to build a certain architecture in my mind, and it occurred to me that since Nat killed no one else, and he killed this beautiful girl, considered one of the belles of the county, the psychological truth was that Nat did not hate her. He loved her, or at least he had a passion for her.

Lewis: He desired her.

Styron: He desired her; he wanted her. She represented to him all sorts of unnamable things. I believe this must have been true. I cannot prove it. I think that if there is any psychological truth in these insights, it partially lies in the fact that one often wishes to destroy what one most earnestly desires.

Lewis: Right.

Woodward: Can we go back to youth and childhood for a moment? In picturing Samuel Turner and his household, did you not have in mind as a model a figure of Virginia history?

Styron: Yes, General John Hart Wilcock. Just by the sheerest chance I read a doctoral dissertation on his life at a time when I was trying to figure out what to do with Nat's boyhood. I had written the first part—Nat's brooding over the revolt in jail—and I came to a dead halt. Almost miraculously, a friend put me onto this amazing doctoral dissertation. It describes a man who was a Virginian landowner, an exact contemporary of Nat Turner's, who despised and loathed slavery with such a passion that it was his daily torment. For me, he was a perfect prototype for Nat Turner's master, and without drawing too heavily on Wilcock, I cast him in the role of Samuel Turner.

Lewis: Did Nat, do you think, never have the sense of being owned? At one point he says he was half deranged at the thought of being owned, and especially owned twice, but that did not come until he was about twenty? In other words, until then, he was a mature, rather educated, intelligent person who had in relative terms, a rather pleasant life.

Styron: I think that is a large part of it. I think that what I tried to betray was the fact that under certain auspices, slavery could be at least a tolerable way of life. I was never trying to argue, naturally, in favor of slavery. I went from the assumption that it was an abomination, but that, given decency on the part of a solicitous master, and given an intelligent and impressionable young Negro like Nat, life was and could have been, as I portrayed it, tolerable. Even more than tolerable.

Yet, insecurity that one lived in during slave times was such that I think Nat snapped into a kind of obsessive fanaticism. Unlike the rest of us, who at the age of twenty one, might suffer trauma, Nat, when he was sold at the age of twenty one, suffered a trauma from which he could not recover. The event was so cataclysmic, so total and so enduring that he could not find the hope that non-slaves might have found at that time in life.

Lewis: Well, I remember that very interesting and moving meditation, the beginning of the third part of the novel, on the relative rarity of pure hatred: he says calm and intelligent hatred is relatively rare. Isn't that what you are saying?

Styron: I think I was trying to say something I believe to be true: that the Negro slave of antebellum years in the South, who was without any contact with white people, was so far down a psychological scale that he could hardly hate in this calm, intelligent way Nat describes. For one thing, I do not think the intelligence of the average Negro who lived in a shack at the edge of a big tobacco or cotton plantation had come to full flower. He had been reduced to the level of an animal, quite consciously so. This sophisticated hatred, I think, must have arisen among Negroes who had been in contact with white people, especially among those who had, like Nat Turner, gained education. The more respect he received from white people, the more he had a desire to cut their throats.

Lewis: Is there an inevitable contradiction here, namely, that the kind of person who had the capacity to organize rebellion, would also have a sensibility which would forbid his carrying it through?

Styron: I think that it is quite apparent that he was a man who had very little taste for blood. I think (again, I am improvising on the actual record) that it is quite clear to me that when faced with the actuality of the blood and exposed intestines. . . .

Lewis: He vomited. . . .

Styron: Yes, he got sick. This is a perfectly good human reaction. It is quite clear to me that historically, the failure of his own leadership was what helped undermine the rebellion.

Lewis: He says at the end, doesn't he, that he would do it all over again, except he would spare Margaret Whitehead. In other words, he would not kill another time.

Styron: I guess so, if you want to look at that little paradox that way. I did not intend it to mean quite that; by the time of the ultimate

moment of his own death, he had come around to a guarded understanding of the quality of Christian redemption, whether he accepted
it or not.

Lewis: Well, it was a unique combination of circumstances and
qualities, and I think that it is a unique novel.

Woodward: I quite agree. I think that this is the most profound
treatment we have had of this very important phase of American
life—slavery—in our literature. Of the many treatments of slavery in
American writing, this is the only one I know which tells the story
from the slave's point of view. Very few novels have dealt with slave
rebellion: the only one I know is Melville's *Benito Cereno,* and that,
of course, is a white man's view.

Styron: Well, I thank you.

Announcer: William Styron, discussing his novel *The Confessions
of Nat Turner* with C. Van Woodward, Sterling Professor of History at
Yale, and Richard W. B. Lewis, Professor of English and American
Studies.

William Styron on
The Confessions of Nat Turner:
A *Yale Lit* Interview

Douglas Barzelay and Robert Sussman / 1968

From *Yale Literary Magazine*, 137 (Fall 1968), 24–35. Reprinted by permission.

In the midst of the defacto cultural country club that is Vineyard Haven, William Styron settles down to his second Bloody Mary, made with lemons sent him every year by his college roommate, Florida's Governor Claude Kirk. His lack of authorial reticence about the *Nat Turner* controversy is surprising; he seems, at times, possessed by a guarded yet almost compulsive desire to purge himself of a residual bitterness towards his attackers. Styron is not a racist, not even an unconscious one. What he is, consciously, is a liberal caught in an intensified, perhaps paradigmatic version of the dilemmas which beset the contemporary white intellectual: how to help the black man without condescension; how to balance the demands of black power with an intellectual and visceral commitment to integration; how to communicate with those blacks who condemn him as a "devil"—as integral a cog in the racist monolith as the most unreconstructed Southern bigot.

Relaxing, Styron recalls his friendship with James Baldwin, who wrote *Another Country* at the Styron home in Roxbury, Connecticut—a relationship which perhaps catalyzed Styron's attempt to project his own consciousness—he does not minimize his WASP, Tidewater Virginia heritage—into that of a black man.

The resultant hostile reaction of the black community startled him: for a long time he has been unsure of how to respond to it. Yet there is a proud, perhaps even haughty side to Styron—indeed, one suspects, the capacity to be obdurate which now expresses itself in a sarcastic contemptuousness for the stupidity of those he feels should know better. He speaks—now with measured contempt, now with a burst of incredulity—of those critics who he feels have not attempted to understand the book, or who have distorted the historical record. His confidence in his own historical scholarship is apparent as he cites planta- tion records and abolitionist accounts in support of the contention that the real perniciousness of slavery lay in the very fact that it was not physically brutal—that in subtly manipulating the relative comfort of the slave, the master was able to induce more psychological debilitation than he could have commanded with a whip.

Yet Styron's serious interest in history and his flirtation with political activism (he was a member of the challeng- ing McCarthy delegation from Connecticut) are both completely subordinated to his dedication to his craft. A notoriously slow, meticulous writer, he does not force his inspiration. *Set This House on Fire,* his third novel, took five years to write; *The Confessions of Nat Turner* has been germinating since childhood. He regrets the con- troversy which presently surrounds it; he is an active man now forced to wait: to wait for an obfuscating controversy to ebb; to wait for the inspiration that may well lead him in an altogether new aesthetic direction.

It was a crisp, clear September day when we inter- viewed Styron. To those who know the Vineyard well— and whose wealth or profession allows them to stay beyond Labor Day—the unnatural calm made this the most perfect time of year.

                                          Douglas Barzelay

Yale Lit: In the introduction to *The Confessions of Nat Turner,* you refer to the novel as a "meditation on history." Does this term define a genre which is different both from the novel that attempts to reflect a specific historical era and, on the other hand, from a novel with no historical context at all?

Styron: I've found that the phrase "meditation on history" has buffaloed quite a few people, and I've never really been able to figure out just what I meant by it. I wanted to take the curse of the historical novel off of the *Confessions*—the curse of the historical novel as romance—and to give it a profounder implication. Using the first person, as I did, allowed me to use the word "meditation" as a descriptive noun. Certainly the first person is an important component of the word "meditation."

Yale Lit: What do you mean by the "curse of the historical novel."

Styron: Perhaps it's a personal tic, but the phrase "historical novel" implies a disreputable occupation—in this country especially. You think of Frances Parkinson Keyes or F. Vanwyck Mason or any of those other practitioners of meretricious romances. I think the historical romance in this country—I don't think anywhere else—has had a bad odor. I wince when I see "Mr. Styron's historical novel." But I should add, however, that I think it is possible for a historical novel, in the best sense of the phrase, to be a great vehicle to transmit all of the things a work of art should: information, emotion, imagination. The historical novel just hasn't been used in this way in this country—with a few exceptions, however. I think of Faulkner at one or two points; I think of Robert Penn Warren. But there are not many reputable writers who have used historical fiction. What I wanted to do in the *Confessions* was to peel off the old connotation and use another description. That's why I called it a "meditation."

Yale Lit: Both Faulkner and Warren have used the historical novel not only to make a statement about an era, but also to make a statement about history and about the processes of history. Does *The Confessions of Nat Turner* make such a statement?

Styron: Yes. Among other things, I was quite specifically trying to transmit, perhaps for the first time, through my own understanding of history and of the era, a consciousness of that time. If there was any feeling of the necessity of the book for me—aside from the art involved—it was to transmit a *sense* of history for our time.

Yale Lit: Given this definition of the purposes of the historical novel, should the story of Nat Turner be viewed simply as the reflection of an historical incident or as a work of metaphorical and allegorical significance?

Styron: Ideally, if the book has succeeded, it should contain elements of both. That is, it should faithfully transmit a sense of the era and also achieve an entirely different, separate sense of the allegorical. I was pleased to note that one critic pointed out that the book is a religious allegory; it is a story of man's quest for faith and certitude in a pandemonious world, symbolized by bondage, oppression and so on. I think, as time goes on, the book will be examined more in this light than as a strict rendition of the history of slavery in this country. In every time, every era we live in, people seek intellectually in books for different things. Obviously, the thing that is closest to us at this moment is the agony of the race problem. So therefore, quite clearly, the book has seized on people's imaginations for that reason. But your question does bring up this other dimension of the book, which is its viability and its meaning as a religious allegory. I think it has to be looked at in that way.

Yale Lit: Perhaps that is as potent an answer to the black critics as you could have; that there is a great dimension of Nat which does transcend race. In that sense, do you think that your Nat is representative of much more than a Negro caught in a particular historical predicament?

Styron: Yes, and I think that's an extremely intelligent approach. Almost no one, in the hysteria and controversy surrounding the book, has even thought to regard it as something else, something besides a political explanation for contemporary problems cast in an historical mode. For instance, among other things, the book is a kind of symbolic representation of the conflict between the vengeance and bloodshed of the Old Testament and the redemption, the sense of peace and renewal, of the New Testament. Anybody who finishes the book, I think, will have to see that. Very few people have brought this up—with one exception, the Dean of the Duke University Chapel. He delivered a few sermons on the book, and, quite accurately, saw the book as a religious problem rather than a racial problem. I don't think any book is of perennial value unless it does contain these other reverberations. If the *Confessions* was purely a book which made an impact because of its apprehension of an era, an historical complex, then—as expert as that apprehension might be—it would not contain those overtones it does have. I don't think art works in this way, however, and this is why it is perfectly accurate and probing to suggest that something else is in the book which people have generally overlooked and which gives it its disturbing implications.

Yale Lit: Along this line, you have referred to Nat Turner as a particularly American type of hero—more or less a-racial. Could you expand on that?

Styron: Nat is a man who could not have existed anywhere outside of America, even if he were white. His problems are truly American; even his sexual hangups and difficulties are American in
outline. . . .

Yale Lit: In what sense?

Styron: In the sense that there is a residual Puritanism, a conflict-
ing Calvinistic sort of frustration, which are part of him because he is
what he is, but also because he is the product of an era in American
history. I would also say that his idiom is American, as well as the way
he reflects a peculiarly frontier sort of experience. I don't like to use
analogies to another writer, but some people have remarked that
some parts of the book remind them of Mark Twain. I think this might
be true. Certainly I didn't try consciously to refract a Mark Twain
atmosphere, but nonetheless, I was writing about the same era which
is Mark Twain's greatest stock-in-trade; it's set in almost the exact
same decade. The book could hardly avoid having that peculiarly
American frontier flavor. To those various extents, I feel the book is
American in nature.

Yale Lit: Returning to the religious issue, do you feel that one of
the reasons it has been overlooked is that religious questions seem to
have retreated from the center stage of American intellectual thought,
and that politics, including the racial question, have taken up that
void?

Styron: I think that that's perhaps a good explanation why the
religious aspect of the book has not been picked up and played
upon. Let's project a moment. The book conceivably could have
been written twenty years ago, given certain factors. After all, it's a
book I could have written if I'd been older then, using the same
material and having the same mind. But let us say that it was written
in 1948, before the civil rights movement started, before the anguish
and the wrench of contemporary events caught us up. I would suggest that critics reading the book then would have said: "This amazing book about a man in religious torment reminds us of echoes of
T. S. Eliot," and is only peripherally about race, and so on and so on.
Certainly, in '48, the religious element would have been seized upon
and emphasized.

Yale Lit: Perhaps it's possible to combine both the religious issue
and the racial issue by saying there is a peculiarly idigenous brand of
Southern Negro Christianity which has a theology all its own. Were

you conscious of the uniqueness of Southern Negro religion and did
you intend to present it as a tradition which White America can learn
something from?

Styron: If you notice from Genovese's review, he mentions that
one of the black critics, Mike Thelwell, faulted me for not having
sufficient understanding of the *purely* religious nature of the Negro in
the South—then and now. I know that I've always been enormously
moved, ever since I was a kid, by the Negro and his relationship to
his religion. Some of it's in the music. I remember, in the late thirties,
listening to a program on the radio called "Wings over Jordan." It
was a concert of spirituals—and they were *beautiful.* They tugged at
my heart; I was getting a message. Now, twenty years later, the idea
of Negro religiosity has vanished as a concept. It's something to be
despised and abhorred because it connotes literally all that Negro
militants see as the worst aspects of the Negro experience in America.

Yale Lit: It's fatalistic, isn't it?

Styron: It's fatalistic; it's masochistic even; it's a prostrate sort of
acceptance of the Negro's miserable existence, with the hope of resurrection being the only thing to give it all some meaning. And yet I
believe that this is how, up until the last few years, Negroes have
survived in this country. They've had other crucial experiences, but
for the Southern Negro—not the removed, transplanted, urban
Negro—religion was a profound and important component of his life
ever since slave times. Without an understanding of it—or at least an
empathy with it—I would not have been able to write this book. You
could not conceive of a Negro revolutionary in slave times in
America—this is a very important point—who was not, basically,
motivated by some earnest, fervent religious drive. This includes the
two other Negro slave leaders we know something about: Denmark
Vesey and Gabriel. They were both men who played profoundly
upon the religious instincts of their followers; this has to be understood.

Yale Lit: Didn't Malcolm X appeal to this religious side from
another angle?

Styron: Yes. His whole involvement with the Black Muslims was
an attempt to find some religious foundation for his revolutionary
impulse.

Yale Lit: His was a less passive and more Calvinistic religion than
Nat's wasn't it?

Styron: And to that extent, very revolutionary. The cleansing Puritanical side of it—its meticulously Calvinistic, if you will, aspect—is very close to the revolutionary bone. I don't know, but perhaps Malcolm X was aware of something in the Negro cultural experience which demanded a religion, even though it was quite the opposite of Christianity.

Yale Lit: In Nat Turner's case, isn't his type of Southern Negro religion profoundly anti-revolutionary? How do you get from a religion built on passivity and suffering and a retreat from external reality to a religion which implies political activism?

Styron: Possibly you can only do it if you're a religious fanatic like Nat Turner—who, I believe, must have had an enormous, innate revolutionary streak in him, a streak of profound, very complex rebelliousness which he had to articulate through this religious rationale without which he could not have operated. After all, any revolutionary—I don't care who he is—is going to peg his program on something that is presumably going to make an appeal to the people who are following him. It would have been very difficult for Nat Turner to have simply said: "Gentleman, this is a social evil we are existing under," and to spout a few pre-Marxist maxims about the whole difficulty. This is why I presumed—there's no one who really knows so I had to imagine—that he said to his followers: "I had a vision; God told me and you must believe it, because you believe in me."

Yale Lit: Is there perhaps any parallel between the relation of Nat to his followers and the more contemporary relation of the late Martin Luther King to his followers? Were they not both revolutionaries whose appeals were grounded in the religious foundation of Negro culture?

Styron: I don't think I ever consciously thought of King, although he would have been part of my over-consciousness. There is a continuity involving Nat Turner and Martin Luther King.

Yale Lit: Do you think that in criticizing the *Confessions*—in indirectly criticizing the traditional religion of Nat—the black critics might be denying the very past which they seek to revere, at least theoretically?

Styron: Yes. This is a very complicated, two-way sort of problem. Jimmy Baldwin has tried to probe this thing. It's as if the black militants were saying, "We must find *our* history." But, faced with that history, they are going to find that it is largely based on this thing they despise: a reliance on what Jimmy has called "the white man's religion." He says—I'm paraphrasing him, of course— "the white man made us kneel at his cross." To some extent this was true, although it was never so simple as that in slave times. There were certain minor areas of slavery in which there was probably very little religious activity at all, depending upon the whim of the master. But, by and large, most masters, because of the time, *were,* if not religious, at least oriented toward religion. Therefore Christianity became an important heart of Negro life. And, in fact, once it got started, it became endemic. Surely Marx was right when he talked about religion as the "opiate of the people," because for the Southern Negro it became a *real* opiate. It *had* to be; it was the only way of life for Negroes which made the *other* way of life, the intolerable burden of working in the fields, bearable.

Yale Lit: Isn't there a special irony, then, in what the black intellectuals want to do with Nat Turner? They want to create a myth around him and make him a heroic piece of the past they can look to, and yet he is so fundamentally caught up with this very idea of religion—the white man's religion—that they're trying to deny.

Styron: Yes. Nat would be the paradigm, in a curious way, of this hopeless problem. For instance, when you read Herbert Aptheker, of whom my black critics are disciples, on Nat Turner, he absolutely minimizes the religious aspect of the man's career; being an old-line doctrinaire Marxist, he would have to. His is a nice, skillful piece of distortion, I might add—which he, of course, accuses me of indulging in. But it is true that the militants are faced with a problem here. They are asking black people to regard their past with understanding, but what they're going to get, if they're looking for *surface* heroes, is too often somebody like Nat Turner, who is a religious fanatic on the *surface*—a complete nut like some crazed Harlem preacher—and a primitive visionary. The facts tell us this: that if you examine the testimony, the original *Confessions,* any intelligent person is going to be appalled by his vision of a heroic figure, because he's not very heroic looking at all. He looks like a *nut* who gathers together several followers, plows through a county one evening, admittedly without even having devised a plan, and kills fifty-some white people, most of whom are helpless children. *Big deal!* Fine hero. And this is what is so *ridiculous* at base in this attack on my book.

Yale Lit: It seems that the militants' standards of heroism are considerably different from yours. What needs are they serving in demanding Nat Turner to be a black Achilles, a hero whose strengths, it would seem, are largely physical and sexual rather than spiritual and moral?

Styron: I don't know what needs they have in mind. Putting that aside, I would only say that their demand for it, for this kind of primitive, archetypal hero, is very naive and unsophisticated. It's intellectually indefensible; it's so completely lacking in what we consider the accoutrements of the intellectual process. It's a childish, infantile yearning for something that didn't exist. It's what Christopher Lasch has called "neo-socialist realism," it's on the level of the *New Masses* in 1930 demanding that writers who didn't write about brave factory workers were not fulfilling their artistic function, and claiming that a writer who, like Faulkner, wrote about monsters and creeps in the South, was simply abdicating his artistic responsibility.

Yale Lit: Isn't the issue simply this: they want a social myth, a political tract, a call to action, and this is totally at odds with what writing a novel, a work of fiction, is all about?

Styron: Of course. That's basically what the problem boils down to. I'm quite amazed that it should have been taken so seriously. After the smoke clears, I think it's going to be regarded as a very simple controversy dealing with outdated principles of Marxist social realism.

Yale Lit: Artistic considerations aside, you don't think that this type of mythologizing can serve a healthy popular cause or a healthy political cause?

Styron: No, because I think it's a balloon; I think that it's embarrassing. I was up at Harvard a while ago for a colloquium on the *Confessions* and there were some black militants in the audience— quite a few. The kind of abusive questions that they threw my way simply made everybody wince. You could see a visible wave of embarrassment go over the crowd, who, one felt, were sympathetic to the Negro cause, probably even to black militancy, and therefore were all the more embarassed when one of these kids would get up and say: "How come you made Nat Turner a *homosexual rapist?*" This is the kind of question which is so ludicrous it's beyond answer. I noticed out of the corner of my eye this shudder of embarrassment going over the white students who, one felt, were saying to themselves: "How can they reveal themselves like this?" It is a question like that of the black student that *does* make you feel that these people are after some impossible symbolic representation and are, concomitantly, unwilling or unable—I don't know which—to plunge into the complexity of a character like the Nat Turner that I created.

Yale Lit: Is it possible to have a Negro art which is at once aesthetically valid and, at the same time, does serve some healthy political or social need?

Styron: I don't think that the sort of art which is being *demanded* by the black militants will ever serve any kind of purpose—because it's not art; it's propaganda. It's been proved over the years that it might serve to make the heart beat quicker or stronger in the sense that a corny anthem does, but that it serves no intellectual or profounder purpose to hold up to view "heroes" who are really plaster saints.

Yale Lit: Can art serve both purposes, especially in this particular case?

Styron: I doubt it. I think the drive here is toward action, toward immediate revolution, and a book like mine is showing a person too complex ever to be a proper model for revolt. It's showing a man who's irresolute, and who is, to be sure, a man filled with weaknesses, self-doubts. A book like *The Confessions of Nat Turner* isn't going to serve—indeed isn't meant to serve—the purposes of revolution.

Yale Lit: Do you think that this revolutionary purpose, the creation of heroes—taken apart from the attempt to force it into a literary context—is something that is valid and necessary for the black man in America today?

Styron: I think that the anguish which has been created by my book is largely due to the fact that I'm a white man and I wrote the book. In your question, for instance, you just emphasized the word "black," unconsciously. You're talking about *black* revolution, *Negro* revolution. Here I am a white man, from middle class Southern origins, and *I* wrote the book!

Yale Lit: In this regard, do you think that your approach toward race is substantially different from that taken by Negroes like Baldwin and Ellison? Do you think that there is a white viewpoint toward racial questions which is not necessarily racist but which is different from the Negro viewpoint?

Styron: I don't think it should be. I don't think that kind of artistic separatism is valid if you're going to use the word "art" to qualify it. I would like to believe—I'm being simple-minded perhaps—that a Negro should be able to come along and write a fantastic novel about Andrew Jackson—maybe even a very funny novel—filled with all the parodoxes. When these people were accosting me up at Harvard, I said to them: "Why are you getting on me? I haven't done all that much; it hasn't been all that enormous. If you want to retaliate, as you seem to, why don't you write a book exposing Abraham Lincoln as a racist, which he was to some extent. But write a good novel. I'm not going to serve as a scapegoat for your own frustrations, your own inability presumably to do such a thing."

Yale Lit: You have mentioned in an article that, in *The Sound and the Fury,* Faulkner chooses to look at Dilsey in the third person, while he looks at all the white characters in the first person. Why, in *The Confessions of Nat Turner,* did you choose to write about Nat in the first person, and what problems of idiom and style did you face?

Styron: That was an almost purely artistic option. It had to do with the fact that I believe the first person to be a peculiarly 1960's form of address. More and more writing is becoming first person today, because of something in the air, some psychic need for writers to address themselves in this very personal style. The second thing was that—at last, as a white man—I wanted to risk leaping into a black man's consciousness. Not only did I want the risk alone—which was an important thing, to see if it could be done—but, by doing so, I thought I could get a closer awareness of the smell of slavery. For some reason, to register, to filter through the consciousness of the "I", the first person, is often a very powerful way of getting at immediate experience.

Yale Lit: To what extent do you feel *The Confessions of Nat Turner* is a continuation of the works of such Negro writers as Ellison, Baldwin and, to go back even farther, of Wright?

Styron: I think the *Confessions* is just a continuation of a tradition which we're going to find more and more of. An important strand of American literature is based on a consciousness of this division in our culture, this racial division. Melville had it; Mark Twain had it; Faulkner certainly had it; Sherwood Anderson had it; and Richard Wright had it. To some extent, it's been a large, important stream in the Mississippi River of our literature. I think that my book will have its place as part of this consciousness that we all share, black and white. Ralph Ellison's next novel, which has been a long time in preparation, shows a daring boldness on his part to penetrate into the white consciousness. Without such efforts, I visualize an America where we will not be able to exist unless we exist together. I fully believe this; I don't believe we can exist apart. The awareness of this, I think, will only come through literature which allows both black and white to courageously venture into each other's consciousness. I think its a denial of humanity, of our mutual humanity, to assume that it is pretentious and arrogant and wrong for a white man to attempt to get into a black man's skin.

Yale Lit: James Baldwin has been conspicuous among black intellectuals in endorsing your book. To what extent did this threaten his standing within the black community?

Styron: Jimmy does have a very enormous, crucial problem; how to be a spokesman for the strong impulse in his own race toward the truly good aspects of black power—that black power which has vocally put me down in the person of Stokely Carmichael and Rap Brown, who've all made public statements against Nat Turner, *my* Nat Turner. It's an enormous problem to wish to support these people and also to give support to me. I think, though, as this controversy wears off, that more and more black people are going to say, "Oh, come off it; don't be so childish. Read the book, it doesn't put us down. Don't be upset because it's written by a white man."

Yale Lit: There has been a great deal of talk about a tradition of Southern writing. Do you consider yourself related to it?

Styron: That goes without saying, really. I don't feel myself committed to the Southern tradition in the dogged and unregenerate way my predecessors have, largely because the South has changed. I don't feel any commitment toward living in the South; although I'm from Tidewater Virginia and feel Southern, I don't feel so Southern that I'm not able to move rather easily out of the tradition. But, on the other hand, I feel a definite attachment to the South; I feel that I know the South and that I'm of the last generation that can know the South as we traditionally know it.

Yale Lit: Southern writing has been defined by its elaborate rhetorical texture, its lushness and sensitivity to the natural landscape, and, above all, its sensitivity to the idioms of Southern speech. Is there anything more in the way of a viewpoint which can be identified?

Styron: I would say that it also has to do with a sense of tradition, of ancestry, of family, a sense of such matters as the importance of the Civil War to the history of the South, and the sense of literature as a continuous, continuing fountain. I don't mean to say that all Southerners are rabid readers; I mean to imply rather the idea of a respect for prose, a respect for literature as it is fed from the Bible—especially the old King James version—as a kind of cornerstone for the Southern ethos.

Yale Lit: Does the Negro have a unique place within the Southern writing tradition?

Styron: He's often been just a comic embodiment. Uncle Remus is certainly a very good example of this personification at the beginning evolution of the Negro in the South. Joel Chandler Harris certainly was not ridiculing Uncle Remus—he had a great respect for him—but that would be one of the earliest embodiments of the Negro in Southern literature. And certainly Faulkner should be mentioned. His Negroes are powerfully seen, beautifully realized. But as I said earlier, if I did do anything original in *Nat Turner* it was to, for the first time so far as I know, plunge a white consciousness into a black incarnation.

Yale Lit: John Hersey's new book, *The Algiers Motel,* was criticized in the *New York Times* for overemphasizing sex as a mainspring of racial prejudice and hostility: some of these same criticisms have been levelled at *The Confessions of Nat Turner.* How central, especially in the South, do you feel sex is to racial conflict?

Styron: I've said in print that I feel it's in many ways overemphasized. It entirely depends upon the context. I think that in the urban South, in recent years—and at present—there has been such a separation of the races that this factor has not been very important.

Yale Lit: How about in the South of plantation days?

Styron: I would say that the closer you get to an earthy proximity, the closer you get to a sexual tension. During slave times the tension must have been constant and enormous because of the structure of the system. And we know enough by now of the admixture of white blood into black blood to know that indeed there was a lot of "action" going on. But I think as the South became urbanized this tended to diminish in urban areas and even in relatively small towns as a polarization took effect.

Yale Lit: More specifically, was it important to Nat Turner's role that his sex life be atypical—or do you regard his sexual tensions and conflicts as typical for a Negro in that setting?

Styron: It occurred to me—when I did any abstract thinking about Nat—that he must be a man of enormous frustration. Given the evidence that he didn't have a wife, this indicated some kind of singleminded, perhaps puritanical revolutionary drive which precluded the idea of fecund sexuality. After all, that kind of asceticism is a common component of the revolutionary temper. I believe—I'm not sure, not being ascetic myself—that ascetics must have fantasies and fantastic, probably unspeakable drives and hangups and desires, and these I felt it was necessary to give to Nat in order to fill out his characterization.

Yale Lit: What is your response to the charge that you distorted the historical record in failing to include any mention of Nat's wife?

Styron: Gene Genovese is absolutely right when he puts down this myth about Nat's wife—that's one of the most idiotic of the criticisms. There's a fanatic named Howard Myer—obviously one of these Aptheker-oriented people, who wrote a book about Thomas Wentworth Higginson, an abolitionist Yankee who led a regiment of black soldiers during the Civil War. Myer quotes Higginson as saying—this is in 1860—that Nat Turner had a wife. Total hearsay. Myer propagated this notion and it somehow gained currency. It shows you how willing those people were to take hearsay as evidence. There *is* in the original *Confessions* a reference to his grandparents, whom of course I did leave out; I changed that around simply to suit myself, and I offer no apology for it at all. It doesn't need apology. But as Genovese said, how incredible that he would mention his parents and his grandparents and not mention his wife. And then to accuse me of falsifying by adhering to the original testimony, and to ask me to accept this hearsay evidence of thirty years later, is just appalling beyond belief. It's so shoddy. And I might add, again in parentheses, a wife was a meaningless thing in those days; it could mean that you had a wife if you had a master who believed that matrimony was a sacred thing; it could mean that you just had a woman—who you just had and vanished—so the whole thing is problematic.

Yale Lit: Would you say, then, that Nat's somewhat pathological sexual behavior is representative more of a revolutionary personality than of a peculiar racial tension?

Styron: That's distinctly what my meaning was. I was very amused in that attack on the book by Richard Gilman where he joined the black philistines so unconsciously by making that remarkable statement that, "There is no evidence that Nat was troubled by sexual desire," which is tantamount to saying the man wasn't human. You can't reply to criticism like that.

Yale Lit: Don't you think that recently the trend in the American novel has been reversing itself in the direction of political and social polemic?

Styron: I think when it does that it's unfortunate, but I think the swing away from too much interior, private, Virginia Woolf-type writing—the novel of sensibility—has been healthy. It doesn't matter so long as a good novel emerges out of any significant social struggle. More often than not, though, they're going to be bad.

Yale Lit: You will be teaching creative writing at Yale spring semester. How do you visualize the role of a teacher of creative writing: what can he do, what can't he do, and, above all, what about the craft of writing can be taught?

Styron: Very little, I think. You can offer students a sounding board for each other, and a kind of inspiration, if that doesn't sound too fancy—a sense of caring, a sense of involvement, a guidance. I think that somebody who's older, who has been in the game longer, is able to suggest certain ways things are written, comprised—to point out obvious error in judgment, error in assessment, and so on. It's a sort of guidance; I don't think anything can be taught. The ability to encourage a writer who has talent, to show him where his strengths are, to have him concentrate on those strengths; to show him where his weaknesses are, to try to perhaps guide him so he will eliminate those weaknesses: that's about it.

Yale Lit: Do you think that in this age, a rather self-conscious literary criticism is impinging on the craft of spontaneous writing?

Styron: I don't think the two are incompatible, but I myself just never bother about criticism. It's a valuable adjunct to literature, I suppose, but I think its regrettable that a lot of obviously honest critics conceive of it as being more important than creative writing.

But most of it gets shovelled down the drain eventually. Obviously you can't damn criticism off hand, because it does have its value. But there are almost no critics of my generation that are particularly good. And basically it's something that doesn't concern me. I just stick close to my last, and try to write.

Yale Lit: In that connection, what sort of things are you working on now?

Styron: I'm trying to crank up a short novel but I'll probably do something on my trip to Tashkent first, for the *New York Review of Books*. I'm quite undecided at the moment. I don't feel any great pressure to write, like some people. The well runs dry, and I just wait for it to fill up—before just needlessly turning out something which doesn't move me and is therefore likely to be empty.

Yale Lit: You've said in conversation that you'd be very interested to see the interaction between Mr. Genovese in his Yale course on black history and the black militants at Yale. What do you feel the prospects are, at least at this moment in history, for creating a meaingful dialogue rather than a confrontation between black and white intellectuals?

Styron: I think that they're going to be very slim unless black people take hold of themselves and start using reason instead of irrational and childish logic. If they cannot, for instance, read a review like Genovese's in the *New York Review* and see the passionate appeal to reason in it, then they're going to be lost. They're going to remain, regrettably—I hate to say it—they're going to remain what white racists have always called them: children. And perhaps some of their distraught reaction is logical in terms of history, but the quicker they take hold of themselves and get out of it, the better it's going to be. And I'm very soon going to get impatient enough that I'm not even going to say that I'm sympathetic with the historical logic behind the position. Other people have been victimized and put upon and they have survived to pull themselves out of their predicament without resorting to this infantile behavior.

Portrait of a Man Reading

Charles Monaghan / 1968

From *Chicago Tribune Book World,* 27 October 1968, p. 8. Reprinted by permission.

Interviewer: What books do you recall from your childhood?

Styron: I loved the Oz books. I adored them. And I had a unique experience with them. One of my young friends was the nephew of L. Frank Baum. I used to read his copies of the Oz books and they all were inscribed "To Bobby, from Uncle Frank." I should have stolen them. I remember reading about Christopher Robin. And then there were things that weren't strictly children's books but that I was precocious enough to read—the Hornblower books, for instance.

Interviewer: Did any of your childhood reading leave a permanent mark?

Styron: Those books conveyed a magic that you never lose. They plunge you into the reading experience. The Tarzan books I devoured. And one of my favorites was *Mr. Midshipman Easy* by Marryat. In fact, most anything at that time that had to do with the sea interested me because I was brought up by the sea in Tidewater Virginia. I loved *Robinson Crusoe,* for example.

Interviewer: How about high school reading?

Styron: High school was a dropout period for me. I went to public high school and in those days public high school in Virginia wasn't very much. There were forty-eight states and I think we ranked forty-ninth behind Puerto Rico. You know, down there on the list with Arkansas and Mississippi. Mostly I just raised hell and read potboilers. I got hooked on mysteries and read a lot of Agatha Christie and S. S. Van Dine. Oh, I must add the name of Mark Twain. He's a great favorite of mine. I think I must have first read *Huck Finn* just before I entered high school, when I was about thirteen. That's the only book I've read almost perennially. I've read it every two or three years since then.

Interviewer: Do you still read mysteries?

Styron: No, I've pretty much lost the mystery bug.

Interviewer: How about your reading in college?

Styron: The first college I went to was Davidson in North Carolina. I didn't get much there either. It was wartime so I went into a V-12 program and was transferred to Duke. This is about 1942–43. That's where I really started to read. I had the good fortune to take courses with William Blackburn, one of the great American teachers. Where he really got to us as students was in his courses on Elizabethan drama and Elizabethan poetry. He infused all the magic and grandeur of the period into your bloodstream. Spenser, Shakespeare, Marlowe, Ben Jonson, John Donne. That's where I was led into the world of literature. And outside my courses, I was reading omnivorously. I read the whole body of Thomas Wolfe's writing in about two weeks. I nearly went blind.

Interviewer: What do you think of Thomas Wolfe today?

Styron: Over all, I find him disappointing. There is a great deal of the adolescent in him that doesn't appeal to mature people. But he has some marvelous set pieces, so you can't completely discount him.

Interviewer: Who else were you reading during your college years?

Styron: Fitzgerald, Hemingway, Huxley, Orwell. I didn't come to Faulkner until a little later, when I was twenty-two or twenty-three. I was paralyzed with awe by Faulkner. For my money, he remains the great figure of the era just preceding this one. About the same time I came to modern poetry. I read Eliot and was overwhelmed by him. Auden, Yeats, Wallace Stevens grabbed me at that time. And I started reading Emily Dickinson, whom I regard as one of our truly marvelous voices.

Interviewer: How about the Southern poets, such as Allen Tate or John Crowe Ransom?

Styron: They never got at me in the same way, though several of Ransom's lyric poems are ravishing. One felt admiration for them, rather than that influential enthusiasm.

Interviewer: How about literary criticism?

Styron: Generally speaking, I wasn't enormously affected by literary criticism. I had no animosity toward it. I thought it was valuable, but I was simply more interested in the creative act. I read Lionel Trilling's *The Liberal Imagination* and admired it enormously.

Interviewer: Then you served some time in the Marines.

Styron: Yes, and then I went back to Duke and got my degree and went to New York, where I got a job as an editor in publishing, a place called Whittlesey House, which was part of McGraw-Hill. It's disbanded or absorbed now. I think about then I started writing myself, aimlessly, short stories. They showed some talent, but didn't hold together as artistic entities. I read Malcolm Lowry's *Under the Volcano* around then and was greatly impressed by it. And I was continuously reading Faulkner. I was very worried that he was going to affect my individuality as a writer. I had to leach him out of my system.

Interviewer: Was it the Southern element that attracted you in Faulkner?

Styron: That was part of it, but mostly it was his fantastic use of language. The white heat it generated. I don't subscribe to the idea that a young writer should not be influenced. I think a certain passionate admiration is valuable. Imitation even, for a time, but you do have to develop your own individuality.

Interviewer: How did you get out from the overweening influence of Faulkner?

Styron: I was also influenced by Fitzgerald, so whenever I found myself working in those heavy tones of Faulkner, I used Fitzgerald things to put on the brakes. Also Flaubert. He brought me back to the idea of discipline. It's dangerous for any American not to read Flaubert. By the time I started my first novel, *Lie Down in Darkness*—I was about twenty-four—I think I had developed a kind of individual way of looking at things.

Interviewer: After you published that, Korea came, and you were called back into the Marines. What did you read then?

Styron: Poetry mainly. Camp libraries can be pretty well stacked. Camp Lejeune had a pretty good library, for instance. And people in New York were sending me books. I started reading Greek drama— Sophocles, Aeschylus. Tragedies mostly, but I did read some Aristophanes. Along about then, I began to develop a rather slow but steady pursuit of reading the history of the ante-bellum South. It's continued ever since. I've read a little about Reconstruction. Largely, though, I've confined myself to the era from 1800 to the Civil War. It's like a little garden and you don't want anyone else there. Oddly

enough, the Civil War itself has never engaged me. Military history
leaves me cold.

Interviewer: Who do you think are the great historians of the
ante-bellum South?

Styron: Stanley Elkins, Gene Genovese, C. Vann Woodward.
They're a triumvirate.

Interviewer: What happened after you left the Marines?

Styron: I went abroad, to France and for a while to Italy. That was
'52, '53, '54. I got enough French cranked up then to read *Madame
Bovary* in the original. I read Paul Valery, but in translation. Gide was
very much in vogue then, and I think I read all of his *Journals*. Gide
has sort of gone into eclipse, but I think he'll be resurrected. He's one
of the archetypal French writers.

Interviewer: What attracts you in Gide's writing?

Styron: His whole approach to his own existence, the intensity of
his living, the ability to filter all the details of life through this absolute
self-absorption. He noticed so many details, yet his daily life was always in conflict with his existence. He's a remarkable writer.

Interviewer: After you returned to the United States?

Styron: I lived in New York for a while, then moved to Connecticut, where I still live. I started reading the Russian novel after I came
back. Dostoevsky. I've been reading him for the last fifteen years.

Interviewer: You are often associated with a certain group of New
York writers who were connected with the *Paris Review*. Did that association have any affect on your reading?

Styron: I don't think of anything specific.

Interviewer: What do you feel is the most important American
writing of the past decade?

Styron: Baldwin's essays, Mailer's better journalism. *The Naked
and the Dead* was an enormously impressive novel. Parts of *The
Deer Park* stand up. But his fiction hasn't been so good recently.
Catcher in the Rye is a gem of a book. John Cheever's short stories.
Phil Roth at his best is good. Some of his new novel that's been
published in the magazines is very funny. I'm a great admirer of *In
Cold Blood*. All that stuff about it being a new genre is just obfusca-
tion. It's very high-level journalism. I like Nelson Algren when he's at
the top of his form. *The Man with the Golden Arm* was excellent.
He's sort of faded away in recent years. William Gaddis' *The Recog-*

nitions is an infuriating book. He didn't leave anything out but what he left in is as brilliant as anything that's come along in some time.

Interviewer: What do you think of Norman Podhoretz' contention that the essay outweighs fiction in our time?

Styron: As you can see, I don't agree with it in the slightest.

Interviewer: Do you read much poetry nowadays?

Styron: My reading of modern poetry is rather sporadic. I admire the Russian poet Andrei Voznesensky. Sometimes I go back to A. E. Housman, who, curiously enough, has an enormous appeal for me. Or I'll read the poetry of Melville. Robert Penn Warren recently published a fine poem about a prison in the South. It was remarkable.

Interviewer: What are you reading now?

Styron: I'm reading Aleksandr Solzhenitsyn's *The First Circle* and a Japanese novel called *The Pornographers.* It's very funny. I feel pretty well taken care of for the moment.

The Uses of History in Fiction

Ralph Ellison, William Styron, Robert Penn Warren,
C. Vann Woodward / 6 November 1968

From the *Southern Literary Journal,* 1 (Spring 1969), 57–90.
Reprinted by permission of the *Southern Literary Journal* and
the participants.

The exchange that follows is edited from the transcription
of a panel discussion at the thirty-fourth annual meeting
of the Southern Historical Association in New Orleans,
Louisiana, at the Jung Hotel, 6 November 1968.

Woodward: In introducing novelists into the formal deliberations
of historians, I really feel no need to apologize, except perhaps to the
novelists. For if apologies are due, they should come, I think, from
the side of the historian. Historians have too long cultivated a rather
priggish, Nineteenth-Century cult of fact, a creed that borrowed its
tenets and prestige from the sciences and the heyday of their ascen-
dency. Like scientists, we said, historians stuck to the facts, preferably
to hard facts. This conception, this prestige of hard facts, derives especially from the English. It was Oscar Wilde who said that the English are always degrading Truth into Fact, and he went on to say that
when a Truth becomes a Fact, it loses all its intellectual value.

Since fiction was conceived to be, in this usage, the opposite of
fact, and since novelists dealt exclusively in fiction, historians were
inclined to be rather priggish about novelists, especially if they ventured into historical subjects. Historians have been much more eager
to claim kinship with scientists, notably social scientists. When the
social sciences turn to historical subjects, historians appear flattered
rather than offended. We were, or have been, inclined to embrace
them as cousins, to offer joint courses, to hold conferences. Our kinship is actually much closer to novelists. We are in fact siblings, historical siblings. The novel is the youngest of the literary forms—the only
one the Greeks didn't invent. It was born only in the mid-Eighteenth
Century, not long before professional historiography first saw the light

114

of day in Germany. Both sprang from a common parentage of story tellers. Both grew up together in an environment permeated with the growing historical consciousness of western man, and competed with each other to satisfy the demand for historical understanding.

In their mutual attitudes there has been a good deal of sibling rivalry—though, it is, I think, more manifest in the historians than in the novelists. Actually, I find among novelists more respect for and awareness of good history than I find among historians a proper respect for and awareness of good novels. Over the last two centuries novels have become increasingly saturated with history, and novelists have been becoming ever more deeply historically conscious.

In a sense, all novels are historical novels. They all seek to understand, to describe, to recapture the past, however remote, however recent. They might all be described by the title of Marcel Proust's great work, *Remembrance of Things Past*. In his own efforts to understand, describe, and recapture the past, the novelist uses no more specialized a vocabulary than the historian. As Isaiah Berlin has said, history employs few if any concepts or categories peculiar to itself, but broadly speaking, only those of common sense, or ordinary speech—in other words, the same speech the historian himself uses. If the historian feels free to borrow concepts and insights from the psychologist, the analyst, the sociologist, in his efforts to explain human motivation and behavior, the novelist is equally free to use the same resources in doing much the same thing.

An historian stands in no less need of imagination than the novelist; if anything he needs rather more. There are firm rules, of course, about what his discipline permits and forbids him to do with his imagination. He cannot, for example, as the novelist can, invent characters, invent motives for his characters. I certainly have no wish to relax those rules or to confuse or blur the distinction between the historian and the novelist. But over the years, as I have watched my novelist friends at their work, as I have read their books and talked with them about their problems, I have learned to appreciate more and more how much we have in common in our uses of the past, our interest in it, our demands upon it, our concerns with it.

This is, I think, especially true of Southern writers, and particularly of the three who take part in this discussion. Allen Tate has spoken of the peculiar historical consciousness of Southern writers, and described their work as a literature conscious of the past in the present. Tate could hardly have called to witness a better illustration of his thesis than his friend Robert Penn Warren. Warren's books have dealt with virtually every period of American history since the time of Thomas Jefferson, including that time and including also the period of Jackson, the Civil War, the early years of the 20th Century, the 1920's, the 1930's, and on down to the present. These books constitute for some of us a good part of our intellectual autobiography. His first book was not fiction at all, but a biography of John Brown. It seems to me that in that book of "straight" history, he announced the basic themes of all his novels: man's confrontation with evil, and the conflict between good and evil within the human heart. Together, these books constitute a moral history of the South.

William Styron's early novels dealt with contemporary themes and characters, though never without a characteristic consciousness of the past in the present. Only in this latest novel, on Nat Turner, has he turned to the more remote past for his subject, and in this "meditation on history," as he calls his book, he comes very close indeed, given the license of the novelist, to doing what the historian does in reconstructing the past. Here he is concerned with the particular, rather than with the universal, which is, I believe, the distinction that Aristotle made between poetry and history.

Ralph Ellison has declared his allegiance to history, as well as his Southern identity, most clearly in his warning to a critic about the abstraction he would impose upon American reality. With characteristic Southern fear of abstraction, and abhorrence for it, he declared: "The Negro American consciousness is not a product (as so often seems true of so many other American groups) of a will to historical forgetfulness." Rather, it is the memory of slavery and the hope of emancipation, and the myths, both Southern and Northern.

I will call on these speakers in the order of seniority, and that will put Mr. Warren first.

Warren: I want to say that I am appalled and honored to be invited to a group of historians. It makes you feel that the writing of fiction is more important than you thought it was, and that your writing is, too. I am honored to be here and it is a great pleasure to be among my friends—three old and dear friends.

What I want to do now is simply to try to state a few principles that occur to me about the relation between history and fiction—in a way, between history and art, as I see the problem, as a background to what may happen later.

First I should like to say that the word History is a very ambiguous word. Clearly it means on one hand things that happened in the past, the events of the past, the actions of the past. And the word also means the record of the past that historians write. So whenever the word is used, we have to sort out its meaning. I myself use it differently, in each sense, as the occasion may demand, and I'm afraid my friends do the same thing.

As Vann has said, history is in the past tense. That sounds simple enough. It is about the past. But it is not simple, because it is not merely about what happened in the past, it is also the imaginative past. History and fiction are both in this past tense. History is the literal past tense. The historian says, "It was in the past; I prove that it happened." The fiction writer says, "I'll take it as it has happened, if it happened at all—which it probably didn't." But the mode of the past tense is the past tense of a state of mind—the feel of the past, not the literal past itself. It is a mode of memories. It's the mind working in terms of memory. The history of the past that the historians write is the racial past, the national past, the sectional past, all kinds of pasts, including economic history—but the past, always. To the novelist, say Thackeray, writing about Becky Sharp, the past may be merely a little personal past. But it is past. Even science fiction is about the past; the writers tell about the future as though it were past. In science fiction, you get yourself to a point beyond the story that you are telling. It is never in the future tense. It is in an assumed future which has become a past.

This fact points to a particular stance of mind: it has *happened,* and we are trying to find its meaning. It's a mode of memory we are dealing with, an actuality as remembered. History is concerned with actuality; its past must be provable. The fiction writer's past is not provable; it *may* be imagined. His characters *may* be imagined. But historical characters are imagined, too. They are brought into the picture of an imagined world. For how do we know the world of "history," unless the historian has "imagined" it?

Now the big difference here between history and fiction is that the historian does not know his imagined world; he knows *about* it, and he must know all he can about it, because he wants to find the facts *behind* that world. But the fiction writer must claim to *know* the *inside* of his world for better or for worse. He mostly fails, but he claims to know the inside of his characters, the undocumentable inside. Historians are concerned with the truth *about,* with knowledge *about,* the fiction writer with the knowledge *of.* And neither of these "knowledges" is to be achieved in any perfect form. But the kinds of "knowledge" *are.* This is a fundamental difference, it seems to me.

This leads to another distinction. Fiction is an art, one of the several arts. I want to read a little passage—the most radical passage I could find—about art as distinguished from other human activities. "Either art is a pure, irreducible activity, one that provides its own peculiar content, its own morality—it includes itself in its own meaning; or art is, on the other hand, a pleasanter form of presenting facts, meanings and truths pertaining to other realms of reality like history, sociology, morality, where they exist in purer and fuller form." This states the distinction quite coldly. For fiction is an art, like painting or music—with one difference. Its materials are more charged with all the human commitments and recalcitrances and roughnesses.

Now here is where the rub comes, I think. The materials that go into a piece of fiction may be drawn from history or human experience, but their factuality gives them no special privilege, as contrasted with imagined materials. They have, as "materials" for it, the same status, and nothing more than that. But they come in with all the recalcitrances and the weights and the passions of the real world. The simplest example I can think of is this. Take *Hamlet,* or any tragedy we all admire and respond to. It is dealing with the recalcitrances of human pain, confusion and error. We know these things all too well: the pain, confusion, and error of our own lives. But we come out of the play not weeping, but feeling pretty good, and we go down to the beer parlor and talk about it. Something's happened to the pain, confusion, error. It has happened only because we put the pain and error into perspective, and look at it—to see it and at the same time not quite feel it. We see it as if it had happened a long time ago—to us, but to somebody else, too.

There is, however, always a point where the exigences and the pains of the materials of fiction or drama or poetry are too great to be absorbed. This recalcitrancy, which is the basis of contention between the form and the content of literature, can become too great. The really bigoted Catholic cannot read Milton; the really bigoted Protestant can't read Dante. In reading literature we have to make allowances for our theories and our beliefs. But there is a point where it cracks. Let's recognize that. There is a form in which the recalcitrant material—that is, the practical commitment in relation to it—violates the vision of humanity, the long-range beauty of contemplation that is art. Let's leave it there for the moment.

Ellison: I think I'll go back and try to talk about American historiography and American fiction. I would start by suggesting that they're both artificial; both are forms of literature, and I would suggest further that American history grows primarily out of the same attitudes of mind, and attitudes toward chronology, which gave birth to our great tall stories. Constance Rourke reminded us that we began to define ourselves and to create ourselves through the agency of the word, of the imagination, the fictional imagination—and that basically we are liars. I would sugget that historians are responsible liars. Liars are not bad people; I am by profession a liar. The role of lying is like the role of masquerading. Yeats has a quotation, which I have used somewhere, about the necessity of putting on the mask in order to achieve one's dreams, one's idea of one's self. So when I put a scar on my face or part my hair, you understand that I'm trying to achieve some idealistic image; or if I wear it in Afro-style or conk it, you understand that that too is simply a human assertion against the flux and flow of time and a desire to modify that which was given. And it is here that the novelist and the historian appear to part company. The historian is dedicated to chronology. He can suppress, he can emphasize, he can project, and he can carve out his artifact; and this helps us to imagine ourselves, to project ourselves, to achieve certain goals, certain identities; but he must obey the order of the calendar and the tides of political fortune. I can't, here in New Orleans, fail to point out that so much of American history has turned upon the racial situation in the country. This is a given and accepted fact now. It's argued over and over again. The problem that we have to deal with on the side of history is: How much did you choose to put in, how much did you leave out, what did it lead to, and how to interpret the results. I'm going to be a little nasty here and suggest that our written history has been as "official" as any produced in any

communist country—only in a democratic way: individuals write it
instead of committees. Written history is to social conduct and social
arrangements in this country very much like the relationship between
myth and ritual. And myth justifies and "explains" facts. Now it's all
human, it is understandable and it has to be evaluated, because complex personal and political interests are involved in such intricate
ways that arriving at objective evaluations is extremely difficult. But,
thank God, there have been a few novelists who decided to tell the
"truth" in their own unique and devious ways. Isn't that nasty?

For here the novelists have a special, though difficult, freedom.
Time is their enemy, and while chronology is the ally of the historian,
for the novelist it is something to manipulate or even to destroy. And
this, I think, is why we wish that historians, within the limitations
which they embrace and to which they dedicate themselves, could
do a little better by chronology, by events as they actually unfold.
Because in certain ways the historians have, thankfully, taken a
broader cut of the American experience than the novelists. By nature
they possess a greater patience before facts, before events. If you
really want to find out what happened in the United States over all
these years, you know that *some* historian has written something
about it. That is one of the glories of historical writing in this country;
there has always been somebody who, for some reason, has tried to
say, "Well, the consequences of this fact actually exist, this event actually occurred, and I think it is related in such and such a way to the
total reality." But too often history has been an official statement, and
it has danced attendance to political arrangements.

Fiction, on the other hand, as it manipulates reality, as it tries to get
at those abiding human predicaments which are ageless and timeless,
has fought with time, has fought with the realities as envisioned by
official history, and by rearranging experience in artful ways it has
tried to tell us in small ways the symbolic significance of what actually
happened. If you want to know something about the dynamics of the
South, of interpersonal relationships in the South from, roughly,
1874 until today, you don't go to historians; not even to Negro historians. You go to William Faulkner and Robert Penn Warren, or you
go to the popular arts. You have to read the latter very carefully of
course, because they are the biggest liars of all. But somehow the
novelists try to deal with unpleasant facts, difficult facts, and Faulkner

dealt with the most unpleasant facts of race. I suppose that's why American history has not been ultimately concerned with tragedy, while literature, at its best, always has. It's always trying to find ways of dealing with the unpleasant facts, and the only way, the profoundest human way, of dealing with the unpleasant, is to place it in conjunction with the pleasant. Thus fiction, at its best, moves ever toward a blending of the tragic with the comic—or towards that mode which we know as the Blues.

I would suggest, then, that American novelists have a special role which should not be confused with the role of the writer of history; which for them is *verboten.* The moment you say something explicit about history in a novel, everybody's going to rise up and knock the Hell out of you, because they suspect that you are trying to take advantage of a form of authority which is sacred. History is sacred, you see, and no matter how false to actual events it might be. But fiction is anything but sacred. By fact and by convention fiction is a projection from one man's mind, of one man's imagination. An American novelist tries to integrate all of the diversity of our people and our regions, our religions, and so on, into an imaginative whole. And through that imaginative integration he attempts to seize the abiding circumstances, the abiding problems, the abiding and time-tested forms of humanity—heroism, truth and failure and love and death—all of the ramifications of those experiences which make us human.

I think that we have something very important going here. We work the same side of the street. So keep us honest and we'll keep you historians honest. I think that Red Warren, who has always been concerned with history, has offered us an example of how to confront the problem of history as the novelist should. I think that when he wrote about a great American politician who governed his state and refused to intrude into the area of the historian, he refused because he was canny enough to realize that he could never get *that* particular man into fiction. And yet, I believe that he did use that man to bring into focus within his own mind many, many important facts about power, politics and class and loyalty. So today we possess an essence of that man presented in a highly imaginative, moving and enduring way, without the novelist having taken anything away from that man and without his having added anything to one who we

know was an important historical figure—except the art-created possibility of looking at him through the enrichening eyes of Red Warren's imagination. Thanks to Warren's art we may now view that
man through that heightened sense of the past which both history
and literature grant to all who are truly involved with the mystery of
human existence.

Styron: I have never talked much in public. I don't mean to sound
shy, but I haven't, nor have I taught, and I admire the eloquence that
has preceded me, and only wish that I were able to speak in an
impromptu manner as well as my good friends have done. As a consequence, I have resorted to a composition, fairly brief, some of it
composed on Eastern Airlines today, with a terrible and ominous
post-election traumatic blues all over me. So I'm going to read it, and
if you shut your eyes, perhaps I can give you a subtle feeling that I
am not reading it.

Last spring in an exchange in the *Nation,* I quoted at some length
from a volume called *The Historical Novel,* by the great Hungarian
Marxist critic, Georg Lukács, in an effort to explain my attitude toward the freedom of movement and choice any good novelist must
exercise when writing historical fiction. Historical fiction has been
largely discredited in this country, doubtless due to the fact that its
practitioners, most of them, have aimed at titillating a predominantly
female audience, an audience one hopes has now been preempted
by the Late, Late show. What I am speaking about, of course, is the
serious historical novel: literature in the tradition of Scott, Stendhal,
Tolstoy, Pushkin, Faulkner, and Warren, and it is to this great genre
that Lukács has addressed himself, in my opinion, with more intelligence, passion, and penetration than any other modern literary critic.
As Irving Howe has written of Lukács, "Unlike so many Marxist
critics, Lukács turns to literature not because it provides him with
political opportunities but because he has been involved with it for a
lifetime and has experienced the passion of the true scholar. . . .
Repeatedly Lukács turns to 'the increasing concreteness of the novel
in its grasp of the historical peculiarity of characters and events,' repeatedly to that self-reflectiveness in the dominant characters of the
modern novel, which he sees as the sense of history become part of
experience and thereby transformed into a dynamic agent reflecting
and acting upon the dialectal contradictions of the outer world."[1]

It seemed to me that some of Lukács' observations on the historical novel and the novelist's responsibility are more trenchant and wise than any I could make about the matter, and certainly record as well as I could my own feelings about the intricate and subtle relationship between historical fact and fanciful conjecture; between historical faithfulness and literary license, along with other troubling problems that beset the unhappy wretch who dares tackle this literary form. Let me then quote again from Lukács, hoping that these maxims will serve as representative of my own sentiments regarding the fiction writer's very difficult obligation to make sense out of history.

"The deeper and more genuinely historical a writer's knowledge of a period," Lukács says, "the more freely will he be able to move about inside his subject and the less tied will he feel to individual historical data." Speaking of Sir Walter Scott, for instance, he observes: "Scott's extraordinary genius lay in the fact that he gave the historical novel just such themes as would allow for this 'free movement,' and so cleared the way for its development; whereas the earlier traditions of his so-called predecessors had obstructed all such freedom of movement, preventing even a genuine talent from developing. Naturally, a special difficulty is involved in the treatment of specifically historical subject-matter. Every really original writer who portrays a new outlook upon a certain field has to contend with the prejudices of his readers. But the image which the public has of any familiar historical figure need not necessarily be a false one. Indeed, with the growth of a real historical sense and of real historical knowledge it becomes more and more accurate. But even this correct image may in certain circumstances be a hindrance to the writer who wishes to reproduce the spirit of an age faithfully and authentically. It would require a particularly happy accident for all the well-known and attested actions of a familiar historical figure to correspond to the purposes of literature. . . ."

In another context, Lukács expands on this theme of what is not merely the likelihood but the necessity of the writer being allowed great latitude in structuring his vision of the past. He says, "What matters in the novel is fidelity in the reproduction of the material foundations of the life of a given period, its manners and the feelings and thoughts deriving from these. This means, as we have also seen, that the novel is much more closely bound to the specifically historical, individual moments of a period than is drama. But this never means being tied to any particular historical facts. On the contrary, the novelist must be at liberty to treat these as he likes,"—and this is an important phrase, I think—"if he is to reproduce the much more complex and ramifying totality with historical faithfulness. From the standpoint of the historical novel, too, it is always a matter of chance whether an actual, historical fact, character or story will lend itself to the particular method by which a great novelist conveys his historical faithfulness."

Finally, quoting Pushkin, Lukács remarks: "Truth of passions, verisimilitude of feelings in imagined circumstances—that is what our mind demands of the dramatic writer." And he declares, "the writer's historical fidelity consists in the faithful artistic reproduction of the great collisions, the great crises and turning-points in history. To express this *historical* conception in an adequate artistic form the writer may treat individual facts with as much license as he likes, for mere fidelity to the individual facts of history without this connection is utterly valueless" (pp. 166–68).

Needless to say, the foregoing thoughts merely skim part of the surface of Lukács' philosophy of history and its relation to literature. Yet in his unyielding insistence that a writer's responsibility is not to the dead baggage of facts, but to the unfettering and replenishing power of his own imagination, that imagination which at its best can alone reveal ultimate truths, Lukács' observations seem to me enormously provocative, and I hope they provide substance for further discussion this evening.

Woodward: Thank you very much, gentlemen. As an historian, I gather from the comments of Mr. Warren that the novelists deal with the inside of history, leaving the outside, I suppose, to the historian; from Mr. Ellison, that historians are essentially liars, and this leaves the truth to the novelists; from Mr. Styron that fidelity to fact is not an obligation of novelists, and this *emancipates* them. Am I too far off base, gentlemen, in saying that it seems to me that you are saying you are going to write a "super-history," or at least a better history than historians can write?

Ellison: No. I'm suggesting that we have reached a great crisis in American history, and we are now going to have a full American history. You, Vann, began to initiate this movement, as far as I am concerned. We're beginning to go back and to evaluate those realities of American historical experience which were ruled out officially. Henry Steele Commager and a lot of other people, such as Samuel Morison, have turned flip-flops in recent years. I used to be outraged when I read some of the stuff that they wrote, because there is, certainly in the Negro part of the country and in the Southern part of the country, a stream of history which is still as tightly connected with folklore and the oral tradition as official history is connected with the tall tale. I think that we are beginning to realize that.

For instance, the only public school I ever attended was named after Frederick Douglass. The people who walked there from Tennessee and the Carolinas have a sense of history which is only now beginning to get into the history books. Part of this is legend. Part of this is myth. But so much of it—so very much of it—is what actually happened, happened to them. And if official history, if conscious historians do not take cognizance of this experience, then what a critic like Lukács says has very little validity. He was, after all, writing about European countries, with no divided history. Of course I know that the Owen Glendower that Shakespeare gives us in the historical plays is certainly not the Owen Glendower of the Welsh, it's the Shakespearean and Elizabethan notion of Owen Glendower. But here we are dedicated to a different kind of democracy. We have all of these things which happened, and they happened in such great variety. I'm afraid to say what Louisiana experience is, what Louisiana history is, even of the period of Huey Long, because I used to hear things—and highly favorable things, about Long, for instance—from Negro students that I attended college with at Tuskegee.

I think that one of the things that we want to discuss here is the rhetoric of fiction. If you project in fiction a version of history, then you have an obligation to think about these other feed-ins from the common experience which are going to put to question your particular projection of history. I don't think that history is Truth. I think it's another form of man trying to find himself, and to come to grips with his own complexity, but within the frame of chronology and time. Here in the United States we have had a political system which wouldn't allow me to tell my story officially. Much of it is not in the history textbooks. Certain historians and untrained observers did their jobs, often very faithfully, but many of them have been forgotten except by scholars and historians, and the story they recorded was altered to justify racial attitudes and practices. But somehow, through our Negro American oral tradition and through the names given to children and to public institutions—those places with which white society was not too concerned as long as they did not challenge the public order—these reminders of the past as *Negroes* recalled it found existence and were passed along. Historical figures continued to live in stories of and theories about the human and social dynamics of slavery, and about the effects of political decisions rendered during the Reconstruction. Assertions of freedom and revolts were recalled along with triumphs of labor in the fields and on the dance floor; feats of eating and drinking and of fornication, or religious conversion and physical endurance, and of artistic and athletic achievements. In brief, the broad ramifications of human life as Negroes have experienced it were marked and passed along. This record exists in oral form and it constitutes the internal history of values by which my people lived even as they were being forced to accommodate themselves to those forces and arrangements of society that were sanctioned by official history. The result has imposed upon Negroes a high sensitivity to the ironies of historical writing and created a profound skepticism concerning the validity of most reports on what the past was like.

And so, when a novelist moves into the arena of history and takes on the obligations of the historian he has to be aware that he faces a tough rhetorical problem. He has to sell *me*, convince me, that despite the racial divisions and antagonisms in the U.S., his received version of history is not drastically opposed to mine. Because I am conditioned to assume that his idea of the heroic individual is apt to violate my sense of heroism;—for instance, Bedford Forrest is considered a hero by many whites but it would be an heroic task for me, or for most blacks, to see him so. I can, however, accept Sam Fathers or Lucas Beauchamp in Faulkner, in ways that I couldn't accept Jim in *Huckleberry Finn*. For me, Jim was not rounded enough. And yet, he was involved fictionally with serious historical matters. But Lucas Beauchamp was involved with serious historical and personal matters—*but* (and this is an important *but*) he was mainly involved in those things which historians would not talk about, and this is one of the important roles which fiction has played, especially the fiction of southern writers: it has tried to tell that part of the human truth which we could not accept or face up to in much historical writing because of social, racial and political considerations.

Warren: Our little girl, who is about eleven years old, was studying for an exam in American History, and she said to me, "Hear my lesson." I heard her lesson and she said things I thought were pretty preposterous, but I didn't say anything about it, but she was watching my face. "Oh, Poppy!" she said, "this is for an exam; this is not the truth. I know better than this."

Now this is not the historians' fault. This is the people who write text books of history. It's very different. Official histories may be tests, or orators at the Fourth of July, or textbook makers, but not historians. They are very different, you see. And girls of ten years old get this point quickly; they understand it perfectly. By the time they are seventeen or eighteen, in college, they may lose it. But they know it at ten years old. They watch things much more shrewdly than their elders; they have no stake in it except truth—truth, and grades. They are quite different: they know this, you see.

The historian is after this truth, and it's a good truth. So is the novelist. They are both trying to say what life feels like to them. They have different ground rules for it. Let's assume that both are conditioned by their societies at every given moment—at every moment in history, in time. Now, the breaking out process is always an act of imagination both for the historian and the novelist. The rules are different, though, in this sense: the historian must prove points, document points, that the novelist doesn't have to document. Yet without that sense of documentation, the knowledge that It Is Possible, the novelist can't operate either. He is conditioned always by the sense of this documentation—that it is historically possible. He himself is tied to the facts of life. He must respect them. Insofar as he departs from them by imagination, he departs in terms of the possibilities laid down by these ground rules of fact—psychological fact, historical fact, sociological fact, all the various kinds of fact. Those are his ground rules. He can take a new view of them, but he cannot violate any one of them to a point which invalidates acceptance. That's the big proviso here. It varies a great deal. The materials that go into his work come from the rough-textured life around him, made up of beliefs and facts and attitudes of all kinds. A bigoted Catholic can't

read Milton, and a bigoted Protestant can't read Dante, but a civilized
Catholic can read Milton with joy. There's a point, though, where
one's commitment to basic ideas and basic materials, by reason of
bigotry or something else, makes one incapable of accepting the total
vision of an art—of a novel or a poem, or whatever. Let's face this
fact. The autonomy of the art is always subject to the recalcitrance of
the materials and to your own lack of self-understanding.

Styron: I don't know what I'm going to say to add to this confusion. We've been dealing in very intelligent abstractions, all of which
make me feel that maybe we should get a little bit more concrete. I
like that phrase of Red Warren's just now: "The autonomy of the art
is subject to the recalcitrance of the materials." This is something that
I have had preying on my mind for some time, in regard to a private
argument, which became extraordinarily public, having to do with a
book I wrote not too long ago. It occurred to me in thinking of this
particular book, *The Confessions of Nat Turner,* that in all of the extraordinary flak and anti-anti-missile barrage that has surrounded it,
no one, insofar as I know (and I don't mean only people who
criticized it from the black point of view, but a number of my white
commentators as well; and I bring this up not out of any immodesty,
but simply because I'm more comfortable in talking about particulars
rather than aesthetic abstractions)—no one has conceived of this
book, which does deal with history indeed, as a separate entity which
has its own autonomy, to use Red Warren's phrase, its own metaphy-
sics, its own reason for being as an aesthetic object. No one has
ventured, except for several people in private (bright people, whom I
admire), to suggest that a work which deals with history can at the
same time be a metaphorical plan, a metaphorical diagram for a
writer's attitude toward human existence, which presumably is one of
the writer's preoccupations anyway—that, despite all the obfuscation
which surrounds the really incredible controversy about the rightness
and wrongness of racial attitudes, wrong readings of Ulrich B. Phillips, Stanley Elkins, and so forth, a work of literature might have its
own being, its own fountain, its own reality, its own power, its own
appeal, which derive from factors that don't really relate to history.
And this is why, again, I'm intrigued by Red Warren's phrase, "the
autonomy of the art is subject to the recalcitrance of the materials."
   I would like to suggest that, in the endless rancor and bitterness

which tends to collect and coalesce around controversial literary works, it might also be wise to pause and step back (I'm not speaking of my own work alone)—and regard a work as containing many metaphors, many reasons for being. This is true for all the literary works I admire. They are works (and I would include, among modern works, books by my distinguished contemporaries to my right) which do exist outside of history, which gain their power from history, to be sure, which are fed by a passionate comprehension of what history does to people and to things, but which have to have other levels of understanding, and have to be judged by other levels of understanding. It may be that in our perhaps overly modern and desperate preoccupation with history, which can be so valuable, we lose sight of the ineffable othernesses which go to make a work of art. At the risk of repeating myself once more, I would like to say that these factors have been forgotten.

Warren: May I say something, Vann? It strikes me that the question is one of the basic tensions of our whole lives. We can't have an easy formulation for this, an easy way out of the question. We are stuck with the fact that life involves passions and concerns and antipathies and anguish about the materials of life itself—whatever goes on in our hearts and outside of ourselves. This is what good literature involves. If you couldn't carry these things into literature, literature would be meaningless. It would be a mere parlor trick. All this—the concerns, the confusion—goes into literature; it goes into the arts. It exists in terms of the experience that the writer describes in literature, presented there in and of himself. They are not the same thing for everybody; a little different, you know, for each person, frequently quite different. But they all go in as passion, as commitments of various kinds. Yet at the same time the thing described must be made objectively itself. Now take Glendower, to whom Ralph was referring. Now nobody here is a Welsh nationalist, I trust. If there is one here . . .

Ellison: Ralph Ellison is.

Warren: No you're not; *you* aren't Welsh.

Ellison: I'm a Welsh nationalist. But I also admire art.

Warren: I'm a Confederate. So here we are. We have personal loyalties and problems, you see. But in *Henry IV, Part One,* Glendower didn't bother us in terms of the great theme of the play. Peo-

ple are not living and dying over Glendower today. This is a purely
pragmatic approach to it, you see; what can we surrender, what immediate needs can we give up, how can we withdraw our commitments in a given region of this play—in materials of the play—to gain
a larger view? Now I couldn't care less who won the battle, at
Shrewsbury, personally. It was a long time ago, and it isn't very important now. . . .

What I care about is the pattern of the human struggle there—as
we know it in relation to Hotspur on one hand, and to the cold
calculators on the other hand, and to Hal, as kind of Golden Mean,
and then, at last, to Falstaff, with all of his great tummy and great wit,
and his ironic view of history and morality—outside of all schematic
views. We are seeing a pattern of human possibility that bears on all
of our lives, a pattern there that we see every day—the Hotspurs, or
those cold calculators like Westmoreland, and then the people like
Hal, who try to ride it through and in their perfect adaptability be all
things to all men, and drink with Falstaff and kick him out at the end
(in the next play, of course). We see this happening all the time.
Shakespeare wrote a great vision of human life, but it's not about
Welsh nationalism.

Ellison: Yes. And I'm all for the autonomy of fiction; that's why I
say that novelists should leave history alone. But I would also remind
us that the work of fiction comes alive through a collaboration between the reader and the writer. This is where the rhetoric comes in.
If you move far enough into the historical past, you don't have that
problem. I don't give a damn what happened to Owen Glendower,
actually, but as a writer, if I were to write a fiction based upon a great
hero, a military man, whose name is Robert E. Lee, I'd damn well be
very careful about what I fed my reader, in order for him to recreate
in his imagination and through his sense of history what that gentleman was. Because Lee is no longer simply an historical figure. He is
a figure who lives within us. He is a figure which shapes ideals of
conduct and of forebearance and of skill, military and so on. This is
inside, and not something that writers can merely be arbitrary about.
The freedom of the fiction writer, the novelist, is one of the great
freedoms possible for the individual to exercise. But it is not absolute.
Thus, one, without hedging his bets, has to be aware that he does
operate within an area dense with prior assumptions.

Warren: Quite right.

Ellison: This I say without any discussion of Bill's personal problem. I haven't read his book, and he knows that—well, maybe he doesn't. Our house burned down so I didn't get to read it at first, and after the controversy I deliberately did not read it. One thing that I know is that he isn't a bigot, he isn't a racist, and all of that. That's beside the point. But there are very serious problems involved. I am known as a bastard by certain of my militant friends because I am not what they call a part of the Movement. That is, they figure I don't cuss out white folks enough. All right; I cuss them out in my own ways. But this isn't the real problem. The real problem is to create symbolic actions which are viable specifically, and which move across all of our differences and all of the diversities of the atmosphere, and allow us to say, "yes," just as Red is saying about Shakespeare. This tells us something of what it means to be a man under these particular circumstances. But at the same time you don't have the freedom to snatch any and everybody, and completely recreate them. This is why you must lie and disguise a historical figure. You cannot move into the area, or impose yourself into the authority, of the historian, because he is dealing with chronology. The moment you put yourself in a book, the moment you put any known figures into the book, then somebody is going to say, "But he didn't have that mole on that side of his face; it was on *that* side. You said that he had a wife; he didn't have a wife. You said that he beat his wife at three o'clock in the afternoon; no, he beat her before breakfast, and they got up at five." Facts are a tyranny for the novelist. Facts get you into all of this trouble. On the other hand, Bill, I would suggest that whether you like the dissonance you picked up, you've written a very powerful novel, and it's very self-evident. Don't kick it. Don't knock it. Just leave history alone.

Styron: I'm not kicking, Ralph. I'm not. No. I'm glad you authenticate what I said through the voice of Lukács, that facts *per se* are preposterous. They are like the fuzz that collects in the top of dirty closets. They don't really mean anything.

Warren: I wouldn't go that far.

Ellison: They *mean* something. That's why you're in trouble.

Styron: I'll dispute that.

Ellison: Okay.

Styron: It depends on what facts you're talking about. Let's pare this down. Obviously when somebody like Lukács, or somebody like myself, claims that it's necessary to dispense with facts, it's not to say that promiscuous blindness, a disavowal of evidence, is what the novelist has as a dirty little secret all of his own. It's not that at all. It's simply to say that with a certain absolute boldness, a novelist dealing with history has to be able to say that such and such a fact is totally irrelevant, and to hell with the person who insists that it has any real, utmost relevance. It's not to say that, in any bland or even dishonest way, a novelist is free to go about his task of rendering history with a complete shrugging off of the facts. This is not what Lukács says; it is not what I say. It is simply that certain facts which history presents us with are, on the one hand, either unimportant, or else they can be dispensed with out of hand, because to yield to them would be to yield or to compromise the novelist's own aesthetic honesty. Certain things won't fit into a novel, won't go in simply because the story won't tell itself if such a fact is there. This is what Lukács meant. It's what I mean when I say that a brute, an idiotic preoccupation with crude fact is death to a novel, and death to the novelist. The primary thing is the free use and bold use of the liberating imagination which, dispensing with useless fact, will clear the cobwebs away and will show how it really was. This is all I mean about fact and its use or misuse.

Ellison: You mean really what was in your imagination, not in historical reality, don't you, Bill?

Styron: Well isn't that what we're talking about? I mean, when we read *War and Peace* we are reading about Tolstoy's imagination. I don't want to make any invidious comparisons; I'm just saying that anybody who deals, any creative imagination which deals with the fabric of history leaves you, if he's a good novelist, with a sense of an imaginative truth which transcends, in this case, what the historian can give you. An historian can tell you just what happened at Borodino, but only Tolstoy, often dispensing with facts, can tell you what it really was to be a soldier at Borodino. This is what the distinction is, and this is what I insist is the novelist's prerogative when he is faced with the materials of history.

Woodward: I'm interested in this question of fact myself. One of our distinguished novelists present, Red Warren, has written a novel

about an historian. I think that Jack Burden was an historian, really.
At least he was the narrator of *All the King's Men,* and he had two
historical investigations in his career. One of them, you'll remember,
was the investigation of the truth about an ancestor, I believe a great-
uncle named Cass Mastern, and he said that the investigation was a
failure. It was a failure because he was simply looking for the truth.
The second investigation was about a man who turned out (though
he didn't know it at the time) to be his father, Judge Irwin, and this
investigation proved to be a great success. And he said that the reason for that success was that he was only looking for facts. The facts
resulted in the suicide of his father, and a tragedy. So an interesting
distinction was made there between facts and truth. Jack Burden,
incidentally, was an historian, a seeker for a Ph.D., as some of us
have been.

Warren: He didn't get it.

Woodward: He didn't get it, and the reason, as you say, was he
did not have to know Cass Mastern to get the degree. He only had to
know the facts about Cass Mastern's world. I would be interested in
hearing you discuss this distinction between fact and truth. I think it's
to the nub of our discussion, perhaps.

Warren: I'll tell you how it happened. I'll do it in two ways. One is
how it happened to me, and the other is what could be said about it
afterwards; they are quite different things. Jack Burden himself was a
pure technical accident, a way to tell the story. And you stumble into
that, because you are stuck with your problem of telling a story; you
have to make him up as you go along. But that's another problem.
The question about his peculiar researches, as I look back on them, is
simply this. Being a very badly disorganized young fellow, he really
didn't want the Ph.D. anyway. He stumbled on his family history,
involving a character in his family, a couple of generations back, who
had devoted his life to trying to find a moral position for himself. And
this young man, without any moral orientation at all that I could
figure out (he's an old-fashioned lost boy, not the new kind—there
have always been these lost boys), didn't want his Ph.D., and he
didn't know what to do with himself. He didn't know his mother, he
didn't like his father, and so forth. At first he couldn't face the fact
that in his own blood, there was a man who *had* faced up to a moral
problem in a deep way. He couldn't follow it through, could not bear

to face the comparison to the other young man. Then, he couldn't face the truth otherwise, without this piece of research. Later, when he had the job of getting the dirt on a character in the novel, he did get all the facts. He gets all the facts, and the guy turns out to be his father, who commits suicide. It's a parable, I didn't mean it to be one; I wasn't trying to make a parable of truth and fact. It just worked out that way. You sort of stumble into these things. It's a parable, as you pointed out to me tonight; I hadn't thought about this before. Well, the facts Jack Burden gets are deadly things. Facts may kill. For one thing, they can kill myths.

Woodward: We're working here toward a distinction between fact and fiction. Fact comes, I believe, from the Latin: *factum est,* a thing done, an event. It has acquired a lot of prestige in historical circles; it gets talked about all the time—facts, something you dig up like gold, you unearth. Fiction is something that's created, something that's made, something that is made up perhaps of facts and a lot of guesses. I think of two protagonists in Faulkner's *Absalom, Absalom!,* Shreve McCannon and Quentin Compson, who are really seeking historical truth, and they are doing it with facts and evidence, and bits and pieces, and they go on and on, trying to create this image and to discover the truth about Colonel Sutpen. What they are trying to do seems to me very similar to what the historian is trying to do. He gets together a lot of evidence, and he "creates" the truth.

Ellison: But they are characters in a fiction, Vann, not historians. so there's a difference.

Woodward: Yes, but the historian seems to me to be doing much the same thing with the evidence he gathers. He puts it together. Cleanth Brooks has put page after page of the evidence of *Absalom, Absalom!* together to show how this truth is arrived at.

There are some people here who came to ask questions of these writers, and I think we ought to give them an opportunity.

First Questioner: I would like to direct my question to Mr. Styron. Mr. Styron, Mr. Ellison said that the novelist doesn't have the right to distort facts completely. He said his power is not absolute when it comes to fact. Then you also talked about imaginative truth, and that certain things don't fit into a novel. I'd like to know about the fact that Nat Turner was married—didn't that fit into your novel?

Styron: It seems to me I've heard this before. I can only reiterate what I have said despairingly in public and even more despairingly in cold print, that in the evidence which was available to me when some years ago I began to collect the few basic materials to write this book, there was no evidence which told me he had such a wife.

First Questioner: Didn't Thomas Gray's *Confessions* say that?

Styron: No. I'm very sorry. Or is that a rhetorical question?

First Questioner: No, I read an article in *Ebony* by Lerone Bennett.

Styron: I read it, too. He's wrong. No, if you read the *Confessions* yourself, the original *Confessions,* this is one of the amazing things about it. He mentions all the rest of his family, but mentions no wife. Once again, in an essay I wrote about this controversy, I said that, without laying aside my belief in the irrelevance of certain facts, this on the other hand would have been so important that if I had been given any kind of substantial evidence that he had a wife, then as a novelist I would have felt compelled to create a wife for him. But I only ask again, certainly not for the last time, that people who, like yourself, constantly castigate me for leaving his wife out, consult the evidence yourself, and use a little reason.

First Questioner: Is Margaret Whitehead, in the evidence, completely obsessed in his mind?

Styron: Margaret Whitehead is a part of my fictional imagination. I have no apologies for her. But as for the fact of a black wife, I submit to you, humbly, that the evidence does not show that he had one; and therefore, I think reason dictates that it was perfectly all right for me to leave her out.

First Questioner: I have a number of other questions, but I'm only going to ask one more. You said that a novel has its own reason for being. What's the reason for being for *The Confessions of Nat Turner?* Because I read it and I couldn't find any.

Styron: Well, I don't know how to answer a question like that. In fact, I don't think I'll try. It's so majestic a question that I don't think I'm able to answer it.

Second Questioner: Seeing as though calling historians liars tonight has been quite popular, I can remember that the last time I called you a liar, it became very bitter. It seems as though we con-

front each other from the North to the South. I met you in Massachusetts this summer, and now all the way down in New Orleans
I'm here to call you a liar again.

Ellison: Which one of us, please?

Second Questioner: I'm primarily concerned with Styron. I met
him this summer at Harvard. I think possibly we need to take a look
at the revolutionary black figure, Nat Turner, to see what he actually
represents to black people. I think when we talk about slavery and
revolution that it has to be looked at from a psychiatric or a psychological viewpoint. Okay, we take a look at the ten blacks who responded to your book on *The Confessions of Nat Turner.* In this
group we have C. V. Hamilton, we have Alvin Poussaint. These men
have really delved into the thing; they have looked at it from a psychological viewpoint.

I heard Warren say a few minutes ago that fact can destroy, that
fact can be deadly. I contend that imagination and lying can also be
deadly and can also destroy. Now let's take a look at this a bit further.
First of all we see two major bases from which this book was written.
We see some religious ties with Nat Turner—that he was a preacher
or something, who had some vision about killing white folk. Secondly, I remember your statement that the white woman was a
higher symbol or goal for the black man or the black slave—something that he looked up to and wanted and desired. Okay, I remember asking you that question up North, and I want you to tell these
Southern whites this same thing. I want to know this: if the white
woman was the symbol for Nat Turner to look up to and this was
why he wanted sexual relations, and had all these desires, then, since
that black woman [in the novel] was below the white man, what kind
of image was she?

Styron: Have you paused for a question now? Well, let me tackle
all of these again, one by one. Indeed you have haunted me. You're
my *bête noire*, I'm afraid. I recall you from Harvard Summer School
with terror. Now here you are again. I won't reply to your *ad
hominem* remarks about my "lies," and so on, but I will try to reply
directly to you about what I conceive to be the essential truth about
Nat Turner's relationship with white women. Forgive me if I para-
phrase you badly, but I think you are asking me if I sincerely believe

that Nat Turner really yearned, carnally and otherwise, for a white girl. Am I right?

Second Questioner: No, you're wrong.

Styron: Well then, would you please rephrase it?

Second Questioner: My thing was, if you placed the white woman above the black slave—the male slave, and said that this was something that he wanted because she was above or higher than him, then how do you explain the white man reaching below him to go back in the quarters, to get the black women out of those slave quarters, which is the cause of many of my brothers and sisters sitting here tonight being of different pigmentation of skin?

Styron: I don't think at any place in the book did I for an instant deny the very implicit fact that white men were down in the quarters at all times. The reason that I didn't necessarily describe this happening in any great detail is simply that it didn't suit my artistic needs. But if you are implying that somewhere in the book there is a vacuum, that somewhere in the book there is an implication that Negro women were not violated more or less systematically by white men who ruthlessly went down in the cabins, then you have totally misread the book. Because it's there.

Second Questioner: You see, the facts you included would *sell.* The whites *wanted* to read that Nat Turner was not a strong, black, revolutionary figure, but that he had certain sexual desires that drove him on. All right, you talk about his killing women and children. Let's take a look at the *Ten Black Writers* and how they analyze that. It seems that most of the men were away at a meeting. This made no difference. You talk about children; you make me believe that Nat Turner walked up and just stabbed babies or beat them in the head— which possibly would have been all right, because possibly he had the insight to know that these same little white babies would one day be the slave masters of his children, wherever they were. So wiping out the white children would be the very same thing as wiping out those adult honkies. When he burned down a house, he got white women and children and anybody else who was in the house. It made no difference who was in the house; when the house went up in flames, everybody and everything in the house went up, not just women and children.

Styron: What is your complaint?

Second Questioner: My complaint is this: don't just say he killed women and children, like the man had a hang-up or was afraid of white men, because explicitly the ten blacks tell you how he knocked some honky down and beat him to death, and then laid his wife down and killed her, right next to him. He wasn't afraid of white men; he killed white men, white babies, white women, white cats, white dogs, everything that was in the neighborhood.

Styron: Indeed he did. I tried to point out something to you, I think. I shall try again. (You reappear in my dreams; I knew somehow that you'd find me here. From Cambridge to New Orleans; it's more than the mind can encompass.) Anyway, if I may quote, in a sort of contradistinction to your ten black critics, one of the people who criticized the ten black critics, in this case Eugene Genovese. I think he pointed out, at least to my satisfaction, that if you will read the evidence—if you read the crude evidence of Nat Turner and his insurrection, and you can read it in twenty minutes—you will get the impression, and any rational person will get the impression when he is finished, of a ruthless and perhaps psychotic fanatic, a religious fanatic who, lacking any plan or purpose—admittedly, because it is in the testimony, lacking any plan or purpose—takes five or six rather bedraggled followers and goes off on a ruthless, directionless, aimless forty-eight-hour rampage of total destruction, in which the victims are, by a large majority, women and little children.

Second Questioner: But *white*.

Styron: No. Wait a minute. This is the crude evidence; this is what Lukács would say. These are the facts. Deal with them. I submit to you—I submit to any rational intelligence in this room who would allow himself twenty minutes—that this is the impression you would get. A deranged—

Second Questioner: It isn't the impression that I got.

Styron: Well, I'm sorry.

Second Questioner: It may be a white impression.

Styron: I don't think so.

Second Questioner: Quite clearly.

Styron: I don't think so. What Genovese was generous enough to grant me, in my dealings with this man, was that I supplied him with the motivation. I gave him a rationale. I gave him all of the confusions and desperations, troubles, worries.

Second Questioner: But look. Let's stop here.

Styron: Excuse me. Will you hear me out?

Second Questioner: He was a slave, and that gave him enough reason.

Styron: All right. Listen to me, will you, please?

Second Questioner: That gave him enough reason, right there.

Styron: All right.

Second Questioner: You didn't have to create anything for him. He saw brothers and sisters being killed all around him. He saw families being broken up.

Styron: The evidence . . .

Second Questioner: I notice your other point, that these were kind slavemasters. It doesn't matter how kind they were; they were slavemasters.

Styron: I'm sorry, you haven't read it carefully. The evidence doesn't show any . . .

Second Questioner: I've read it quite carefully.

Styron: Well, then, we're at an impasse, my friend, because you say it's one way, and I say it's another.

Second Questioner: Yes, but everytime we meet, you always jibe, and say that I miss your point. You ought to stop lying.

Woodward: Are there other people who want to ask questions?

Third Questioner: I have a question about another Southern novel, an older one. Perhaps I have read you, the panel, wrong, but I gather you would be willing to predict that in a hundred years *Gone with the Wind* will be an obscure or forgotten novel. From listening to what you have said about using historical facts and about catching the essence, I gather that you would think that *Gone with the Wind* has failed.

Styron: You must be crazy; I didn't say any such thing. I admired *Gone with the Wind* very, very much. I reread it about four years ago. It's a remarkable novel. I don't think it's a great novel, but it's a remarkable novel, precisely because this little woman from Atlanta had a fire of an imagination, which captured her and somehow allowed her to breathe some kind of miraculous spirit through and around the rather threadbare facts about antebellum Georgia. I certainly would not say that it's going to be dead in a hundred years. If I led you to believe that, you misunderstood me.

Woodward: Yes sir?

Fourth Questioner: As long as we call ourselves black and white, then even if we gain black power, unless we censor that movie I'm sure all white folks will go to it. They love that myth. But I think it's slightly beside the point. [*to Styron*] I would suggest, by the way, that I'm very sorry that Mr. Ellison didn't read your book. I'm extremely sorry, because of the putdown that you did on the young man. I think that intellectually you would have had a little bit more trouble with Mr. Ellison. I didn't stand up here for a putdown, so I'm not going to ask you anything at all. I have a whole lot of trouble with that book. I must say that, like every other black man, I resented it. I do think that the book must not be valid if all the black intellectuals put it down. If it salves the conscience (salves; how do you spell that word?)—if it salves the conscience of whites, and they want to read it, well, then you can make some money. But in view of this, I want to ask Mr. Warren this: since we all felt that *All the King's Men* had to do with Huey Long, why didn't *he* say Huey Long, or King Fish, or something like that? I wonder what would have happened to *The Confessions of Nat Turner* had it just been called the *Confessions of a Revolt Leader,* or something like that. I doubt if anybody would even have paid any attention to it. So I'd like to ask Mr. Ellison—he disguises his characters—

Ellison: I made them up; they were all me.

Fourth Questioner: Yes, I know, but you've lived through [the period] since Rinehart, you've lived through Malcolm—

Ellison: Yes.

Fourth Questioner: We've had some different experiences [since then.] I don't suggest that you follow in the footsteps of Leroi [Jones] really, as a lot of my militant friends would suggest, but since you are older, and you did live through something, I'd like to know—I mean, it was different, you know; everybody was trying to get along with whitey during that time, and now it's kind of six one way, half-a-dozen the other. But since you've lived through Malcolm, and I've heard that you are writing now, how do you see guys like Rinehart? Would you fictionalize Malcolm, disguise him, or would you feel free to say, well . . .

Ellison: I would be ashamed to tell the truth about Malcolm in fiction.

Fourth Questioner: Ashamed to tell the truth about him?

Ellison: Yes. Well, I think you're getting at a much more important problem which . . .

Fourth Questioner: You see, I'm concerned with *using* work . . . Malcolm versus fiction for instance. I'm saying, leave off the word Nat Turner on that book, and just make it the *Confessions of a Slave Leader,* and nobody would read it. (Which I don't think they should, anyway.) But what would you do with Malcolm?

Ellison: Well, wait a minute. You throw too many things at me at once, when you're really bouncing them off me to hit Bill.

Fourth Questioner: Yes, I'm trying very hard.

Ellison: All right . . .

Fourth Questioner: He [Styron] put down that other young man so skillfully. I think I'd be a little bit more trouble because I don't think that that young man was aware of the fact that Mr. Styron was trying to put him down.

Ellison: Maybe the young man . . .

Fourth Questioner: I thought that was cute and extremely unfair. Nine million people in this country voted for Wallace—I take that rather seriously. A fascist. I mean, you see, we haven't accomplished the revolution—

Ellison: May I . . .

Fourth Questioner: Yes, please.

Ellison: I think that there is a basic question of what all arts attempt to do, or what art should attempt to do. Through depicting the real, fictionally, imaginatively, by abstracting from the historical process, reducing it to a controlled situation where the imagination can load each character, each scene, each mood, even each punctuation mark with the individual writer's sense of life, art can give man some transcendent sense of his complexity and his potentiality—of his possibilities—and convey something of the wonder of human life, and I must say, without reducing man to what Malraux would call a handful of secrets . . .

Fourth Questioner: That's why I'm sorry you didn't read the book.

Ellison: . . . posited in his negative potentialities. I think that there is something else here which *you* might think about. I don't know whether you are a writer, or whether you should write, intend to write, or what not. But I think that there is a world of art, a world of fiction, and this must be protected against assaults. Not because we are black or white, or because we are oppressed and fighting for more freedom in this country, but because we seek to express ourselves. I want to say, I want the freedom to depict, to recreate Robert E. Lee in terms of my own vision of human possibility, human failure, and so on. So we cannot reduce this thing, really, to the struggle, which is very important on the political level. This distinction is very important, and I point out that two of the ten critics tried to stick to the literary, to the artistic problems involved. Beyond this, of course, as you and the other young man have dramatized so vividly for us, there *is* a problem. Damn it, there is a *problem* about recreating historical figures. That's why I said it's poison to the novelist; he shouldn't bother them. Don't appropriate the names. Don't move into the historian's arena, because you can only be slaughtered there. But you can also be very, very powerful, and I think that this should not be missed: this book, whatever its literary qualities—and I will stand up for Bill's personal qualities and his . . .

Fourth Questioner: Malcolm said that most whites in America, deep down in their toes, are racists, even when they don't think so.

Ellison: I would suspect that all Americans, black and white, are racists.

Fourth Questioner: Well, we . . .

Ellison: That isn't the problem here, you see. You asked me then what would I make of Malcolm. Well I wouldn't dare to tell the truth about him, because it would destroy the same myth, and this myth is a valuable myth. But I don't want Malcolm telling me what American history is, and I don't want him to tell me what my experience has been, and so on, any more than I want or I would allow Bill or anybody else to do that. You see, there is a world of fiction, and there's a world of politics. I think it's very important for your own position that you keep these things in clear perspective.

Fourth Questioner: Are you suggesting that we are still invisible?

Ellison: I am by no means. I was not invisible, and I would think that you, speaking with your inclination, would remember that old joke: The Negro is unseen because of his high visibility.

Woodward: Well, I hope that enigma will satisfy questions. There are people here who have been standing patiently for over two hours, and I feel that I am obliged to bring the meeting to a close after one more question.

Fifth Questioner: I was going to ask two questions, but I'll condense them. Mr. Styron has stressed several times what I think is probably the quintessential bone of contention this evening; he said—I think I quote him accurately—that the fiction writer's obligation is to make sense out of history. I was going to ask whether he thinks that is the fiction writer's primary, or one of his primary, obligations. I'd like to address my central question to Mr. Ellison, and step back to a novel that is not as recent and, at present I assume, not as controversial as *The Confessions of Nat Turner.* Mr. Ellison, you said that Jim of *Huckleberry Finn* was not rounded enough, and I think many of us would probably agree with that, but I'd like to ask whether you feel that this was because of a failure of creative imagination, or a failure of historical imagination, on the novelist's part. Or do you see the two as one problem?

Ellison: I think the author was too much a victim of the history of his times. Artistically, you see, fiction isn't written out of history, it's written out of other art forms. The going art form for depicting Negroes, the one freshest on the minds of people during Mark Twain's time, was the popular art form of the blackfaced minstrel, and it was that tradition which Mark Twain was very much involved in. His own values managed to project through Jim, but I still insist that it was not grounded enough in the reality of Negro American personality. I know of no black—Negro—critics (I'm a Negro, by the way) who wrote criticisms of *Huckleberry Finn* when it appeared. It was all a dialogue between, a recreation, a collaboration, between a white American novelist of good heart, of democratic vision, one dedicated to values—I know much of Mark Twain's writing—and white readers, primarily. What is going on now is that now you have more literate Negroes, and they are questioning themselves, and questioning everything which has occurred and been written in the country.

Fifth Questioner: Well, then, in a sense his creative imagination was limited in fact by the historical moment, and that is what has changed.

Ellison: Limited, too, by his being not quite as literary a man as he was required to be. Because he could have gone to Walter Scott, to the Russians, to any number of places, and found touchstones for filling out the complex humanity of that man who appeared in his book out of his own imagination, and who was known as Jim.

Fifth Questioner: But were any of the, let's say, less socially favored characters of novelists who were his contemporaries or his predecessors any more fully recreated historically than he managed to do with Jim? You know, with someone with whom he could not directly identify?

Ellison: Aren't you making this too much of an objective matter? It's a collaboration. It was a successful book. I read it years ago. In fact, it was so successful and so painful that they made it a boy's book, a children's book, in order to be able to deal with the moral pain which it aroused. Nevertheless, part of the discomfort which we feel—and the questions which those slaves (when was this? the 80's), those people of my background, would have asked about it—was not Mark Twain's central concern. What I am suggesting is that *everybody* reads now. *Everybody* is American whether they call themselves separatists, black separatists, secessionists or what not. And everybody is saying: Damn it, tell it like *I* think it is. And this is a real problem for the novelist.

Woodward: Ladies and gentlemen, we are limited to two hours and we have exceeded our limit. Let me thank you for your patience and good humor, and our fellow members for their contribution.

1. Irving Howe, preface to Georg Lukács, *The Historical Novel*, trans. Hannah and Stanley Mitchell (Boston: Beacon Press, 1962), pp. 9–10. Subsequent quotations are from this edition.

Intolerable America

Michel Salomon / 1969

From *Magazine littéraire*, March 1969, pp. 24–25. Reprinted by permission.

MS: What is your view of America today?

WS: I believe that one of the main reasons for the frustration and unhappiness in America is the chaotic urbanization which has completely swallowed us in the last twenty years. As for myself, I live in a rural area. I don't farm, but I like this way of life. It's very quiet and isolated. My first experience of New York was immediately after World War II. Of course, it was a large city even then, but as anyone will tell you it was not *this* large, *this* noisy and dirty, and it was not a hotbed of crime and frustration. You could walk anywhere in New York, at whatever time, day or night, without fear of being attacked. Now I wouldn't dare venture along Park Avenue after midnight. I think that, in a subtle way, a large part of our national tension derives from this anarchy, this gigantic urban octopus which wraps itself around us little by little. Too many cars, too many people, too much of everything joining forces to create loneliness and frustration. Yet, the reverse may not be true. I believe we've had our fill of bucolic imagery. There are also farmers murdering each other, country people who hang themselves. Still I believe you tend to be more satisfied with your lot, more at peace with yourself, as you move farther and farther away from the centers of these enormous and chaotic American cities which, I might add, are becoming uglier and uglier.

MS: What do you think of the drug phenomenon?

WS: There's no ready answer to that. Twenty years ago, during my first stay in New York, drugs were a minor problem. The causes for the enormous outbreak of drug use are complex. They even include the Mafia as one element in a network of very diverse causes. There is no drug problem in Nebraska.

MS: There are no blacks either.

WS: But neither are drugs very widespread among blacks in Alabama. It's an urban problem essentially. I was not born in a large city, but I have lived in New York long enough to feel a deep modification in the atmosphere, to feel the absurdity of the pressure the city exerts, and I don't think it comes from ourselves. I believe its causes are exterior: the plethora and the enormity of things in all large American cities—Chicago, Los Angeles, even Atlanta. And I believe that therein lies the main problem of American life: how to succeed in making the place where you live a pleasant community. Some people are quite content with life in the cities, but they are usually people who have the means of living very well. At a much inferior level, urbanization leads to the miserable state of mind we are describing. America has changed deeply. We no longer live in a rural world, nor even in the world of, let's say, Sherwood Anderson or Theodore Dreiser, admitting that these authors were speaking about other cities. When you consider New York in the works of Henry James, it's again something different. Even when James just describes the atmosphere, the geography of the place, and does not mention the manners of the well-to-do, he speaks of a community where it was possible to live with some refinement and style. When there are more and more cars, trucks, buses adding to the confusion, it leads any person sensitive to noise to the edge of neurosis. Like several of my French friends you may have noticed that, unlike Paris, there is no law here strictly forbidding the use of horns. During a stay in Paris, two months ago, I noticed the absence of this very real aggression on the senses. Of course I detest the traffic in Paris, I find it frightful, but at least this law against horns is enforced. I believe such a small thing can be a very important factor. New York is unlivable—no doubt about it. Most of my friends are city dwellers and do not share this feeling. They are immune, capable of facing the city. But for me the problem of urban horror is the central problem in American life.

MS: Do you think there might be a sort of quiet black power movement developing in the United States? Certain blacks sympathize with the black power movement but believe that its objectives will not be attained through violence and terrorism. Instead they will proceed by playing the game, participating in the bureaucracy, being elected mayor in some cities.

WS: The situation of blacks in the cities being what it is, the fact that Cleveland has elected a Negro mayor is very meaningful, since Cleveland is the sixth or seventh largest city in America. That shows extraordinary progress. Yet my friend Jason Epstein of the *New York Review of Books,* who has many contacts among the Harlem population, is thoroughly convinced that next summer we will see true open war in Harlem which, up to now, has escaped large-scale riots such as those in Watts and Detroit. My deep sense of despair about America stems from the fact that we are no longer controlling our environment, that we are allowing a kind of surreptitious ugliness to invade our landscape and, consequently, our minds.

MS: It's because you have too many things, like a child who has too many toys and whose room is cluttered. The appearance of America could be symbolized by these enormous junk yards that spread over several miles.

WS: Yes, it's very sad. But everyone cannot afford to live in the country. Our landscapes are among the most beautiful in the world. A spread of unspoiled land in New England is magnificent, but only a few are lucky enough to live in it. Vermont is, I believe, one of the most beautiful places on earth and yet, perhaps because of this, it occupies among the states a rank next to last in terms of population. It takes people to succeed in spoiling a place. The more numerous they are, the more complete the mess is.

MS: What do you think of the student movement, of the hippies, etc.?

WS: I don't know, I'm not close enough to that generation to be able to understand it. I don't know what that generation really seeks.

MS: Don't you visit universities?

WS: Very seldom. Sometimes I go to Yale because I am a fellow in one of its colleges, also because I don't live very far away. But I don't undertake extensive tours of universities; therefore, I've remained quite ignorant of the hippies' goals.

MS: But what do you think about the student movement as a phenomenon? Do you believe it to be as important as we do in Europe?

WS: I learned today from one of my doctor friends, who also teaches at the Cornell Medical School of the State University of New York, that the radical movement has even insinuated itself in the medical schools, which is really extraordinary. Medical students have started rebelling against traditional methods of teaching. This doctor thought the revolt was interesting because, for the most part, the

teaching of medicine had become frozen. Up to a point, this movement was quite refreshing to him. I believe that there are many valid
things in this revolt. In certain cases, protest has run wild and de-
generated into the ridiculous, but I think that, in the beginning, the
impulses were very positive.

The generation to which I belong went through World War II. I did
most of my studies after being discharged. That particular generation
must have been the most conservative and boring group of young
people this country has ever known. It's understandable. Like so
many other countries, America had waged a really very trying war,
and young people had no more time to waste. For those Americans
who had participated in it, that war was in fact the first this country
had experienced outside its own territory. It was also a murderous
war. We lost many men, and this experience marked the survivors for
many years. Personally, I was in the Marines and served in the
Pacific. When we returned we were very anxious to complete our
studies and succeed rapidly in society. Among other things, we young
men got involved in a blind struggle for wealth and social position. It
seems to me that it is those values that are rejected today. I believe
that, to a large extent, the young scorn the anti-intellectualism which
marked not only my own generation but previous ones as well—the
generation of people who are now in their fifties, for example.

MS: What do you think of the Jewish intellectual community and
its role?

WS: Its role in intellectual life is undeniably very important. Even
though you'll find a few eminent Jewish intellectuals among con-
servatives, like Sidney Hook or Lionel Trilling, you can say that the
Jewish intellectual community has always been liberal and that the
people at the *New York Review of Books,* for instance, are without a
doubt, from an American point of view, radicals (although none is
communist). A man like Benjamin Spock, a leader of the anti-Vietnam War movement, is a Jew. I do not involve myself personally in
all those activities but, at the same time, I do not disapprove of them.
It's really not my area of interest, but you could say I'm watching
from the edge of the racetrack. Actually I refer less to Spock and the
anti-Vietnam War movement than to the groups of intellectuals who
criticize the establishment from a more or less Marxist point of view,
without embracing communism.

MS: Is New York still the intellectual center of America?

WS: Yes, New York and Cambridge, I think. The University of California may be in the forefront as far as scientific research is concerned, but in the area of ideas I'd say that New York sees seventy-five percent of the creativity, Cambridge and Harvard twenty-five percent. In that community, you would find that fifty percent are Jews, that ninety percent of the people are leftists or centrists, and ten percent blend rather easily into some kind of conservatism—at least respectable conservatism, not the Goldwater type.

MS: Isn't such a division rather simplistic?

WS: It's often a practical means of describing a community, especially when speaking to a journalist.

MS: Do you think that the intellectual community is entirely divorced from the administration or isn't there a kind of myth about the Kennedy era, a purely sentimental disillusion?

WS: Without a doubt, all intellectuals agree that Johnson is not their man, when compared to Kennedy.

MS: But was Kennedy really their man? He was also a very good actor.

WS: But he was more than that. As I see it he may have been presented a little too insistently as an intellectual, but you should not underestimate a man who, on entering a room where I was, as he did two weeks before his death, was capable of coming straight to me and asking: how are you getting along with the book you're writing about rebellious black slaves? I had mentioned that subject to him only once, several months before, but he remembered it perfectly. You shouldn't neglect the value of such an incident with a man who was a political leader. Johnson, on the other hand, wouldn't even have known my name.

MS: But the average American likes Johnson, finds him a good Yankee representative.

WS: I'd really like to see the results of the opinion polls. Maybe the average Texan likes him, but I've heard taxi-drivers criticize him roundly. Recent statistics show that twenty-one percent of the population approves of the current policy of the government toward Vietnam. You'd have expected at least forty or fifty percent. This shows that currently there is a very great dissatisfaction in America.

MS: Are you working on a new book?

WS: I'm soon to begin work on two short novels, and I also write articles for the *New York Review of Books* and for *Harper's.*

MS: Are you on good terms with the literary world?

WS: I'm really not a part of it. I live on the fringe.

MS: A little like Salinger? Do you think he really exists, or is he a myth?

WS: I have never met him. He has not written anything in the past five or six years. He may have cracked, or he may be on the edge of madness.

The Editor Interviews William Styron

Philip Rahv / 1971

From *Modern Occasions*, 1 (Fall 1971), 501–10; republished in
Intellectual Digest, 2 (March 1972), 82–84. Rahv submitted
questions to Styron, who answered them in writing. The holograph manuscript of his responses is among his papers at Duke
University. The text published here has been corrected against
the manuscript.

Q: As I recall, your first novel *Lie Down in Darkness* appeared in
1951, and you will no doubt agree that the American literary situation has changed considerably and perhaps in very surprising ways
since then. What changes have particularly struck you—changes in
the qualitative productivity of writers as well as in the mood and general atmosphere of the literary life in America? Have we been witnessing a falling off in the quality of imaginative writing or merely a shift
to new techniques, assumptions and goals?

A: Random House has published two issues of a periodical devoted to Negro writing called *Amistad*. Despite the hope-inducing title
the overall tone of this venture is truculent and racist, and I was especially taken by an essay in the first issue entitled "Southern
Hegemony" by a professor of English at City College named Addison Gayle, Jr. It was not the attack on Faulkner and myself as apolo-
gists for the plantation tradition and creators of black stereotypes that
struck me about the professor's essay—this is old hat to me by now,
and besides I've resolved to try to touch as little as possible here on
the wearisome imbroglio surrounding *Nat Turner*—but what must be
one of the most remarkable statements about belles letteres to be
published in recent years: "It is no misstatement to say that American
culture today is little more than a fiefdom of Southerners who exercise more despotic control over the national literature than their
forefathers exercised over their plantations." This, from a professor of
literature, writing in 1970! Incredible as it was, I believe I had a
sneaking sense of confidence such as I haven't felt since those grim
days—dating back, I think, to the appearance of Malamud's first
work and the publication of *Augie March*—when I began to realize

that the tradition from which my own writing derived was no longer the hottest thing around.

It's not news anymore, but certainly the most dramatic change in the American literary situation has been the efflorescence of Jewish writers in all fields—not just the novel but journalism, drama, and criticism. In poetry the record has not been quite so spectacular. I wonder why. But indeed, there have been occasions when upon reading an issue of the *New York Times Book Review* I have gained the impression that *all* the new and interesting novelists were Jews. The sheer numerousness of Jewish writers has of course often been misleading because these writers are by no means of similar quality, and doubtless such a renaissance—like the erstwhile Southern renaissance—gives a certain feeling of sameness. Over recent years one senses a terrible monotony about the work of the lesser of these novelists: the same heroic-pathetic protagonist hemmed in by suburban blight and his own neuroses, comically grappling with a loveless marriage, a psychiatrist, a sadistic gentile boss and all the other twentieth-century horrors. This semipicturesque mode—not long ago it used to be called black humor—has become a kind of cliché. But the very best of these writers—and I'm thinking of Philip Roth, of course, and Bruce Jay Friedman and Irvin Faust and Leonard Michaels— have brought a personal vision and originality to their work, which in general has been of a high order. There are I'm sure many reasons for this phenomenon, but one of the most important is certainly the shift in America from the pastoral, small town life-style to the urban equivalent with its weird and singular frights and tensions. They in turn comprise such a set-up for the Jewish sensibility: that comic awareness so exquisitely poised between hilarity and anguish which seems the perfect literary foil for the monstrousness of life in big cities. This is of course not to say that the WASP consciousness has been lacking in a comic spirit to exorcise its own frights and tensions: it pervades the work of every good writer from Mark Twain to Faulkner to Sinclair Lewis to Ring Lardner to Peter de Vries—a WASPified Dutchman. In fact, it is hard to think of any American writer of consequence who is downright humorless, with the possible exception of Dreiser. But I think one can say that, generally speaking, the major work of every major American until recently has been tragic, at least *serious* in tone, adumbrated by Hawthorne's forest-gloom. The unique, wrenched comic cry of the Jew is certainly a new sound in American literature, and coincides with the rise of our intolerable cities, in which the Jew as denizen is the perfect witness—at least until the blacks find their real voice. Even Bellow, who I suppose is the most "serious" of our Jewish writers—as well as being one of our best writers—strikes some of his truest notes when he is being simply funny, as in his play *The Last Analysis*. At the same time, what I consider Bellow's most perfectly formed work, *Seize the Day*, is hardly funny—though streaked with mad flashes of humor—yet I know of no American narrative that leaves one with such an excruciating sense of the city as an awful presence.

Q: What do you feel about another well-known Jewish writer whom you haven't mentioned—Norman Mailer?

A: I think Mailer is the best journalist we have, a man of spectacular gifts, possibly a true innovator, and a showman of a very high class. For his own peace of mind I fervently hope that he wins the Nobel Prize. He has written some scurrilous things about me in the past, upon which I will not take this opportunity to retaliate, being a Christian. Apropos of which I'd like to add that, despite all the foregoing, I don't see any necessary end or even decline of writing by us uncircumcised dogs. In Moscow several years ago I was asked to discuss informally the subject of contemporary American writing before a small gathering of members of the Soviet Writers Union. In regard to certain trends, I made the mistake of asserting much too facilely that the Jews had a firm grip on the literary scene; "firm grip," I discovered later, was transmuted through my interpreter into the Russian equivalent of "stranglehold" and I could tell from the perturbed eyes and murmurations in the group that they thought I had dipped my toes in the dark waters of anti-Semitism. I hastily extricated myself by pointing out that I only meant that Jewish writing had "arrived" in the same way the other more or less clearly defined schools of literature had come to prominence during the history of America—a new country which allowed for very little stability or permanence in anything and whose very splintered and complex nature seemed to espouse the notion of regionalism. I said that modern Jewish writing seemed to me to represent a distinct outcropping of cultural regionalism, phenomenally vital at this particular moment but no more to be wondered at than its immediate predecessors—the

South of Faulkner, Warren & Company; the literary resurgence of the
Twenties whose most gifted exemplars were uprooted Midwesterners
like Hemingway, Fitzgerald, Sherwood Anderson and Willa Cather;
the Chicago school; and of course, far back the New England of
Hawthorne, Melville, Thoreau and Emerson. I said that there was a
certain amount of generalization involved in making this analysis, and
that the analogy was in any case imperfect since there were at all
times too many notable American writers who fitted no school or
regional classification, but that nonetheless it did appear to me that
Jewish writing as an entity was simply taking its place in the literary
mainstream at a fortuitous time in history. At this point I was asked:
did this mean that Southern writing had run its course, or was
finished? And I confess that for a long moment I was at a loss for
words. I think I must have said then what I still believe to be true
concerning the South and its literature. There was an Old South
which of course was a universe unto itself, and was quite unlike any
other geographical or cultural organism on this continent. The complex amalgam of its laws, its traditions, it codes of conduct, its religiosity—all mixed up with the hideous wound of the Civil War and
the agony of slavery—caused it to be immensely *different* from the
rest of the country, created a regional exoticism that virtually cried out
for treatment as literature. Much of the power of writers like Faulkner,
for instance, or Flannery O'Connor, derived from their ability to see
the bizarre connotations of this *difference* of the South, to perceive
the ironies and contradictions involved when people inheriting so directly the manners and mores of a nineteenth-century feudal, agrarian society collided head-on with the necessities of an industrial
civilization. The result of the collision—and I might add the collision,
with all of its ironies and contradictions, is not unlike the collision of
the modern Jew with our urban civilization and its discontents—may
have been comic or more often, with Faulkner at least, tragic, but it
did give rise to a rich, viable literature. Yet now as this difference is
erased and the contradictions smoothed out, now that the South to
everyone's amazement proves to accommodate itself to racial integration far more gracefully than the North, now that Atlanta resembles Detroit and industrial plants sprout like mushrooms up and
down the seaboard and the girls wear hot pants on the streets of
Nashville—now that the difference has gone, and no one save a few

antiquarians and scholars and readers of Faulkner can know what the Old South really was; now, in short, as the South is truly absorbed into the substance of the rest of the nation, I think that Southern writing, if it doesn't fade away altogether, will certainly no longer correspond to anything we recall from its illustrious past. Possibly the works of Walker Percy give a clue. I think it's fascinating that he and Flannery O'Connor, two of the very few really interesting Southern writers of the post-war period, are both Catholics with a skeptical turn of mind. But to get back to my original point, I'm sure that writers like Percy will coexist handily with the Jews in their great resurgence. In Nixon's paradise, there should be plenty of *Lebensraum* for everybody.

Q: There is a general impression abroad that the novel as a creative genre has seen its days and is now in a state of decline. It is being said that the national existence is so fabulously dramatic and bizarre in many of its manifestations that the novelist cannot be expected to keep up with it. Hence it is claimed that so far as intrinsic interest is concerned the journalistic article is superior to fiction; and people cite such books as Truman Capote's *In Cold Blood* and Mailer's *Armies of the Night* as examples of how fictional techniques can be applied successfully to the account of actual events. In other words, what is being asserted is that history has overtaken the novel and left it in the rear.

In your opinion, is there any validity in these claims of the novel's decline? Or are the obsequies read over it altogether premature in that they are based on a fundamental misconception of the relation of the imaginative act to "real life"? Can it be said that there is a specific area of experience, actual or potential, which is open to the novelist and which is by definition closed to the reporter or journalist, however avidly he pounces on the raw actualities of "life" in its sheer immediacy and amorphous condition?

A: Haven't the obsequies been read over the novel since time immemorial, really? The short story seems to have suffered a mysterious decline, but I don't really think the novel has. I remember that as a very young writer twenty years ago, right after *Lie Down in Darkness* was published, I participated in my first literary symposium. It was sponsored, I recollect, by the P.E.N. Club. The subject even then was tired: "Is the Novel Dead?" I don't recall what I said, or much of

what was said in general, but I do think I remember that the participants concluded that the prognosis for the health of the novel was
tentatively hopeful. I think I would conclude the same today, with a
few important qualifications. In a negative sense, I no longer can say
that I really feel the same excitement I once felt upon reading a
novel—any novel, including not very good novels. I remember the
avidity with which I pounced on novels fifteen or twenty years ago,
devouring several a week sometimes. Whether the change came
about in me or in the temper of the time I don't know, but I certainly
no longer pay novels the passionate court and attention I once did. I
think that all this somehow does have to do with the dramatic and
bizarre quality of the national existence that you allude to—the sheer
distractedness of life—yet I am still far from ready to sell fiction down
the river. A number of years ago Norman Podhoretz wrote an essay
(or perhaps several essays) which held the point of view that fiction
was substantially moribund, and that expository writing such as that
represented by the best essayists and journalists was supplanting
fictional narrative as a viable art form. I think Podhoretz wildly over-
stated his case, for reasons I'll try to touch on in a moment, but along
the way he did make what I thought were some astute observations—observations which at the time helped explain my own dimin-
ishing interest in the general run of fiction. Where I agreed with him
was in his point that in this fantastic world the claims on our emotions
and our intellect are so urgent, so persistent and clamorous, that it is
no longer either sufficient or rewarding to curl up with yet another
cleverly written, well-crafted novel which describes, say, the beginning and the end of a love affair. During the novel's serene heyday
the changes and variations on this theme—and a score of other
themes—might readily engross the reader's attention, but in our day
they no longer suffice; we've been there too many times before. But
the undoubted decline of interest in the kind of novel Podhoretz was
citing seems to me in the end to be literature's gain, for it more and
more demands of our best writers that they seek arresting new
modes—and I don't mean tricks—and, even more importantly,
significant themes. At the same time it should encourage mediocre
writers to go back to turning out advertising copy. For while
Podhoretz is right, I believe, in his claim that essays and journalism
can now best handle much of what once lay exclusively in the prov-

ince of fiction (Baldwin's noble *The Fire Next Time* is certainly worth
a score of "problem" novels about the racial conflict, and Mailer's
operatic style was perfectly wedded to his subject matter in *The Armies of the Night*) I am still convinced that at its best the novel has a
poetic and moral dimension, an imaginative thrust, a transcendental
reality that simply renders even superlative journalism inferior by
comparison. Off-hand I can name at least four novels—all of them to
my mind genuine works of art and all of them of the post-war period—which illustrate what I mean. That is, besides being works of
art, they all fulfill that ancient definition of the novel as a medium
which "brings us the news." The books I have in mind are *All the
King's Men, The Tin Drum, The First Circle,* and *Lolita.* No work of
reportage could ever equal Warren's brilliant revelation of the career
of a Southern politician; although of course his novel is much more.
Grass and Solzhenitsyn have told us more about post-war Germany
and life in Soviet Russia than any number of journalistic think-pieces;
and as for one aspect alone of American life in *Lolita*—that marvelous portrayal of life in motel rooms and on the open road, all coun-
terpointed against Humbert Humbert's blissful erotic
crucifixion—what journalism could possibly hope to match it? What I
think I'm trying to say is that some of the best novels have always
had a large element of the journalistic embedded in them; the novel's
poetic and imaginative freedom allows the writer to use and at the
same time to transcend the journalistic, and in fortunate cases to produce something more lasting. I might add that I think *Nat Turner* is a
case in point. I might surely have been able to write a creditable
piece of historical journalism around the Turner insurrection; after all,
it was a real event. But it was the imaginative potential of the event
that challenged me, and only a novel could have allowed me to
dramatize the event and at the same time to create a synthesis of all
the various aspects of slavery and the ante-bellum South that I
wanted to get down on paper.

   Q: From your point of view as a novelist, what do you make of the
impact of so-called youth culture on the literary life in America?
There is the cult of the movies, for instance, by which many young
people are now caught up, and there is also the McLuhanite trend to
elevate the media of sheer visuality above any kind of verbal expression. Do you think of these as long-term phenomena that tend to

undermine the literary effort or do you regard them as mere transient enthusiasms? Do you believe that some of the techniques developed in movie-making are transferable to the fictional medium?

A: One thing I'm often baffled by is the solemn attention paid by such organs as the *New York Times Book Review* and other journals to the matter of what young people seem to be reading. To be sure, most of them don't read much of anything, but I'm constantly amazed at the concern displayed at what reading habits they do have, as if whatever latest cult-hero they idolized might be in itself a fact of far-reaching significance. About ten years ago it was Salinger. Now we have it on very good authority that just at one university— Yale—a year will go by without the name of Salinger ever being uttered. Then there was Kerouac, then Golding, then Tolkien—all fads, all faded. Certainly Salinger, at least, deserves better! I myself have been occasionally pleased to find that I'm on the reading list at such-and-such a college, but it's now clear that it must literally be a fate like death to be the object of a cult. I hear that Richard Brautigan is the newest arrival; I extend him my condolences. I suspect that *Catch-22,* which is enormously popular, will survive on its own merits, but the continuing admiration displayed for John Knowles' *A Separate Peace* simply eludes me since I cannot understand how that vapid prose could appeal to anyone, no matter how young. However, I suppose we should be thankful that they're reading something, and I think it might be much healthier that they passionately read even a writer who tends to reinforce their most unsubtle prejudices, like Vonnegut, than they be force-fed courses in the minor Victorian poets, as I was.

A graver development among young people, in my opinion, is their increasing disregard for history—either as a college discipline or as a general field of interest. A recent *New York Times* article noted that in high schools interest among the students in history was practically nil, while the overall enrollment in history courses in American universities and colleges during the past few years had diminished by a third—astonishing and sinister if true. All of this of course is directly linked to the mystique of "Now," the principle of instant gratification and the consequent abhorrence of anything traditional that has so firmly seized at least a large segment of the young. I doubt if all of this could be blamed on the decade-long atrocity in Southeast Asia.

The whole cultural revolution we are going through—including its faddism, its sexual liberation, anti-intellectualism, and scorn for the old and the past—is the result of irresistible pressures against so much that was stupidly puritanical, stifling, hidebound and square in American life, and a great deal of it I find healthy and exhilarating. I suspect that the younger generation would be very much the same even without the present war. But certainly the war tends almost to validate even the worst extremes of the youth culture, including drugs. In the face of the very real possibility of personal annihilation in a totally immoral conflict, how could the pursuit of any discipline—history perhaps above all—have any meaning?

As for the effect of the movies and the other media upon our literary life, I have never really considered them a major cultural threat. It has been posulated that the influence and power of the mass media have caused them to siphon off great talent from more serious endeavors—literature and the arts—but this is palpably not so, if you consider the general sleaziness and mediocrity of what turns up on television or at the local movie house. I think I have a higher regard than Mary McCarthy for movies as a medium—at their rare best they can convey a wonderful immediacy and excitement—but I do share the feeling she expressed in these pages that they are not an art-form. I believe it was one of the greater exponents of the medium, Jean Renoir, who got to the heart of the matter when he said that movies date more quickly than any other form of communication. I would certainly agree, for although they can often vividly refract the surfaces of the contemporary they are almost never able (except for an instant or two in Bergman and perhaps Fellini) to evoke the timeless.

I recall that about twenty years ago, in the early fifties, there was a great stir and alarm in intellectual circles about something called "mass culture"; the idea was feverishly spread that high culture as we know it—literature, music, art—was in imminent danger of destruction by the proliferating vulgarity of the hoi polloi. But two decades later I can't really see any significant change; things are perhaps a little bit better and hardly any worse. Television is still the abomination that it was and Broadway still cranks out tawdry musicals; but books get published, good music is still performed, and the cultural scene in general is much more lively and interesting than it was when

the literati were broadcasting their fears, back in Eisenhower's fifties.
There are some causes for concern, of course: the decline or disap-
pearance of so many magazines is one. But the McLuhan bugaboo
has never frightened me, really. I think that the so-called "high" and
"low" cultures, while perhaps tending to overlap in some ways more
than ever before—the influence of movie technique on the novel IS
an example—will in general remain discrete and parallel forces as
they have always been, basically independent of each other, to
everyone's satisfaction and relief.

Q: Pornography is now to all intents and purposes freely available
throughout the United States. In fact in the name of freedom of expression anything goes, so that nearly every kind of pornographic
material, no matter how obscenely perverse, is being widely distributed. Now quite apart from the sociological implications of this state
of affairs (i.e., whether or not pornography promotes juvenile delinquency, etc., etc.), what if any are the specific effects on the writing of
serious fiction at a time when the explicit or clinical sexual scene has
become virtually mandatory? Or to put it even more plainly, does the
recourse to the formulas of pornography and its characteristic obses-
sions and compulsions tend to liberate or, conversely, to coarsen and
cheapen the literary faculty?

A: A distinguished British critic told me not long ago that he had
publicly advocated the free dissemination of pornography mainly because he felt it was a superb aid to masturbation. Since we were not
intimately acquainted I failed to ask why a healthy-looking man like
himself, and one so imaginatively gifted, should require the aid of
pornography in his autoerotic seizures. I was further puzzled when,
not too long afterwards, I was made a present of a great deal of
hard-core pornography, both written and visual. I must confess that I
perused this mammoth collection with eagerness, discovering in the
process that pornography (a) satisfied my curiosity about certain
things, (b) almost never stirred me to the same libidinal response as
the British critic, (c) frankly repelled me in many of its manifestations,
and (d) caused in me no impulse to see more. Only (a) was a positive
response and I would like to suggest that the curiosity-satisfying aspect of pornography may be its chief and perhaps its only value. For
those of us brought up with all of the Calvinist repressions it is
cathartic if nothing else to discover that a six-person orgy looks like

nothing so much as a plate of macaroni rather than the stirring Dionysian frieze that one had imagined; that a significant number of male pornographic participants have penises that are limp or, if erect, seem to be gratifyingly no larger than one's own; that if you have seen one act of fellatio you have, almost literally, seen them all; that buggery looks truly painful; and so on. When pornography has either refuted or corroborated one's fantasies it has served its function and may be put back up on the shelf. I cannot possibly imagine it harming anyone, although some of it could make a very sensitive person nauseous.

I think that the general relaxation of taboos on language in books has been a very healthy thing, allowing writers at their discretion to use words and to evoke situations and attitudes which even twenty years ago would have brought down upon them the wrath of the law. Without this new freedom a book like *Portnoy's Complaint* could never have been published, nor could I have gotten by with some of the scenes in *Nat Turner.* But this has very little to do with pornography. Many serious writers in the past (like painters) have secretly created pornography to stimulate themselves or their friends; now that pornography is virtually legal I doubt very much that good writers will resort to it in order to stimulate the general reader.

Conversation: Arthur Miller
and William Styron

Rust Hills / June 1971

From *Audience,* 1 (November-December 1971), 4–21. Reprinted by permission.

Arthur Miller, the playwright, and his wife, the photographer Inge Morath, live in a large, comfortable house on a hillside overlooking the farms and woodlands of Roxbury, Connecticut. Not far away live William Styron, the novelist, and his wife, Rose, an associate editor of *The Paris Review.* The two couples are good friends and see one another often. One afternoon in June, 1971, I drove over from my own home in Stonington, sent by *Audience* to listen to the two men talk, and very kindly invited by Mrs. Miller to stay for dinner with the four of them. The conversation took place in a small study with a big desk which Miller uses "just to pay bills"; he has a separate studio to work in. Styron settled into Miller's desk chair and Miller straddled a chair in the middle of the room. We had two tape recorders going.

PARTICIPANTS
AM Arthur Miller
WS William Styron
IM Inge Morath
RS Rose Styron
A *Audience* (Rust Hills)

IM: I just wanted to take a couple of pictures. I'll take them quickly, then I'll be out. Okay? Just while you're starting?

WS: What kind of questions you going to ask, Rust?

A: Well, I think one of the things I want to ask you is advice. It was all Inge's idea originally—

IM: I said, "Writers should talk to each other."

AM: Yeah, and they do—

WS: I think it's a good idea.

A: Well, you know, interviews have kind of run their course. I mean, everybody's sick of interviews: the people who get interviewed, the readers, maybe even the interviewers. And, but—you guys must *talk,* and if we could—I know it's hard to simulate that, but, uh—One thing that surprised me when we cast about for people to do these *Audience* "Conversations" with one another, we kept coming up with names of writers. Maybe it's just that I don't know any musicians, or something like that, but it doesn't seem to me that painters or musicians or anyone *talk* as well as writers, which is kind of an irony.

WS: Musicians talk well, painters don't, I've found. Would you agree, Arthur?

AM: Painters are impossible.

WS: They really are, verbally, with a few exceptions, like Bob Motherwell. On the other hand, I've known some marvelously articulate musicians. People like Sam Barber and—well, Lenny Bernstein, and Aaron Copeland, are truly gifted conversationalists. But painters, generally speaking, are—*(breaks off, laughs, starts again)* I think I decided not to live out near East Hampton because I'd have to listen to all these painters.

A: Another thing I don't have an idea about is whether these conversations should have a central theme for each one, or a theme that continues from conversation to conversation, or just be the kind of interaction that occurs between the two people involved—have it shape its own form. *(to Miller)* I should think it would be a little like putting two characters together on a stage, or is that presumptuous?

WS: No, I think that since you're trying this out and don't know what form it is going to take, you should just let it have its head and see what comes out of it.

A: What do you two normally talk about? You're neighbors here, and you get together—

WS: Well, I guess over the years we've talked about just about everything.

AM: Yeah, including, uh, well, sometimes local stuff.

WS: Connecticut politics, the arrival of the Connecticut state income tax—

AM: Taxes in general.

WS: God, taxes in general.

A: And real estate, surely real estate?

WS: Land, carpentry, construction, buildings.

AM: I don't know, I think that, uh, the issues of—if there are any—of *writing,* come up least of all.

WS: Just about, I think that—without being necessarily boorish—that writers conversing with one another tend to talk about *non*-literary matters probably more than . . .

AM: *(interrupts)* Unless it's the critics.

WS: Yes. *(both laugh)* The critics always come in for a rough time, especially if it's around the time a work is appearing, right?

AM: Yes. In fact I was just over in the bookstore this afternoon to pick up a book I had urgently ordered three months ago and completely forgot about. I thought I couldn't live without it, and I just remembered today that I'd ordered it. And there was Bob Anderson . . . in the bookstore. And in two minutes what we were talking about was who was going to succeed Richard Watts on the *Post,* and—who's the other guy?—somebody else who looks like he's going to be succeeded. And I've heard this disastrous conversation all my life.

WS: Well, it's especially true, I think, Arthur in the theater. We fiction writers bitch as much about literary critics as you playwrights do about drama critics, but I think they don't have this overwhelming power in the world of books that they do in the theater, and that's why playwrights tend to carve them up—

AM: Well, they kill you. They can really destroy you. But that's a funny thing—I remember Chekhov writing somebody a letter saying that if he had listened to the critics he would have died drunk in the gutter.

WS: True.

AM: I guess it was a different situation in Moscow in the nineteenth century than it is here, but it doesn't matter.

WS: You mean *(pause),* it doesn't matter in what way?

AM: I mean that, uh, presumably they didn't kill off any other Chekhovs. *(pauses)* I guess *(pauses again)* in the long run. Or Ibsens, or anything of the kind. Ibsen—I was just reading a biography of Ibsen, in which he was inveighing against critics in the same way. They exercise, they *import* trouble, I think. But in the final analysis maybe they're not as important as we make them out to be. I don't think twelve people in this country could name the Norwegian critics at the time of Ibsen *(Styron laughs)*, and yet they were the real bane of his . . .

WS: Bane of his life. Well, my feeling about critics is very interior, and it has to do with maturity and growth and one's own self-confidence, because when I was a young beginning writer, the slightest slur could just cause me the most horrible despondency.

AM: Yeah, cringing.

WS: *Cringing,* that's what I wanted to say. And as I've gotten a bit mellower, I would still have to be frank to admit I still don't *like* harsh criticism or those attacks that writers always get, but I've found that I've developed a very thick skin over the years. If one is subjected to the kind of vituperation that, say, *Nat Turner* received, one's epidermis has to become calloused. And I do tend to agree with you that perhaps the first thing a young writer should try to do is remember that critics really do not count for a whole lot.

AM: I think, though, they mean a tremendous amount to a young writer, because in effect they launch him.

WS: You mean in the positive sense?

AM: Yes. Without them it's pretty hard for a man who's never been heard of to make any impression, because the public doesn't know his name and has no reason to buy his book or see his play. You're so to speak born under a curse in these fields: you enter by virtue of their support, more or less, or at least their negligence.

WS: Well, certainly to be cast into total oblivion like so many young writers are by the book reviewers, as distinct from the critics, is an unfortunate thing to happen—especially when the young writer happens to have talent. Most full-fledged critics, of course, don't pay much attention to new writers per se anyway, unless . . .

AM: Right. They're busy with established people.

A: Has a critic, as against a reviewer, ever pointed out anything to you in your work that you didn't know was there?

WS: Never! (Audience *laughs*) I honestly don't think so.

AM: I never had that experience. In fact, I've talked to numerous writers in my life and I've never heard one say that, even the ones who were favorites of the critics. I think that what we call criticism is most of the time just a projection of one man's—is just what the work reminds the critic of—in one way or another. I had one—I wish I'd

saved it, it must exist—it was a review by George Jean Nathan, who
was then finishing his career, when I came in, and he reviewed—I
can't remember which play, I think it was *All My Sons*. And the
whole review—it wasn't a condemnatory review and it was sort of,
uh, interested in the work. But all he did for a double column in the
Hearst paper which he was then working for—the New York *American*, I think it was, or the *Journal*, or the *Journal-American*, whatever
it was called, was: he listed all the plays—and there must've been
one hundred—which in some way, shape, or fashion this play of
mine evoked in his mind. Not saying it was copying them or anything—all it was was a display of his memory. And I would say, of the
hundred, eighty-five I had never heard of, or of the authors. Many of
them were Hungarian plays that had never reached Budapest
(laughs). That was the archetype of that kind of criticism for me. He
was quite open about it, though. He felt, I think, that his audience
expected erudition and would sit there and marvel at how much he
knew. I never did understand what his influence was. *(pause)* But I
guess that twenty years earlier, when he was a great partisan of
O'Neill's, and—on the whole, I guess his taste was to—he was a
debunker of the ordinary theater.

WS: Yes. I think there is something to be said for the craft of criticism when it is addressed to the task of illuminating and elucidating
work. I think this can be a very high-level sort of activity. And if done
by the hand of a master—like an Edmund Wilson or a Leavis or a
Rahv—it can really bring us into a new awareness of the work. And
this is what the high function of the critic is. Almost all valuable criticism seems to me an attempt to do this. Negative and destructive
criticism is of almost no value whatsoever, it seems to me.

AM: Well, they're interested, aren't they, in telling you what's in or
out? What's to be admitted into the halls.

WS: Yes. This is what makes critics like that of very little value.
They remain essentially hack reviewers with fancy prose styles to give
them a kind of fake cachet. But basically, because as Arthur says, it's
a matter of letting a writer in the hall or out, their function is that of a
flunky, a doorman.

A: *(laughs)* But they'd say they were keeping up the standards.

WS: Well, they're not, because their personal esthetic is too degrading, too antipathetical to literature. There are undoubtedly cer-

tain critics who've become famous as practitioners of hatred and destruction. I could name a few—but won't. This is not to say that literature shouldn't always be under examination. One does not wish for shoddy goods to be accepted as fine material. But the distinction I'm trying to make is between the doorman—and the true critic, who is usually a man who has dedicated himself to the task of showing us what's of value in a work. Valueless works do not usually need to be torn down; they are already on the junk heap.

AM: Yeah, well, the whole thing is in a context, in this country anyway, of a dwindling audience. Perhaps this is true for fiction, it's certainly true of the theater. In other words, the importance of the critic to the survival of the work is in proportion to the social debilitation of the art. Where you have a thriving theater, which is inexpensive, easy to get into, and is a part of the lives of the people, then the make-or-break power of the critic is minimal. Those who are more fastidious in their tastes might consult them for their opinion or to buttress what they already think. But in times like that criticism doesn't have any effect on the art of the time. There is no gatekeeper because there is no gate. It's rather a flow of life that goes in and out of these playhouses. For example, in England until recently the critics were self-consciously aware that the American critic had a power that was inconceivable in England. There was no critic or group of critics in England that could literally close a show, and the reason was simple: the price of the thing was so minimal, even in an inflated economy, that people would go to see a play because they thought there was an interesting actor in it, or because there was a good scene in the play, or because the idea appealed to them—and even though they knew the play had been dismissed by many critics. But you'd spend the little ticket price there was, if you were interested in the theater, just to see what it was you wanted to see about it. Now when that price starts rising, as it has in England, people begin wanting some kind of guarantee that their six or eight bucks, as compared with two dollars or a dollar-and-a-half, is not going to be thrown away. Then the critic becomes the gate-keeper.

A: In the same way the price of the average first novel has made the gate-keeper almost necessary there too.

AM: Yeah, sure. The publishers all tell you now that to publish a new and unknown work of maybe doubtful acceptability grows

harder and harder by the day and in some places is impossible anymore, simply because the cost of production is what it is. *(to Styron)*
We've got an example here, in the book you reviewed only two
weeks ago, on the front page of the *Times Book Review.*

WS: Jim Blake.

A: Jim Blake's letters from prison, mostly to Nelson Algren?

WS: Right, it's a fascinating book.

AM: But there is apparently no advertising budget for it of any
description.

WS: None at all. It's a felony.

AM: There just isn't any at all. Blake said he nearly got in a fist
fight with the Doubleday advertising manager. Now here they've got
a front-page, positive review by William Styron, and I understand
they simply have not got—in other words, that was not the horse that
was going to run.

WS: It was dead before it started.

AM: It makes you wonder why they published the book at all.

WS: It's too bad. *(A pause)*

A: Do you ever, when you're talking, talk about what you're working on? I mean, do you know what Bill's working on? And do you,
Bill, know what he's working on?

AM: I know Bill's working on a book.

WS: I know Arthur's doing something called a play. *(both laugh)*
No, I think we wait until the moment of fruition before that. I can't
say it exactly bores me to talk about work in progress, but after a
while if you talk about it too much, it becomes a very tiresome subject to yourself. And therefore I think it's often advisable just to shut
up about it and talk about other things and just wait for the moment.
(to Miller) Because I think I've been to all your first nights in the last
six or seven years, and this is where you learn what it's all about.

AM: Although, you know, I was going to say it doesn't do any
good reading things to people, excepting I was just thinking the Russians were always reading things to each other, and I suppose they
still do.

WS: I remember you read a couple of short stories to us one
night. I think short stories make the perfect readable commodity—a
manageable length, and one does not drone on too long.

A: Willie Morris told us that you have a short story about your
grandfather arriving in this country?

AM: Yeah, my father.

A: He says it is absolutely marvelous and that we must move heaven and hell to get you to let us have it.

AM: Well, it was part of something else, that's why I didn't let it go. I wanted to do more with it, and I haven't had time.

A: Is it related to the play? It seems to me that Morris told Geoff Ward that it was related to the play, the one you're working on.

AM: Well, in a way it is. But only remotely. That wasn't the reason that I—I thought I would write a large kind of memoir, which I started to do, then stopped doing. I haven't decided quite what form to do it in. It's not quite ready. Willie read sort of the raw material, which is—it could be published.

A: Lord knows, we'd love to do it. Is it true you sometimes write a short prose version of what later becomes a play?

AM: Well, that happens. But I generally don't publish them, because it gets broken off somewhere, and suddenly I realize I'm writing a precis of what I feel I can do better on the stage. It seems to me that there are a lot of words on the prose page *(laughs)* and sometimes with five exchanges of dialogue it seems to me I make it come to life, you know. Whereas on the printed page it doesn't quite do that.

A: *(to Styron)* You can't agree with that.

AM: No, no, I mean for me. I'm looking for an audience, I suppose.

A: You're imagining an audience.

AM: Yeah, yeah.

WS: Well, I've noticed just recently in writing this movie script I've been working on with John Marquand—it's my first attempt since college to do something in dramatic form—it's not for the stage, it's strictly for film. But I feel the enormous sense of immediacy and aliveness. . .

AM: *Isn't it!?*

WS: It's such a sense of freedom to be unshackled from the restraints of those formal, stately, Latinate . . .

AM: It's vulgar! It's vulgar!

WS: *(laughs)* Yes, but . . .

AM: I mean vulgar in the *old* sense, it belongs to the people.

WS: Yeah, yeah, you're *talking* here. These lines are just rolling out from your characters, and they have such a sense of freshness, even when possibly they're not very good. Nevertheless, you're not sitting down with that ghastly moment, the famous moment Paul Valéry describes, when he says he *could not write that line.* That's why he never wrote a novel. The line being—what is it?—"the duchess went out at five in the afternoon—" I mean, that is the bane and horror of being a prose writer. The furniture. Moving people in and out of rooms.

AM: *(laughs)* To me, there's a screen—I love prose, I love to write it and read it—it is a different screen, though, between yourself and the reader or the audience. And I always feel the screen is down—in other words, that dialogue is evidence. It's a delusion, of course, because after all you're creating the dialogue too. I mean, if a man comes to the door, you can describe him, but suddenly he says something, and it all changes. *He is a witness to himself.* And you're standing aside and not there.

A: But aren't you just giving over the aspects of delineation or description to the actor for appearance, and to the set-designer for the room?

AM: Excepting you're in great control. You could argue that you're in as much control as you are on the printed page, because how many misinterpretations—*(to Styron)* as you can be the witness—can there be to a novel. I mean, the reader's left to his own devices. And he hasn't *got* control you could exercise over his imagination by selecting the actor, and by inflecting the lines. The controls are there. The problem is that most playwrights vacate because they're overwhelmed by the professionalism of other collaborators, like the director and the actors, and they simply walk away from the whole business. But you don't have to necessarily.

WS: That's I think the strength and the weakness of drama, of the *task* of playwrighting, if I get it correctly. The weakness being, okay, you've written a masterpiece, but a masterpiece can be destroyed by a horrible performance. Whereas a work of prose—fiction, let us say—doesn't yield itself to that kind of destruction. You have a bad reader, but that's the reader's fault. The work itself—

AM: Stands there.

WS:—has its own integrity.

A: *(to Styron)* You had a lot of bad readers with *Nat Turner,* didn't you?

WS: Well—it's complicated. *(laughs)* Yes, I guess I had a lot of bad readers.

A: Did you ever do that piece called "Nobody Knows De Trouble I Seen" about it?

WS: Well, someday I'm either going to do it myself, or—a lot of people have said they wanted to do it and have asked if I have the information. I have a bushel basket full of stuff that I would love to give to somebody I trust someday to put together in a way that would put it all in perspective. There's probably been more controversy on *Nat Turner* than any American novel since Harriet Beecher Stowe's. In fact, there are now two books out on the controversy itself. But what they are, are merely collections of essays that have been written about the book.

A: Yes. *(to Miller)* Have you ever had a missed reaction? Did *The Crucible* have any of that kind of . . .

AM: Oh, sure. So did *Salesman* to a degree, but that's all been forgotten. But *The Crucible* was certainly completely dismissed by a large part of the people—and in anger, too. Because it was regarded as a specious defense of the Communists, namely that: there were no witches, but there *are* Communists.

WS: Uh huh, I remember that.

AM: A lot of angry stuff came out of that.

A: Did you answer at the time, the way Bill is considering an answer?

AM: Yeah, I did. I had some interviews and tried to answer it. But of course at that time the furies were riding high. In the McCarthy times the winds were blowing so fast you couldn't hear yourself think. And I don't recall any important person coming to the defense of even the principle involved, let alone the play itself.

WS: You mean, when you say that, there was for instance no long responsive essay in the Sunday *Times,* saying: let's put this matter straight.

AM: No, there wasn't. They would have just as soon forgot the whole thing. It took about four to five years before the play was done again, off-Broadway.

WS: Then it damaged the play at the time?

AM: Oh, definitely, definitely. You see, I'd just had *Death of a Salesman* on, which was an immense hit. And this play came in, and it wasn't all that long later. As soon as the sense of what it was about became apparent, you could feel a coating of ice over that audience. It was just thick enough to *skate* on. It was sheer *terror.* It was *real* terror. I had been in the theater a long time by that time and I'd never experienced such a sensation. In fact, people I knew quite well—newspaper people and so on—when I was standing in the back of the theater and they came out, didn't turn to nod to me.

A: *(whispers)* Wow!

AM: It was as though I—It was at the Martin Beck Theater, I'll never forget that evening—and, you know, newspaper columnists and people I didn't know all that well, but I *knew* them, they'd interviewed me, and we'd shaken hands a few times. And they walked right past me as if I was another post holding up the ceiling. It was quite something.

WS: Yes. Well, that must have been at least as unsettling to you as it was to me when I had my reaction, because yours was coming not from a minority group as mine was, although—alas!—it was coming from the minority I had written about. Nonetheless, the hostility *you're* describing was coming from your peers, so to speak.

AM: It came from almost every quarter. And it was frightening to me because at that time no one could tell what the end result of the McCarthy movement would bring. There was no real resistance to it. The youth were inert. The trade unions were as much with it as anybody else. Where could you look for any ally? You know what I mean? Well, man alive. To tell you the truth I stood back there and I thought: well, if this is the way it is, then the jig is up. No one knew he was going to die . . .

WS: We were saved just in the nick of time.

AM: Right, right.

WS: This can be a very disheartening thing to have happen—to have a work of literature attacked on ad hominem and at the same time political grounds . . .

A: Well, you both chose to write—historically, admittedly—but about contemporary issues and you didn't conceal their relevance, and you both *got* a reaction . . .

AM: Oh, sure, sure we did. You know, the final pay-off to this was that I was in England, and Olivier did *The Crucible* about—oh, I can't remember now, it was in the middle sixties—and I happened to be there, so we went to see it. I sat behind two youngish people in their late twenties, and after the first act, as we were getting up, the girl turned to the fellow and said, "I heard this had something to do with McCarthyism." And he said, "What was that?"

WS: *(laughs)* That's beautiful.

AM: I thought to myself: no wonder it's impossible for scholarship ever to re-create the conditions under which a work is done.

A: But I think to feel disheartened is—You know, if you're going to write *engaged* art, you either have to not do it, or stay out of the kitchen. What I mean is: there's going to be some *heat*.

WS: Well, there's always going to be some heat. But I don't think I'm mistaken to say that the intensity of this kind of heat was such that other controversial works do not generate, not like *Nat Turner* and *The Crucible*. And when I say "disheartening," I mean it in a temporary sense, because as Arthur is clearly pointing out, these things *are* temporary, that works of literature, as distinct from polemical works or works of propaganda, have their own life. And this is what the hope of every writer is: to create such a work. But the disheartening part in my own case is that the hysteria of the attacks by blacks has tended to cause young black people either not to read the book at all, in the last couple of years, or to read it with such hostility that they get a warped version of it. And I think that this is unfortunate, because *unlike* Arthur in the case of *The Crucible*, I had eloquent and noble defenses by totally detached and dedicated people—historians, left-wing historians, too, like Genovese, and Duberman who maintained in strong and uncompromising terms that *Nat Turner* was historically sound. But it's hard to get such a message through to people who've been brainwashed.

A: So it appears the critics are maybe of some use sometimes, in a case like that?

WS: Yes, well, I guess so. *(laughs)*

A: Well, if you discount the professional critics as obviously having really no influence on either of your work, and if you don't swap manuscripts between yourselves, do you just work *entirely* alone, or is there any sort of influence before it comes—?

AM: Well, I work alone. But in the last years I've had a strong friendship with Bob Whitehead, Robert Whitehead, who is my producer. And I do read to him in the course of the work. I like to do that because I—Well, we both want the same thing, see? It comes to that.

WS: Sure, you have a vested interest. I have the same relation with Bob Loomis at Random House, almost exactly.

A: I see: the producer on the one hand for the playwright, the editor on the other for the novelist. Same function.

WS: In my mind, "editor" is just a catch-all word for a friend, and Bob Loomis happens also to be a friend, besides being an editor. I feel an empathy with him, and this allows him to be one of my best audiences. I'm sure it's the same way with Bob Whitehead and Arthur.

AM: Oh, yes.

WS: Bob never fails to call me on something he doesn't feel is working. I remember I read him a scene, which more or less is in *Nat Turner,* in the final version, and I knew it was somehow going wrong the way I was writing it—it was getting wordy and inflated and so on. So I read it to Bob, and he saw the trouble immediately. After I'd read it, you know, I waited for his reaction, and he said, "That's the only scene you've read so far that doesn't ring true to me." And we talked it over and we agreed it had to do with the fact I wasn't close enough in this scene to Nat's point of view to make it really ring with the verisimilitude that the other scenes had. It was a matter of merely shifting a few little stage directions, so to speak. I did it, and it's one of the scenes that has been quoted in critical articles as one of the better scenes in the book. I feel that shows the value of being able to bounce your work off a receptive person.

AM: I think it can be important, but I can see where somebody wouldn't need it at all. That's possible.

WS: An editor could be your wife, or any kind of interchangeable person that happens to be sympathetic to your work.

A: But in both your cases it happens to be the person who sees your work through production. That's good that you're hooked up that way. *(to Miller)* You would then change scenes or something, at the suggestion of Whitehead?

AM: Well, he wouldn't suggest a change. What I can do is look into his eyes, see? *(Styron laughs)* And see whether that arrow *(claps hands, smack!)* has hit anywhere. It comes to that. Or sometimes I'll be writing a scene for Reason A, and the real strong effect of that scene is a result of B, which I'm completely overlooking. This will happen rarely, but often enough to make reading it worthwhile. I think more than anything else it's a—*(pause)* It's a break in the loneliness of the whole business.

WS: Yeah, that's another thing, it's . . .

AM: It's a lonely job.

WS: Well, you eventually come to a point where all of this—especially, I think, if you're writing a novel, although certainly it must be the same with a play—where you have all this dammed-up stuff you have put down on paper, and something in you in a very human way simply yearns for it to be spilled out.

A: Well, that's what I would *think:* that you'd talk with one another about it, and talk with others . . .

AM: Well, you know, except that I've found, and I think Bill has got the same feeling, that—You know reading something is a lot of work, or even discussing some work in progress. It's not anything but labor; it's a creative thing. And I think that at least at this stage of the game you tend to conserve a lot of energy—you know what I mean?—*that* kind of energy, you tend to kind of hold onto it. And, you know, if I were to listen to something another person wrote, I would feel obliged, willy-nilly, to say: well, what can I say that could be of use? And not just sit there and say, you know, "I like that." I mean, what the hell is the point? *(Styron laughs)* You see? In this stage I don't read it to Bob to have him say, "Oh, I like that." Basically I read it to him to say, if anything, "Gee, I don't dig that at all. I don't see what the hell you're—? What's it all about?"

WS: Yes. This is a very professional working relationship. You read it to your wife, who says she likes it. *(laughs)* And you read parts of it to your editor or producer as you go along. But then you wait for the moment you have the thing pulled together and, okay, you print it or put it on the stage. And *then,* then is when all the yearned-for—and anyone who says he doesn't yearn for it is a liar—all the yearned-for appreciation hopefully comes.

A: You don't miss any of the interaction of a literary community? People reading one another's stuff in the coffee shops of London in the eighteenth century or whenever it was, that kind of writers-group sort of thing?

AM: I *used* to do that. When I first started out I knew a half-dozen

playwrights, guys all roughly my age, all unproduced. And we used
to read plays to one another.

A: It may be something you need more when you're beginning.

AM: I think that's true.

WS: I think so. There's a terrific community of interest among
young writers. They all tend to huddle together. And I claim—very
unfashionably—that no harm can come out of these classes in creative writing. Of course, much of it is ludicrous and silly: I mean, you
can't really teach a person how to make a fine novel, in any direct
sense. But I went to several of these classes when I was very young,
and I can remember nothing but good things about them. If for no
other reason: I, as a sort of lonely young fellow managed to get with
a community of like-minded people. Had I not been with them I
would have been even more intolerably lonesome.

AM: I was in a play-writing class at the University of Michigan. As
Bill says, you don't learn how to write a play. But at the age of eighteen or nineteen, the idea of becoming a professional playwright was
like becoming an astronaut or something. It required an assertion of
will and identity then that was just unbelievable. I emphasize *then*
because there was no off-Broadway then. You either went on Broadway or you didn't go anywhere. The universities by and large didn't
produce any plays except those that *had* been on Broadway. So you
had to in one fell swoop scale that impossible fence.

A: Gosh.

AM: There were no try-outs, no anything.

A: Off-Broadway sort of serves like the Little Magazines for a
fiction writer.

AM: Right, right. But you know, I think there is a danger in these
writing programs if you get a director or a teacher who is too—I don't
know how to put it. I think that it would be a terribly destructive
experience to be put in the hands of a playwright who in his own
work is very good, but the very fact he is that good and is that much
of a personality would make it difficult for him as a teacher to open
his arms to work that aesthetically contradicts everything he stands
for and has worked so hard to form. It's a dangerous business.

A: But that's like a strong director for you, or a strong editor for Bill,
isn't it? When you were working with Kazan you were already established as a playwright?

AM: Luckily when I came to Kazan I'd written about sixteen plays. But if I'd come to a strong director very early it would have been a deforming experience. An artist, especially in his youth, is exposed, up there naked, and somebody can just give him a wrong look and he can *blush* himself into oblivion. Because you're most impressionable then. When you've just written your first things, if someone coughs, you know *(laughs),* at the wrong moment, you sink through the floor. *(Styron laughs)* That's why the best writing teachers are probably those who are most bland about it all. They wouldn't necessarily even be good critics. But they'd be good receptors. They'd be terribly excited about anything that had some value. I remember I used to rail in my heart against one or two of the teachers I had because they weren't tough enough on the others—

WS: —On your fellow students? *(laughs)*

AM: Yes. I'd say, "Jeez, he hands out this praise too easily." But then, even then, I realized: well, that's really his job; his job is to support somebody, not destroy him.

WS: This is the great thing about William Blackburn, with whom I studied at North Carolina, and, I might add, about Hiram Haydn, later at The New School in New York. As teachers, both of them created a *broth,* an environment in which young people were allowed to get truly excited. And I think, in retrospect, that both Blackburn and Haydn lavished in a sensible way, possibly too much praise. But *far* better that, because at this impressionable age you want a *festive* attitude towards life. I mean, with all the shit it is to be young, you want to have the attitude that literature is a feast, a thing to rejoice at. Far better to create this excitement—even if it's slightly promiscuous—than to get one of these goddamn awful sour, negative, academic . . .

AM: I once asked Professor Rowe—Kenneth T. Rowe, who was my teacher at Michigan—about all this, because it seemed to me that people were reading and submitting stuff that was of just no value. And he said, "Well, you know, these people aren't ever going to be playwrights"—by this time I was convinced that I would have to be a playwright—"but," he said, "they are going to learn to be better theatergoers."

A: A lot of people learn to read from creative writing classes.

AM: Sure. A lot of people came from all sorts of remote places to the University of Michigan, and these were little seeds he was sort of planting all over the United States. And in the long view he had confidence that if you had talent he couldn't hurt you—and if you didn't, he wouldn't hurt you either. It's a kind of mini-world, which a writer one way or another has to have early on, I think. Maybe he has to go and seek it himself, and if he's lucky he'll find it through another writer, or an editor, or a friend, or his wife, or a girl friend, or some damn thing.

A: Nevertheless, you are in Roxbury, Connecticut, both of you, and there is a fairly close concentration of talent around here. And it may be that when you get together all you talk about is carpenters and taxes, but you are *here* with one another, not living out in Montana or somewhere all alone.

WS: I think it is part of our Philistine heritage in this country that we adopt a pose of the non-community of literature, as if there were something somehow offensive about writers knowing each other. The idea of the sturdy individualist takes over when it comes to what a writer should be and do. The cliché runs like this: "I wouldn't like to live in New York City as a writer, because I myself prefer living here in Montana. Who wants to go to those literary salons?" As if there were something pernicious about salons in themselves. I myself, living in Connecticut, don't want to go to *many*, but occasionally I find it refreshing to be invited by a friend like George Plimpton to go down and come to a party at which I happen to see maybe ten other writers, many of whom I enjoy the company of enormously. This notion about avoiding other writers smacks of Philistinism, nothing else.

A: *(to Miller)* I don't mean to make it seem he's attacking you, but you never *do* go to parties in New York.

AM: Oh, I do occasionally, yeah. But you see my field is nomadic. People disappear into the wilds of Hollywood. The theater has never created much of a circle in this country. I often wish it had. But now it's a one-shot thing: you rent the hall, you put on the show, and then when the show is over everybody disperses, and that's the end of it.

WS: I noticed that, at some of the first-nights of your plays I've attended. As celebrant as many of them have been, there's always a sense of "Good-night, good-bye, that's all."

A: You don't all go off to Sardi's?

AM: Yeah, but it's for two hours, and then you've had it. There is nothing more.

A: Speaking about New York parties and the literary life makes me think of Thomas Wolfe's marvelous evocations of dreams of success, but then when he actually wrote about these salons and the parties, it would be bitterly, satirically.

AM: Well, going back to what we were talking about before, he had a profound relationship with Maxwell Perkins, who was his alter-ego almost.

A: Yeah, but who's to know what Perkins cut out of all those novels? They're still too long. Was the stuff cut any better or any worse or just the same?

AM: God knows.

A: The Perkins writers: Wolfe, Hemingway, Fitzgerald. How romantic and tragic the lives of the last generation of American writers were.

AM: Well, this country kills writers, at a great rate. That's an old story. But I'm not sure it's all that different anywhere else, except maybe France.

WS: Well, they embalm them in France. The difference in being a writer in France as against being a writer here is just astounding. I never feel that I am "a writer" here, in terms of the public. I mean, I check in at a motel, and they don't—no one ever—

AM: No, no, never.

WS: On the other hand, if you get off at the airfield in Orly, you're surrounded by reporters and photographers.

A: I remember your once telling about the great reception you had in France for *Set This House on Fire* as against here.

WS: Oh, yeah, in France, in France they know who you are. It's the same way with Arthur. It's heady stuff after living in a country where you're always having to spell your name out.

AM: Let me tell you a funny story. It really is a funny story. When I first knew Inge. I guess we were just married. And she didn't know New England, so I said, "Well," I said, "let's go up to Boston, I'll show you all the Revolutionary Towns"—you know, Lexington, Concord—I thought she ought to know about these. And I said, "Gee, do you know we're near Salem? Why don't we go there?" Now when I was preparing *The Crucible* I went to Salem, which has the greatest witchcraft library in the world, which nobody goes into excepting a few scholars who are interested in the field, and I had spent about three weeks in that library. They've got stuff there that isn't even reprinted; there are manuscripts in there; it's a *marvelous* library. There are two old ladies running it. And I said to Inge, "Maybe those two old ladies'll still be there." Now at this time it had already been ten years since I'd been in there. So, as we're driving along, I notice she's fixing up her face. I said, "What're you doin'?" She says, "Well, there'll be a reception." I said, "A *what?*" She said, "Well, you're going back to this place I never would have heard of if you hadn't written about it." She'd seen *The Crucible* with Yves Montand and Simone Signoret in Paris, see? So I said, "No, no. You got it all wrong. They're not going to know who I am." Well, she wouldn't believe it. Well, we went in there—now mind you, there are probably three customers a month in this library, this is not a public library—so I walked in, and I said, "I want to show this lady some of the prints"—they had marvelous contemporary prints of the witchcraft, woodcuts and so forth—and we walked around, and she *would not believe (laughs)*—

WS: What happened? You mean?

AM: Nothing happened. I mean, we just went through like Sam Doakes of Lower Forks, Indiana. *(laughs)*

WS: *(laughs too)*

A: Surely neither of you, though, would prefer less anonymity. Surely you like to be able to live a regular life without crowds howling at you and like that?

WS: Oh, sure, there's a great advantage in—

AM: Oh, yeah, I was just going to add I'm not so sure that's all such a bad thing.

WS: No, it falls out in different ways. It is a good thing. Like the French respect to a great degree is a bit phony—not all of it, but some of it. Because most of those Frenchmen haven't read the work. But you acquire a kind of cachet . . .

AM: Yeah, it's a bit of a game there. They always have to know what's on, so they can carry on about it. I used to think it was terrible in America, but now I don't know. The only part of it—*(pauses)*. If there could be a system whereby the writer remains anonymous—which I like—but that the public would know that some of the troubles they had, and some of the problems they've got, *are* being dealt with in works of art. Let them know some of their bewilderment is being worried about.

A: But in the case of *Death of a Salesman,* that's certainly a celebration of the bewilderment of the ordinary man.

AM: Well, that penetrated. I'll tell you a story about that, in the boon-docks. I went over to Waterbury . . .

WS: *(To Inge Morath, who has just looked into the room)* Inge, could I have another drink?

IM: Yes? I'm checking every so often, spacing myself rightly, I hope.

WS: You're very sweet.

A: I'm passing on this one.

WS: Did you get Rose?

IM: I got Rose, she said she'd been on the phone. So she's coming.

A: Would you begin again, Arthur?

AM: Well, you got it on the tape.

A: Yeah, I know, but I've forgotten. I've lost the trail.

WS: This is his story about going to Waterbury.

AM: Yeah, about Waterbury. Speaking about the penetration of a work. I went over to Waterbury because I'd bought a Studebaker and I went to the dealer—it was a new car, a new beautiful green convertible—to get it serviced. And there was a man sitting there waiting for his car to get serviced. So, we got talking a little bit, and I said, "What do you do?" And he said, "I'm a salesman." I said, "What do you sell?" And he said, "Church bells." And I said, "Really? Are there that many church bells? I wouldn't think there'd be a living there." He said, "Oh, you'd be amazed—the number of church bells crack, congregations want to get a new church bell, a bigger one, they get richer, new churches are built," he says, "I'm busy all the time. It's great—great field. What do you do?" *(Styron laughs)* So I said, "I'm a writer." He says, "Oh, what do you write?" I said, "I write plays." He says, "Well, what's the name—what kind of plays?" So I said, "Well, I wrote a play called *Death of a Salesman."* *(Styron laughs)* Well, *he simply got up.* And he walked away and sat in a different part of the show room. He wouldn't *even* discuss the whole thing.

WS: Now when was this?

AM: This was forty—*fifty!* The play was just on. Isn't that marvelous?

A: But he must have thought you invented that, right?

AM: No, he knew about it. I could tell. It's forgotten now, but a lot of salesmen were very upset by that play.

WS: But it really got at him, huh?

AM: Oh, it frightened him.

A: That's more like Bill's reaction from the blacks, what you got from the salesmen.

AM: Yes, you *do* penetrate sometimes.

A: But it seems to me that when you do penetrate, really get at them, then you worry about it?

AM: No, no. Not me. I think the best thing that could happen is when ordinary people know something is there. It means something to them, even if they kick it around. I have a romantic faith in the truth. I feel something sticks somewhere in the mind, that it becomes some way of forming a symbolic conception of what happens to them. Because the problem most people have is the fragmentation of their experience: they can't make any sense at all out of anything that happens, excepting in a retrograde way—you know, they figure this is all because they've sinned, or some crap of this kind—instead of trying to make a conceptualization on some life-giving level. It would be marvelous if they could be more open to art—even medium art.

WS: Yes, but it would be great if they could discriminate between that medium art and real art, distinguished art. If they could realize, for instance, that a movie like *Easy Rider* has its place in the scheme of things, but it's not art, it's not even remotely art, even though it's fine and fun to go see.

AM: That'll never happen, though. That'll never happen.

WS: Well, it's the thing that bothers me most about kids today: that they don't distinguish . . .

AM: The best example I have of what it means to kids: we went to see—what was that movie about a photographer?—*Blow Up,* and we went into this delicatessen about a block away—Third Avenue there?—sat down at the counter to get a quick sandwich after the show, after the movie. And there were three young men dressed exactly like the hero of *Blow Up* with Leica cameras *hung from their necks.*

A: It happens that quickly.

AM: It was right there. And I said to Inge, "Baby, it's all an act—"

WS: You think they had consciously just donned this outfit?

AM: Oh, it was obvious! He had a certain kind of sunglasses. It was the *same* sunglasses. They were carrying the camera that way; they were wearing the jacket he was wearing. And the manner and everything. *(pauses)* I guess it's always that way, though. I guess a lot of people imitated the way they thought Hemingway was like.

WS: Well, I know this for a fact, because I used to go into The Dome in 1951, and there were several Hemingways who would drive up to The Dome on motorcycles, all Americans, all probably in their late twenties or early thirties, all with a mustache, at a time when mustaches were out of fashion. All of them would sit there silently, in The Dome on the terrace there, having their Pernod, and all of them thinking that they were Hemingway.

AM: Well, you know Tolstoy collected all these types who grew long beards and visited him.

WS: Oh, really?

AM: Sure! They'd sit on his porch, it drove his wife crazy, they'd all come and stay for months.

WS: *(suddenly) Hello there!*

RS: *(enters)* Hello! You're not finished?

AM: Finished? Well—

RS: I'll sit out there, and—(Everyone: No, no.)

WS: Don't you think we're sort of finished, Rust?

AM: We've got two tape-recorders going here.

A: Sit down and be recorded.

RS: Well, thank you. I thought you'd already be at the dinner table.

AM: You know what we should discuss though, if we can for a minute, a thing I think is very confusing to the young, is this whole question of this business of relevance, what various generations think is relevant.

WS: Is this thing still on?

A: You don't mind it still being on, do you, Bill?

WS: No, no, of course not, except—*(to Miller)* but *extend your-self*, Arthur.

AM: Well, I think we've gotten back to the crudest form of relevance. When Godard makes a movie he stops it in the middle and someone starts discussing the Chinese Revolution. You know? The theater's been full of it—relevance to Vietnam, and like that.

A: Isn't this kind of interruption part of the modern idea of fiction and drama deliberately setting out to destroy the illusion? Trying to introduce politics *unabsorbed* in a work of art.

AM: But this whole business of relevance to political and sociological fact is disastrous. In the theater, anyway, everything gets vulgarized, made more crude. They've taken from Brecht all his dross—that is to say, all the stuff he was stuck with, at the moment he was writing—and eliminated the poetry. And they call that a statement of some kind.

A: *(to Styron)* You've written perhaps the most celebrated political novel of our time—or anyway, you got the most reaction.

WS: But that's what Arthur's talking about. Because there's no recognition on the part of the attackers that the work has any literary merit whatever, which is almost a demonstration of how incredibly weird the whole situation is.

AM: That's right. Ultimately it comes to be an aesthetic question. I found in talking to some young people that they have no awareness of the articulation of a *central* concept. In other words, if you point out to them that something in a play or movie or book is utterly unmotivated, that it has no *textual* connection with what went before, what comes afterwards, their reaction is: "Well, why not?" You see? The idea of a *whole,* or any organic unity to a work of art, is not only rejected, but seems to some of them even strange. They don't see why *anything* can't be in a work *at any moment.* It sort of reflects the unexpected in society, perhaps, or the feeling that there is no unity in experience. It reflects the influence of surrealism too. The *surreal* quality was to break up relationships that "appear" to be logical or "appear" to be inevitable, so that that which is unrelated is exactly that which is related. You see? To put a wooden leg on an elephant, to put together that which is irreconcilable, is the essence of reality. And if it's done by somebody who has an organic sense of what is unified, so he can dis-unify it, that's one thing; but what has hap-

pened now is—and you *see* it in the young movies that are made—
as soon as something gets contiguous and continuous, *smash it up,*
lest it become linear, lest it become realistic. Which is a whole other
convention. And yet the same people when you sit with them and
they start talking about their lives, they tell continuous stories. In
other words, they tell about how they were in love with this girl, and
then *not,* and then it goes along, and you find out cause and effect.
It's another art form, but they don't recognize that. They think it's a
naked rendition of reality.

WS: You know, did you see *Easy Rider?*

AM: Yes.

A: No. I'm proud of myself for having gotten to see *Five Easy
Pieces.*

WS: Well, no, that's almost a masterpiece. But *Easy Rider isn't,* in
my mind. It exemplifies all the good things about our culture, namely
our technological ability to do fantastic things easily. And yet it has an
almost total lack of any moral or dramatic sense of what makes life
what it is. And when you were just now talking, Arthur, I couldn't
help but think again: *Easy Rider*—which was fascinating, but totally
devoid of any moral tension, moral center.

AM: You know what I think it is?—I think it's the new Naturalism.
That is, Naturalism in its worst sense: where you get the whole thing
no matter how *boring* the damn thing was. *Nothing* was going to be
left out. You never got into the people. And *Easy Rider* is that way.
These are displacement figures—that is to say, they're up there having *scenic* adventures. Which is perfectly fine, but to attribute to it a
deep artistic value is a sign of the moment—that is, that a lot of
people who felt it was of the first importance do feel about life that it
has surfaces but no depth, that it has consequences but not causes,
that there is no center, it's simply that you do get on the motorcycle
and go from one place to another.

IM: *(enters again and speaks to Miller)* Jim Proctor on the phone.

AM: *(leaves to talk with him, or, uh—exits upstage left)*

WS: Jim Proctor?

IM: Arthur's publicity man, a marvelous incredible person. But
you know what was interesting to me with all you were saying—I was
just now down in Miami lecturing to students of photography, and it
was just very interesting. Their whole approach is again different. You

know? Finally one said to me, "How do I find my identity? I can do physics, I can do photography, I can do plastic styrofoam sculptures." I said to him, "You have too much money. It's very simple. You know, you wouldn't have so much money you'd have to stick with one thing and try to find yourself in it." He said, "You know, you are right." And it's *true*. It's like those modern painters who have so much money to buy these enormous canvases. If they would have smaller canvases they would do better work."

RS: You know, it's true. We know someone who does six paintings a day because he has these millions of canvases.

IM: You know, I knew a lot of painters including Picasso very well, and Braque, and they were really friends of mine. And often they would have just that much of a canvas, and it was *expensive*, so Picasso would do something marvelous on it.

A: It's a funny idea. Suppose you were to think that way about paper, Bill?

WS: *(long pause)* You mean? Well—*(laughs)* The analogy—I don't think it works. Paper's, we know, another medium.

IM: Even film, I hate to waste film, because—

AM: *(returns)* Jim Proctor's going to bring Katz's frankfurters.

IM: He's coming Saturday?

WS: He's going to do what?

AM: *(to Morath)* Yes. *(to Styron)* He loves to bring loads of delicious Jewish delicatessen frankfurters.

A: Oh, yeah, Kosher frankfurters.

WS: Well, they have some great ones in New York.

AM: Garlic in them. Oh, they're fantastic.

A: In our Finast there are nine different kinds of hot-dogs and not one of them is good.

WS: *(to Miller)* Save one of them for me.

A: Any of you read *The French Lieutenant's Woman? (Everyone: No.)*

IM: I must read that. Everybody says it . . .

A: Oh, no. I mean it's kind of a spellbinding thing the way Fowles does, but it . . .

IM: I think very soon we have to have the talking over dinner.

A: No, no. I'm not really *talking*.

AM: It's an historical novel, isn't it?

A: Yeah, it's a sort of an attempt to write a Victorian novel *now,* but the point is he *stops* every three chapters and destroys the illusion. Now it's quite true, I mean Fielding will stop and destroy the illusion, and so does Trollope, and so on. But the way he does it, it's just *total,* a total break. Just like putting in a lecture on China or something.

RS: But that breaking of the surface you were describing in the movies is exactly what occurs in most very young contemporary poetry, where they *cannot* allow an image or a thought to go through to three or four lines. They've got to break it and fill in with all these naturalistic details, throw it in and break the consciousness and move along to some paradoxical thing. You're not allowed to see anything whole.

AM: Yeah. Partly it's the whole surrealistic thing inherited from Europe. *(pauses)* It does reflect a reality among us. In other words, when you hear somebody's tale of woe or happiness or something, you end up saying, "I wonder what really happened?" (Everyone: Yes, yes)

The interpretation, which was formerly embedded in the way the story was told, as in Tolstoy—although he of course broke it up too, by suddenly launching out on a vast essay on Napoleon and the nature of war, let's not forget, it just seemed like a part of the tale because it's so long ago—the interpretation, the *stand* of the author is now of the first consequence. What his position is in relation to the material, so that he creates a kind of confrontation, *personally,* apart from his role as storyteller, with the reader.

WS: Pardon a personal reference, but this is what I've been trying to do in this thing I'm writing now. It's not all that original by any means, but it's the only one I know in recent American writing which simply starts out telling a story—*(breaks off)* I don't mention myself, by name. I do say, though, that this concerns the Korean War and my involvement in it and my training in North Carolina. I say I have written a novella about the Marine Corps, which some people will remember and I proceed to say: this is what happened to me. Okay, the alert reader, the one who has any acquaintance with my own work, will read this and say, "Well, this is old Bill Styron; it's a little bit of autobiography."

A: Here he comes again.

WS: Yeah, here he comes again. Trotting it out. *(laughs)* But the point is that what I'm writing is fiction. Except that everything that happens, that most of it, well, that a tiny bit of it, is true: I *did* go down to Camp LeJeune in 1951, I *was* called back in the Korean War. But I'm conning the reader into believing *all* this really happened to me and the events described really took place.

A: The author using his own known identity to establish realism.

WS: Exactly.

AM: Yeah, well I think there's a reason for that. You take what your audience reads, it's basically news magazines and newspapers and television—*factual* reporting, supposedly, of life. Now, inevitably you are trying to offer your bona-fides as a counter-authority on the basis that "I too have felt the whip of this experience on myself." I mean, if I write an article about My Lai, inevitably in the back of your head you're saying, "Well, what the hell does he know more than I do?—He wasn't there." This is a profound problem which is very contemporary. The author today is up against the necessity to establish his authority as he never was before.

RS: A perfect example is what John Corry was telling us night before last. He'd been asked to do two pieces on vanishing wildlife for *Cosmo*. He didn't know anything about these two particular pieces, but he was quite capable of researching them . . .

IM: *(who has been out of the room)* Will any of you forgive me if we go on talking at the table?

AM: We'll have to move all our apparatus.

A: Yeah, but let me just hear what John Corry said.

WS: Let's just finish this.

IM: Oh, I'm sorry, I didn't—

RS: He did not know from personal experience about either of these two wildlife situations he was writing about, but he sat in this friend's house in Virginia writing the two of them. And when he was finished, he went back and re-did them, saying, "Standing on a cliff in Colorado, I *heard* the vanishing wolf"—and he'd never been to Colorado, and as it turned out there weren't any wolves in Colorado. But he'd had to lend this whole thing an authority, and he did it quite successfully, although it was totally untrue. It worked.

WS: It's capturing your imagination. It's going to any trapeze length to—

AM: The author—he's the horse's mouth.

WS: Precisely. You know, it's just the *way* you do it, and this is very very important. It's been done before, but it takes new forms. What I want to do is make it look like autobiography, but then make it *fiction* on top of that in some curious way. Say, aren't we finished now, Rust?

A: Oh yeah, yeah. And I think it has a focus about writing and the writer and that sort of thing. And in some wild way I think it's about *reality*, to try to establish that authenticity and authority you spoke of. But when you two talk alone together, you probably avoid talking this way about literature and writing and all.

AM: No, we talk like *this*. But not about our own work.

WS: Except in a peripheral way.

IM: They tell each other whether they get on with it or not.

WS: "How'd it go today?" is what we say.

AM: There's two tape cassettes. I'll mark this one side "one" and the other side "two." The one that's in now will be "three."

A: That's a professional touch I'd never have thought of.

WS: Astounding that they could be this small.

AM: Well, you know that whole thing about literature in tape cassettes? This is the new book. The cassette rights to a book are going to be a big thing.

A: I don't know that I like that.

AM: Well, nobody's going to ask you. *(laughs)*

WS: But here, can you imagine all of that conversation in a couple of these?

An Interview
with William Styron

Ben Forkner and Gilbert Schricke / April 1974

From the *Southern Review*, 10 (October 1974), 923–34. Reprinted by permission.

Last April, in response to an invitation from the University of Nantes, William Styron made a week-long tour of several French universities. His first book, *Lie Down in Darkness*, had been named on the prestigious Agrégation list in English literature for the university year 1973–1974. Styron was the only living author on the list this year, a list that included two other Americans—Hawthorne and Poe. Organized primarily by the American Embassy in Paris, the tour included—along with the University of Nantes—the Universities of Paris, Rennes, and Bordeaux. The interview developed out of the last leg of the tour, amid a hectic scramble between Nantes and Rennes. Only Styron's patience, generosity, and vitality made it possible because it had to be arranged during the few moments left to him by enthusiastic students pressing the windowsills during the talks and crowding around listening to long discussions afterward. It should be mentioned that the French gave Styron one of the warmest receptions accorded an American writer in recent years, and yet even after hours of lively discussion, he was able and eager to face still more questions and another whirring tape recorder. It was during a fine, lively dinner given by Dr. Alexander Mavrocordato, Director of English at Nantes, that the idea of the interview took final form. Since Styron's talks and his discussions with students had usually centered on his early work, *Lie Down in Darkness* in particular, it was decided that the interview would begin with *Nat Turner* and go on, as the spirit moved us, to touch on his work in progress. It was conducted in two parts, the first in Styron's hotel room in Rennes and the second in the study of Professor Michel Rezé's hillside home overlooking the Loire valley near Nantes. In both cases, the questions followed already exhausting performances. In Rennes, an energetic discussion had taken up most of the afternoon, and at the Rezé home we had all just finished one of Colette Rezé's splendid meals. It was as we were watching the thick white clouds move over the Loire piling up like the oyster shells we had just left on the table when we began again to talk about Styron's new work, an afternoon much like the one he describes in Poland toward the end.

BF: I want to start off with something about Nat Turner. It seems that in all your novels almost every character that is doomed to failure is doomed because of some abstract creed, some ideal. In *Nat Turner* were you interested in showing or exposing the effects of a singleminded abstraction on a man's life?

WS: I don't know if I was doing that because I don't think a good book is consciously thought out that way. I see in retrospect that the themes of all my books do somehow revolve around the idea that people act out of selfish and willful and prideful motivations without realizing that the universe is fairly indifferent and doesn't care, and that more often than not these willful acts will result in some kind of catastrophe, especially if they're directed in terms of violence against other people. And certainly in *Nat Turner* one of the revelations to me of the book as it evolved was that I suddenly realized that I was writing about a man who, in a kind of pathetic way, was ignorant of his own pride, was ignorant of his own undertaking, was ignorant of the enormity of what he was doing—mainly this horrible act of violence in the name of retribution which—well-meant or not—resulted in catastrophe, not only for himself and of course the white people, but especially for his own people, the blacks. The irony of course being (and it was not mentioned in the book) that this insurrection did seal the fate of the black people in Virginia up until the Civil War. I think a good case could be made for the fact that if Nat Turner had not fomented the insurrection, then Virginia might easily have freed its slaves before the Civil War. It was on the way to doing so; they were having great slavery debates, and it's an interesting sidelight, I think, that when Nat Turner's insurrection was revealed and the horror of what he had done was realized, especially when all this became clear in the legislative debates over slavery just a few months later, it was clear: we *can't* free the slaves, they'll kill all of our white people. And so instead of liberalizing the atmosphere, the insurrection made it far more severe. If the insurrection hadn't occurred, there could have been very likely an emancipation before the war. And if that had happened, if Virginia had freed its slaves, it is quite probable that many of the other southern states, especially North Carolina and Tennessee, would have followed suit and that the whole idea of the Civil War would have to be rearranged as a concept because it's mostly likely that North Carolina and Virginia, if the Civil War had begun, would have been on the Union side and there would have been a quick and easy defeat of the other southern states.

BF: But was there any alternative for Nat Turner other than to idealize the revolution? Or is there any alternative for any kind of revolution except to become single-minded, like Yeats's Irish revolutionaries, to become stonelike and in so doing kill yourself and a number of people, but effect some change?

WS: Nat Turner's era was a time of noncommunication compared to what we're accustomed to. The insurrection itself took a number of days to be reported. In modern times of course you would hear about it within minutes. For that reason, the whole event was distorted and exaggerated. Its full impact was never really understood. Some reports said that thousands of blacks had risen and of course this was not true; it was only a handful. In any case, it had very little effect on the North. There was some abolitionist literature fairly soon after that, mentioning that there had been an insurrection in Southampton County, Virginia, and it was slanted toward the idea that the slaves in general were so discontented that they were uprising all over the South, which was not true. But in general it was overlooked, forgotten.

GS: If a Catholic said that the catastrophe came from a too free and independent reading of the Bible, what would you answer?

WS: I think it came from a naïve reading of the Bible. You see, I think that the real Nat Turner as opposed to the one I created were and are two different people. It's impossible that my Nat Turner could really resemble the real Nat Turner, for as a novelist I had to create an entire human being out of nothing. I wrote part of Nat as a projection of my own character of course, like any creation of a writer, but he had to differ from the historical figure as we know him. Otherwise I would have been forced to write a nonfiction biography. I think the historical Nat Turner was an almost insanely motivated religious fanatic, and that he took literally certain messages of the Bible to be an indication that he must be a leader of an insurrection, that he must go through Jerusalem and slaughter and all the rest. And he did so, and his real insurrection was a terrible fiasco because it was a result of a deranged mind trying to work miracles at a time when miracles could not be worked. I took the perfectly legitimate liberty of humanizing this man, or monster, by giving him a rational revolutionary plan, plus other talents.

GS: A superior mind?

WS: Yes. In other words, as a writer I think I gave this man a dimension of rational intelligence which he most likely did not really possess, and as a result smoothed down that stark fanaticism I think was deeply buried in the man's real nature. You don't really have to be a Catholic to ask the question or to understand the answer, or a Protestant either. I think he read the Bible closely; he read the mandates which told him to destroy; he took this literally; in addition he had hallucinations, religious hallucinations which instructed him to set out on his mission. But it was not simply a matter of religious hallucinations. In fact, as some friendly historian pointed out in a review, there is nowhere in the original "Confessions" any mention of a rational plan. If we're to put any credence in the original "Confessions" and believe them, we have to accept Nat Turner saying in the most amazing way that only the night before does he meet with two of the other blacks to discuss the route of the insurrection because up until that time *they had not any plan.* My fictional Nat Turner as you remember steals a map from Mrs. Whitehead and he conceives this idea of an empire in the Dismal Swamp when in reality there was no such thing, if we trust that original document. So that's one of the distinctions that's important: the difference between the real Nat Turner along with his unredeemed fanaticism, and the enlightened if misguided human being I tried to make out of the character.

BF: Why did the blacks attack you so violently? Did it have something to do with the fact that Nat Turner realized the whole thing was a failure, and that all revolutions are necessarily failures?

WS: Yes, that was mentioned. In '68 they could draw parallels, especially when their hopes were so high and the violent immediate effect of a revolution was so vivid; they could say that a honky white man had come along and written a book which indicated, by indirection at least, that such a revolution was going to fail. Well, the point is that as a matter of fact it *was* a failure. I did not actually intend to stress that fact—that was in the history books; we know it was a failure, and it was not among my ambitions in the novel to underline the aspect of failure in the story. But I certainly would agree with you that if I were reflecting or meditating on this, on revolution in general, it would include the tragic notion that men in revolutions destroy so much of the thing they love; namely, they destroy their own notions of humanity by committing acts of violence against humanity. It's a paradox; it's totally unresolvable and no revolution has ever been free of it. That's why most revolutionaries are zealots who are able to put the idea of vengeance vis-a-vis its consequences out of their minds, and are able to kill and destroy without blinking an eye. But the point seems to be that Nat Turner, the Nat Turner I created (and perhaps too the Nat Turner I believe might have existed), failed for the very reason of his humanity. He failed to carry out a more successful revolution largely because his own leadership deserted him at a time when it should have been at its height. He was unable, in effect, to kill—to kill with his own bare hands; he was unable to strike the first blow. I did not invent that—again if there is *any* truth in the original "Confessions." In the original "Confessions" he says: "I strived to strike the first blow." But as you remember he invades the bedroom, he raises the ax and it misses. He can't *strike* the first blow, and so this strange savage creature Will instead strikes the first two victims dead, kills them both. This failure occurs over and over again. Nat mentions it on several occasions. So, the nature of his revolutionary zeal seemed not to include the necessary component which is the ability to be as ruthless and as cruel and as bloodthirsty as anybody you in turn ask that quality from.

BF: So you're saying that Nat Turner is somewhat, I don't know if redeemed is the word. Both his ideal and his humanity are called into question because his humanity is to a point controlled by his ideal but at the last moment that humanity resurges to make the ideal meaningless, but that's not. . . .

WS: No, I understand. It's quite true that revolution is almost the center of the human paradox. It's where all the contradictions do meet in the market place and where you cannot really be dogmatic about anything. It's where all human emotions tend to fly apart and where right and wrong become the most fiercely scrambled. And as I read Nat Turner's original confessions I became more and more convinced of the beauty of what I was dealing with. Because I'd never seen a situation in history in which *so little* is actually known of the central figure, this allowing the writer to use his own intuition and imagination. This was very important to the creation of the book. As I said today, if I'd been asked to do a novel about John Brown or Robespierre or anybody like that I would not have done it because too much is *known* to make any fiction credible.

GS: I'll come to the last question now. One thing that struck me in all your books is the concern with the vividness of boyhood life, and I find the same quality in Proust. For example, Nat Turner's experience at twelve when he spells the word columbine and he's so happy, or when as a boy of seventeen, he's tormented by the flesh. Is there any particular reason these scenes of youth seem to stand out so significantly?

WS: Yes, let me try to explain. After I finished Part One of the book which has to do with Nat just before his trial and which I wrote with relative speed, I came to a dead halt. I had this guy, I had this guy in a jail cell, ready to die, and if you recall any of that first part it was memories of Judge Cobb and recent matters: living at Travis' and so on, and all of these things had made him a slave and angry and despairing and all the many, many other things, building up to the moment of agony when he knows that God has deserted him and he's going to die. And all that, I think, works very well aesthetically. But when I finished that part I had no notion of where to go. The reader at the end of that part wants to know what the hell caused this man to be brought into this extraordinary situation, in this little courthouse in Virginia with all these troops around and these frantic crowds. And I was frankly in despair because I didn't know how to go on. I had the vague idea: well maybe I'll now just start to describe the insurrection as it happened only a few days before. But that left me unhappy, and then a very funny thing occurred. Someone had brought up to my house in Connecticut a sixteen millimeter print of the movie *Citizen Kane*. You know *Citizen Kane*, you know the story, and you know that it has to do with a sled, that on the sled is painted "Rosebud," a word which is so haunting. And not that this is the only thing, other things must have been working on my mind, but I remember after seeing *Citizen Kane* and being so impressed by it, I remember that "Rosebud" motif and suddenly it all became clear to me that what I had to do to fill this gap was to write about this man Nat—this now grown-up man, thirty some years old—write about him as a boy, as a child. When you mentioned columbine it made me think of that, because columbine was my equivalent of "Rosebud." It became a sort of plunge into memory and I distinctly remember starting off with an enormous sense of enthusiasm on this new part which, as you remember, begins something like: "And I was a child living down on the plantation and I was serving at the table and there was a travelling man. . . ." I suddenly realized I had that part all sewed up though it wasn't as simple as that, the way I'm describing it. It involved a lot of information. I had to dig up on my own background about slavery, what slavery was like. But it occurred to me that once I was able to leap into an imaginative re-creation of his boyhood and his childhood, this would be the really major and most important part of my understanding of why he was a revolutionary, especially in relationship to his surrogate white parents, you know, the fact that he was taken over and educated by white people. The blacks, my black critics hated that. But it's impossible to believe that he was not at some place influenced by white education; impossible. Of course to me it was an imaginative leap but nonetheless this was a very important thing to do. I had to get to the roots of this boy . . . I think the tape's stopped. Anyway that's the story. *(Laughs.)* Maybe we'd better shut it off for a minute, yeah. I'm so wound down. I'm running out of calories or something.

BF: After you finished *The Confessions of Nat Turner* and finished answering all the attacks and the criticism, favorable and unfavorable, what did you start working on next? And did it have anything to do with *Nat Turner*?

WS: Well, I officially began to write a novel having to do with the Marine Corps and I'd written a great number of pages, but somewhere along the line I got totally sidetracked curiously because I suddenly realized that what I was doing wasn't motivating me deeply enough. So I had to interrupt this work to do something that I'm doing which is the work I told you about, the book about Poland.

BF: Almost all your other works, your three major novels and even your rather shorter novel, to some extent deal with a tragic situation. Will your new novel be a tragedy as well?

WS: Well, the new book starts off very light in tone, not light but with a sort of ironic humor involved in it. But it touches on very tragic scenes and in a curious way is an extension of *Nat Turner.*

GS: In *Nat Turner,* one of the themes you were leading up to was the theme of betrayal. Nat Turner is betrayed by the Bible, as we discussed last time, but worse than that, as a young man he was betrayed by his master when he realized that Willis, his friend, had been sold. Does the theme of betrayal which was already lurking in *Lie Down in Darkness,* which came to the fore in *Nat Turner,* remain an important one in the new novel?

WS: I think that betrayal itself, to use one word, is not central to the book, but insofar as betrayal is part of some tragic statement I have to make, very definitely yes, it's a part of this book. The book has to do with the concentration camps, which in a sense is a sort of metaphysical betrayal beyond all comprehension, betrayal of the human race, and I don't mean to be stretching the definition too much. But even within the framework of the concentration camps, my specific story is the story of a Polish girl who has been the victim of the concentration camp. It's a very, very particular betrayal that I'm talking about and therefore will be a significant theme in the book.

BF: Does life in the concentration camps figure largely in the novel or does it mainly concern the after effects, with the characters looking back on their lives there?

WS: Well, I felt in this theme that it would be presumptuousness of a large order to try to re-create life in a concentration camp in any way. I'm simply not going to do that. We all know the bare outlines of this thing. But it's too horrible to even contemplate. So, what I've already done is merely to suggest the horror of the place by recording in an almost documentary way certain points, some of the recorded statements made by the victims, and some of the statements and diaries of the S.S. men that ran the camp, doing this simply to suggest the horror, because you can't really do justice to the horror by attempting to say that one's fictional character did such and such a thing and was victimized to this extent on such and such a day because, as I say, it would be almost sacreligious to intrude on that kind of extreme experience.

GS: I wonder if you saw the beginning of the film of the Nuremburg trials when they started projecting a film about Dachau to show to the Nazis who were being accused and the film was first projected upside-down, and I saw, and I wonder if you did, Goering and the other Germans laughing aloud because the picture was upside down. You didn't happen to see that did you?

WS: No, I can well imagine. . . .

GS: Yes, it was wrongly projected and they laughed and laughed until the film started really, and on the right side, and then suddenly the room stopped to dead silence.

BF: So even though you're not going to treat life in the concentration camp directly as you treated the slave system in *Nat Turner,* you yourself have already made a kind of parallel between the two systems. They're both extreme systems of enslavement, one with some, I guess some moments, of redemption. But it seems to me that the concentration camp has absolutely no redemption about it at all. What are the parallels between the two situations, and had you been thinking of the concentration camp when you were writing *Nat Turner?*

WS: No, but there have been interesting parallels made between the two. Bruno Bettelheim of the University of Chicago who was in Buchenwald, I think, has made an interesting parallel. He himself did not so directly make such parallels, but others have used what he said to make parallels between slavery and the concentration camp, namely in attempting to explain why the victims of the concentration camps did not revolt, rise up, just as why the slaves didn't rise up. He suggests that the people who were transported from all over Europe—the Jews, the Gypsies and everyone else—simply could not believe the condition into which they had been thrust; psychologically, they were so traumatized by their new condition that they had no opportunity, given the brief time they had to collect their wits, to truly organize a revolt. This is only one parallel because we know that the slaves, generally speaking, did not revolt. It's an analogy that is perhaps somewhat strained because the two systems were different; the slaves were there for hundreds of years, the victims of the con-

centration camps were there for just a brief time. But nonetheless, to
my mind it's a fairly valid comparison. The degradation of slavery
and of the concentration camps was equally and almost totally complete. Earlier today I remember we were talking about the factories of
nineteenth-century England. But I think, as horrible as they were,
they were really not institutionalized in the same way. They seem to
be part of the historical process, part of the long system of feudalism
or an extension of feudalism that happened rather than was imposed.
Whereas both slavery and the concentration camps had the quality of
institutions, despotic institutions.

BF: In *Nat Turner,* Nat Turner becomes, because of the extremes
of his situation, to a degree that which he hates. He is molded in
terms of the slave system and becomes an inhuman abstraction, almost as devastating as the slave system itself, although he realizes or
begins to realize this before his execution. In your new book, are
there any characters who, because of their time in a concentration
camp, are shaped into fanatics?

WS: That's not a factor in the book as far as I can tell. I do have a
character who is very important to the book. There are three characters and one of them, a Jewish boy who is very much involved with a
Polish girl named Sophie, is deranged and certainly a fanatic,
troubled, probably schizophrenic.

BF: Had he been imprisoned?

WS: No, he hadn't been. As a matter of fact he wasn't even in
Europe. He was an American Jew and one discovers that his character and fate are not bound up in any direct way with the idea of
fanaticism. It's a difficult story to talk about in an abstract way. But it's
a triangle. The narrator is in love with Sophie, as is the other young
man, Nathan.

BF: I wanted to ask: you mentioned earlier in giving us a brief
summary of the book that you as a fictional character were in the
process of writing what is the real *Lie Down in Darkness.* Is there any
connection between the themes you were struggling with in *Lie
Down in Darkness* and the process of learning Sophie's story and the
development of your relationship with her?

WS: Yes, that's important and I should emphasize that because
part of the story is that of the young kid who's desperately yearning
to write. He wants to write so bad his teeth ache. He wants to pub-

lish, he knows he has something churning in him, about a family in the South and about the death of a girl. And incidentally, his father sends him a clipping ("him" being of course *I*, the narrator, whatever you want to call him) about the death of a girl who kills herself in New York. This girl, the narrator realizes, was the same girl he was in love with some years before and consequently this starts other things churning in his head because he realizes that his novel could have the theme of a girl who commits suicide in New York and is sent to Potter's Field and is buried. And all these things begin to percolate in his head, but he has an impossible time putting it down on paper for reasons he is not really aware of yet, of course, simply due to the fact that—I hate to cast it in this terrible cliché but I will: he has not experienced enough. At least he has not seen enough of life, so that the events of the summer of his love for this girl and her tormented relationship both with him and Nathan and their eventual deaths, enable him to apprehend things, to be able to start to write. It's a catalytic event or a series of events which give him self-knowledge at the very end and which enable him, as the reader I presume will see, to go on and write a book which has not been called *Lie Down in Darkness* but will be called *Lie Down in Darkness*.

GS: Students remarked, some of them, that you had forgotten about Peyton Loftis but obviously she's still vivid in your memory.

WS: Yes, yeah. How do they mean I'd forgotten . . . ?

GS: That you had discarded her. You know, Peyton was there, but now she's somebody else. I've given life to Peyton and now let her lie in darkness. But this new novel. . . .

WS: I don't see how that's valid because the book ends and what can you do with your people who die? You can't resurrect them.

GS: But the tragedy of this Polish girl is not unlike, I mean is related to that of Peyton. . . .

WS: I begin to see what you're saying, in fact. That in a sense this is a resurrection. I mean again the story I'm telling is, well, it's half-real and half-fictional. But this girl—the one whom I knew and upon whom my fictional Sophie is based—did go to Auschwitz, she did lose her father, her husband, and her two children to the gas chambers and I'm writing about her. But the way that these things happened are fictional because she told me no more; she vanished from my life for one reason or another. I didn't pursue her any longer. She did not have any such relationship with the Nathan I've alluded to. But the agony of her life as it must have been is something I'm seeking, these many years later. And in that sense you're absolutely right.

BF: You're over here in France responding to an invitation to give a series of lectures on *Lie Down in Darkness* which is being studied by French Ph.D. students. Is there anything else that brought you to Europe?

WS: Well, I mean quite clearly I wanted to go to Poland, which I'd never visited, because of this story I've just spoken about. I went to Warsaw and Crakow, and I went to Auschwitz because I'd reached a place in the story where I felt it was awkward for me to try to give any sense of reality to the narrative without at least having seen the place where all this happened to Sophie. So I went there to see what it was like. And I saw it and it's horrible beyond belief.

GS: Twenty-five years later it is horrible beyond belief?

WS: Still, perhaps more so. I mean, the story's not a fantasy, it's a reality to me. But it had to be fleshed out, it had to be given perspective by my going and seeing the places where it happened.

GS: It's necessary to see and touch those places. . . .

WS: Sometimes. It depends. I have never felt, for instance, this need for research that impels some writers to go to the source of everything about which they write, to smell the place; because I think that imagination is often sufficient. I mean Saul Bellow wrote a book called *Henderson the Rain King* about Africa. It's a good book and he wrote that without ever going to Africa. But in this particular case I felt that I could not possibly get the sense of this locale unless I saw it. So I had to go and I'm glad I did.

BF: When is the publication date?

WS: I don't know because I haven't finished it yet. I was having trouble. I realized the reason for my difficulty in going on was my inability to conceive of what hell looked like, and that in order to go on with some sense of felicity I had to go there. And by chance I realized too that the book is going to take a kind of nice narrative turn, namely that both the maître and the assistant are going to be characters in the book, because I'm going to describe this particular visit in Europe. And the middle-aged successful writer twenty-five years later, guess who, walking alone, among other things, coming down from Warsaw, you know alone, going to Crakow alone, going to Auschwitz alone, and suddenly contemplating at one moment as I did on an unbearably beautiful spring day—which it was, they had a very early spring—contemplating this hell and being absolutely unable to fathom any meaning in life, in existence, you know. And so knowing that that was a kind of funny reaction that should have been predictable, but a reaction which I rejected because of its predictability, until it actually happened. And I sensed it in this brief flash, in this beautiful, these cherry blossoms coming out. . . .

A Bibliographer's Interview with William Styron

James L. W. West III / 21 December 1974

From *Costerus*, N.S. 4 (1975), 13–29. Reprinted by permission.

Most published interviews with William Styron are predictably similar. Certain topics are inevitably brought up: the reception of *The Confessions of Nat Turner*, race problems, history vs. fiction, the South, critics and reviews, Faulkner and other early influences, and literary contemporaries. The interview below is of a different type. I have attempted to phrase questions which a textual bibliographer or editor might wish to ask Styron about his habits and methods of composition, his treatment of his texts in pre-publication stages, his attitude toward ordering post-publication alterations in his texts, and his working relationships with his editors. The interview is patterned on the composition-revision-publication process. Questions deal initially with the inscription of the holograph manuscript, then progress to intermediate prepublication stages (typescript, galleys, and page proofs), and finally move to postpublication textual considerations.

Manuscripts, typescripts, and other important production materials for Styron's novels are housed at the Manuscripts Division of the Library of Congess and at the William R. Perkins Library, Duke University. I have illustrated this interview with facsimiles of documents from among the Library of Congress holdings. For permission to reproduce these documents, I am grateful to Mr. Styron, to Random House, Inc., his publisher, and to the Library of Congress. This interview took place in Styron's home in Roxbury, Connecticut, on 21 December 1974.

JW: You have often characterized yourself as a slow worker. Can you explain why you work so carefully?

WS: For me, it's just an endless matter of moving very, very painfully and tortuously up on my subject. I have a terrific resistance toward getting into the act of writing. For me it's almost an inspirational thing, in that I often have to play music for an hour in order to feel exalted enough to face the act of composing. I suppose its a perfectionism—a fear of not being up to the demands of my imagination—that causes me to go at it every day in such a hesistant way. I find usually, however, when I'm in it deeply, then I'm okay—I'm moving, and, not to say that it's any easier even then, but once I've broken through the sound barrier, so to speak, and I'm in the act of composition, I feel somewhat more at ease. I wish I did have an incredible facility which so many writers do seem to have, an ability to just plunge in each day without any reticence. As I say, this—I presume you might call it perfectionism—inhibits me so much that I just cannot do that. I have to walk around the subject, creep up on it.

JW: Once you begin composing, is there any hesitancy, or very much crossing out and revising, as you inscribe your initial drafts?

WS: I do a great deal of crossing out, interlining and erasing. Although there is no consistency in the process, I sometimes have so many corrections on a page that it is nearly illegible and so, fearing that the typist won't be able to read it, I rewrite (or copy) the entire page. Thus the "clean" look of many of my holograph pages is deceptive. A lot of them were originally a mass of corrections.

JW: You have spoken to me before of your need to have the total pattern—the "metaphor"—of a novel firmly in mind before you can proceed with it. Has this necessity ever caused you to abort a novel?

WS: Yes, more than once. One manuscript, now at the Library of Congress, was going to be a short novella about the Marine Corps—about life in a Marine Corps disciplinary institution. That didn't come off. And then even more recently, there has been the book which I began called *The Way of the Warrior.* I suppose you might call it aborted except for the fact that I do not believe it's truly aborted. It's "interrupted." I hope to get back to it, and fully intend to, because I think I've got a strong subject. But there intervened, when I was fairly well along in the book—several hundred pages—together with a sense of confusion as to where I was going, there intervened this new vision which was so demanding: the novel that I'm now writing called *Sophie's Choice.*

JW: About how much prose do you produce in a normal composing stint?

WS: It varies radically from a few words sometimes—twenty-five words?—to, in the past, incredible stints for me of maybe as much as two or three thousand words. But they are the extremes. I would say that the good average, when I'm working with some degree of control, might be about seven hundred, eight hundred words a day.

JW: All of your holograph drafts that I have examined are inscribed in black No. 2 pencil on long yellow legal-pad paper. Do you use these particular materials for any special reason? Is it a mental thing?

WS: I've always just had a—I've never been able to, for instance, use a typewriter for composition. I can type with some rapidity—not a touch typist skill, but I can two-finger, four-finger it; but I've never, to my knowledge, ever composed anything of what I consider any importance on the typewriter. I've written many letters on the typewriter—that sort of thing. In fact, I do, I suppose, maybe half of my correspondence on the typewriter and half longhand, depending on when, but I've never written any prose fiction on the typewriter. I've just always had a very comfortable relationship with No. 2 pencils and these yellow sheets, which I might add vary also in quality. Some you get are abominable: you can't erase on them, which is something that I like to do. I would be almost in deep despair if I found myself on some island on vacation and unable to get yellow sheets. I *could* compose on white sheets, in longhand, but it would be an added handicap. I think I could certainly get it down without those yellow sheets and No. 2 pencils, but I would be uncomfortable.

JW: Do you prepare your own typescripts from your holograph drafts?

WS: Not usually. If I am writing a very brief thing, a very brief piece, for instance, maybe like an Op-Ed piece for the *New York Times,* I do my own typing there. But I have had a series of professional typists who have done my work, and my wife Rose did most of *Set This House on Fire.*

JW: Do you check secretarial typescript drafts, word for word, back against your holograph drafts to be sure that the transcription is accurate?

WS: No. I rarely do that. I'm so much acquainted with the prose that I have written that I don't have to check the holograph. I've probably missed a few things along the line, but nothing of very much importance.

JW: Do you normally put a draft through more than one typescript stage?

WS: Almost never.

JW: Then you revise very little in typescript.

WS: Yes, once the typescript is there. Of course, ultimately where there is some editorial consultation, with Bob Loomis or somebody like that, we'll make changes, but I'll almost never make initially any changes myself in the typescript.

JW: Do you ever revise in galleys or page proofs?

WS: Very rarely. In *Set This House on Fire,* I did make more extensive changes in the typescript and proofs than in any of the other books that I have written. There was a great amount, an enormous amount, that was cut out of *Set This House on Fire.* I say enormous: for instance, a paragraph where I would read it and see that it was repetitive. There was so much in it that was repetitive, and I rather ruthlessly excised lines all through *Set This House on Fire.* I think the book is stronger for that. I remember I became aware that Peter Leverett, the narrator, was often gratuitously, in I thought an annoying way, commenting on his own actions over and over again, when silence would have been more golden. So there must have been dozens of places where I cut out little observations he made.

JW: Can you describe your working relationship with your first editor, Hiram Haydn, who worked with you on *Lie Down in Darkness* and *Set This House on Fire?*

WS: Well, initially, I had a very good working relationship with him. He was just the kind of editor a young man should have. I know that the British, for instance, sneer at the idea of the American writer's relationship with his editor, but actually there is nothing to sneer about at all. An editor of the kind Hiram was acts in the same function as a very good friend. Indeed, he was a good friend. And I don't see that there's anything really odd or laughable at all about such a relationship.

JW: Did you work closely with Mr. Haydn during the actual composition of *Lie Down in Darkness?*

WS: Well, not at all in the composition. I was my own man. And he was an enormously capable editor, not only practically but psychologically, and had this marvelous ability of keeping his hands off the book as it went along. I imagine I gave it to him in, oh, four or five installments. I wrote maybe one hundred fifty pages, showed it to him, he loved it, but offered no suggestions at that point. Then I'd send another one hundred fifty pages and maybe I did that three or four times. Let us say the manuscript perhaps was six hundred pages. I sent it to him in quarters of one hundred fifty pages each, or something like that. And when finally it was done, I remember how I found truly remarkable his ability then to exercise the editorial prerogative and point out where *he* thought things had gone a little haywire. There were never any major things at all in the book, as I recollect, that he changed; but certainly there were a myriad of little tiny points where he had this marvelous ability (and I've always used it as a kind of touchstone for an editor's ability), that is, the moment which comes when the editor, and Hiram in this case, asks "What were you thinking of here?" And you remembered back to the time you were writing that part and had said to yourself, at that time, "What am I thinking here?" In other words, his ability to detect you at your weakest little moment where your phrase was not felicitous, or accurate, and you thought you could get by with what you put down. He had an uncanny ability to detect you in those impostures. He was truly a fine editor.

JW: Mr. Haydn made some editorial changes in the typescript setting copy of *Lie Down in Darkness.* Can you describe his editorial method when you and he worked over that typescript?

WS: I recollect being pleased at what he was doing, because he was not, in any sense, tampering with my creative process. He was not altering the nature of the book, or even very much of the prose, but was catching me out in inaccuracies and grammatical errors, and an occasional badly chosen word. And I think this is beautiful when an editor can do this. It can only improve the book, without compromising the author's intent.

JW: Did you sit down with Mr. Haydn and approve each of his alterations as he made them?

WS: Oh yes.

JW: Then each of his individual changes had your approval?

WS: Oh yes. There was no place where he didn't very solicitously

ask me. I want to say unequivocally that there was no point at which
he changed something without my *full* approval. And, in fact, I want
to add that there were a number of times where he suggested
changes which I refused to let him make. I obviously can't point them
out—they are too far back in my memory—but I will state that.

JW: I know that you often read aloud from your manuscripts to
your present editor, Robert Loomis of Random House. Did you also
read aloud to Mr. Haydn?

WS: I don't believe I read much of what I was writing to Hiram
aloud. In fact, I don't believe that I did hardly at all.

JW: Can you describe your working relationship with Mr. Loomis?

WS: Very much the same. I have the same kind of faith in Bob's
judgment as I did in Hiram's, with that minor difference that I do
often read out loud to Bob, who is a very good listener, and who
deals in changes or suggestions in the same way that Hiram did—un-
obtrusively and gracefully.

JW: Do you ever read aloud to other people?

WS: I read to Rose occasionally, yes. I think I've read to my friend
Bob Brustein, Dean of the Yale Drama School.

JW: Do you read to any of your writer-neighbors here in Roxbury—to Arthur Miller, for instance?

WS: No. I've read nothing to any of my immediate neighbors.

JW: Are you a careful proofreader of your own writings?

WS: Pretty careful, especially on something I've taken a lot of pain
and trouble with, like a novel—a full-length novel. I'll be pretty accurate with the proof. I don't know how good I am, but I give it a very
hard try.

JW: Do you read both galleys and page proofs of your books?

WS: I go over the galleys pretty conscientiously and carefully, and
by the time it gets to page proof at Random House, there has always
been this extraordinarily good copy-editor named Bertha Krantz who
I have great trust and faith in. She's not flawless, but no one is. Once
it gets to page proof, I leave it in her hands.

JW: Do you insist on seeing proofs of your magazine work?

WS: Yes, always, if I can. Now, for instance, the *New York Times*
has a policy that they don't show you their proof. So you can't do
anything about that. But on the other hand *The New York Review of*

Books always is very, very careful to send you proof. Magazines like
Esquire, Harper's also. I think it's a good policy.

JW: What is your attitude toward small changes, whether they be
intentional or unintentional, made by copy-editors, compositors, or
proofreaders, in your actual wording?

WS: I think that's inexcusable unless they ask your permission. I
think it's their duty to suggest changes if they feel something's unin-
telligible. But I think they should always ask the author.

JW: How about changes made, without your being consulted, in
your accidentals—that is to say, in your punctuation, word division,
capitalization, and spelling?

WS: That's more of—Again I think that—Well, there again, if you
have a chief proofreader like Bertha Krantz at Random House whose
judgment you trust, then at that point you certainly let her have full
head and full authority on such things, because she's actually much
more skilled at it than I am. I think it's best to be consistent if one
can, and that's why a good copy-editor or proofreader is a very valuable asset to a publishing house—because they do have, usually, an
almost neurotic obsession about such things, and I think it's all for the
good.

JW: Once a book of yours is published, do you ever have second
thoughts about passages or words in the text, and do you then ask
for alterations to be made in the plates?

WS: Here's an example: in *Nat Turner,* toward the end, describing
the insurrection, the insurrection itself, I had not in the book been
obsessed by absolute accuracy. Indeed, as I have said over and over
again, I think that an obsession with absolute accuracy is impossible if
you are writing a novel dealing with history. It becomes ridiculous,
simply because you are writing a novel. You're not writing prose nonfiction historiography in which you would have to be accurate about
facts. But at the same time, I kept saying to myself in the writing of
Nat Turner, "Why not be consistent with the facts as we know them
whenever I can, in relatively minor matters." Now I remember, after
the book had been locked in print, I remember that the insurrection
meets its Waterloo at a place called (I forget what I called it in the
book), but in reality, it was Dr. Blunt's place, and I put something
else. I said Ridley's, I think, Major Ridley's. Now, it just always

bothered me afterwards that when I knew the real history of the account—the plausible part of the history as opposed to so much that
was implausible—that we know that the insurrection foundered at Dr.
Blunt's place, and I always wished that I had been able to make that
change. It's still in the book, and it's inaccurate. It's not a major inaccuracy, and no one, except those obsessive critics of mine who worry
about such things, would really care, but things like that have
bothered me.

JW: But you never ask for plate changes that have to do with
wording—with style?

WS: I have never done so. Once a book has been absolutely
locked into plates, I always feel it's like a cast iron monument.
There's little you can do to change it.

JW: I've been asking you about plate alterations—changes made
within an edition of a book. But what about a fresh typesetting—as,
for instance, when *Nat Turner* was reset for the Signet paperback
edition. That textual situation allows for extensive post-publication
revision. Do you ever introduce revisions into your texts when they
are freshly typeset?

WS: I would say quite the opposite. I just would hesitate—really
would have an active distaste—for going over and changing in any
way something that had already been in print, except maybe if someone pointed out some incredibly glaring inaccuracy or error.

Lest from the above I be accused at the outset of sounding too portentous, I will say that these events were a murder
and a rape which ended, too, in death, along with a series of
other incidents not so violent yet grim and distressing. They
took place, or at least had their origins, at the Palazzo
d'Affitto ("a curious group of Arab-Norman structures rendered
specially picturesque and evocative by the luxurious vegetation
by which they are framed. The garden-terrace commands a wonderful panorama.") and they involved more than a few of the
townspeople and at least three Americans. One of these Americans, Mason Flagg, is now dead. Another, Cass Kinsolving, is
alive and flourishing, and if this story has a hero it is he,
I suppose, who fits the part. It is certainly not myself,
whom the events in Sambuco touched only tangentially. I am
self-possessed enough not to despise myself, which is something.
Yet while I have a hunch that in some unforseeable mettle- and
spine-testing situation I would acquit myself as well as many
of the people I know, I have strong doubts as to the limits of
my endurance. This alone, I suspect, is enough to disqualify
me from the hero role. Let us say that I am not of the heroic
mold — a solid middle-class American of the twentieth century.
Gallant struggles are not for me, I observe and I record.
Although I am uncertain of myself, I am a member of that
very communion of young men who like to say: "I wish I were not as
glib and sophisticated as I am." When in many ways, really, I'm
quite shaky. I have the feeling already, for instance, that this
story is going to be cumbersome, disjointed, and certainly in
an age of digests — overlong. I ask you to stick with it. It is
private. In another time I would not have to ask you that.

Figure 1: Page 3 from the printer's copy for *Set This House on Fire*. The page
shows two levels of cutting, both of which eliminate comments by the narrator, Peter Leverett.

is at once subtle and majestic and fascinating, still works its

own ~~good, gray~~ music upon the minds of men. Or at least I hope to

think so. (Incidentally, do not be cowed by my way of expression.

Most young lawyers read nothing but Time magazine. I will do

better as I get away from myself and draw closer to the things I

have really felt and seen and understood.)

A few years ago, when I came back from Italy and Sambuco and

took a job in a New York firm (somewhat second-rate, I must admit,

and not on Wall Street yet laggardly nearby, which caused our

office wits to suggest the slogan, "Walk a block and save") —

several years ago I found myself in a really rather bad state. ~~felt myself situated in the precise center of hell.~~ The death of a friend — especially under the circumstances

~~(I will say that they were sordid and appalling and for the moment~~

~~leave it go at that)~~ that befell Mason Flagg, even more especially

when one has been on the scene, witnessed the blood and the tu-

mult and the shambles — is not something that can be shaken off

easily at all. And this applies even when, as in my case, I had

thought myself alienated from Mason and all that he stood for. I

will come to Mason's ending presently, and it will be described,

I hope, in all its necessary truth; for the moment let me say ~~again~~

only that it left me quite desperately stunned. ~~aflounder in the blackest and most suffocat-~~

~~ing sort of depression. What had happened in Sambuco inhabited my~~

~~days and haunted my dreams; it was a ponderous and godawful weight~~

~~upon my spirit and I could find nothing to distract me from it.~~

~~I tried to lose myself in work, in movies, in books, in booze, in~~

~~anything; indeed — and I am not being facetious — I even went to~~

~~the extreme lengths of trying to lose myself in marriage, when~~

Figure 2: Page 5 from the printer's copy for *Set This House on Fire.* Styron condenses and tones down Leverett's narration.

212

soil, Rye, New York, I believe, but it doesn't matter. I knew that
the Italian girl he had been accused ~~(too late for his own recog-~~
~~nition, for by then he was already dead)~~ of raping and beating
had also died (I had seen her for several seconds that night, and
she had been beautiful in a complete and stunning way, which I
think accounted for much of my later distress). And I knew that the
case — the tragedia, the Naples papers had called it — was closed,
there being little aftermath for snoops and gossips and the simply
curious to feed upon when the two principals were so firmly and
decisively dead. Even the New York papers had given the story
small play, I discovered — and this in spite of the Flagg name
with its more or less glamorous attachments — possibly because
Sambuco was, after all, a faraway place, but more likely because no
one remained to expose his shame and guilt to the vulturous limelight. So, save for the exceptional fact that I had been in Sambuco at the time, (in many ways) I knew no more about the horrifying mess than
the lowliest straphanger.
     Except that I <u>did</u> know, something, and this was what continued to bother
me, and long after the time of those funereal blues I have just
described. ~~Do I sound once again portentous, maybe vulgarly mys-~~
~~terious, or just plain commonplace when I say that I thought I knew~~
~~something that no one else knew at all? I really don't mean to~~
~~sound anything but truthful and exact, and if already this story~~
~~has begun to take on the tones of a narrative of detection, filled~~
~~with hints and rumors and jaunty private eyes, put it out of your~~
~~mind: this is no whodunit.~~ I did know something, and if that something was not much, if it was more in the nature of a strong

Figure 3: Page 8 from the printer's copy for *Set This House on Fire.* Styron
removes a passage in which Leverett declares: "this is no whodunit."

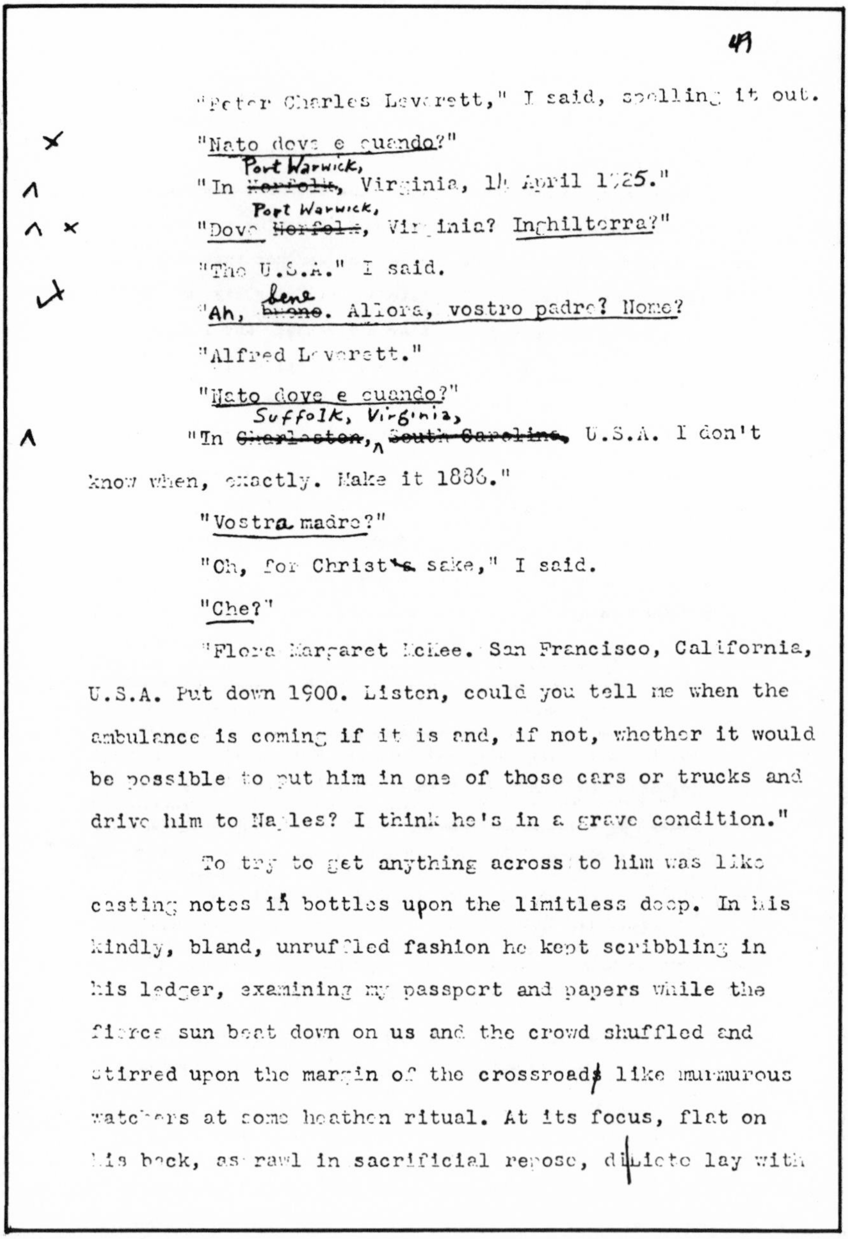

"Peter Charles Leverett," I said, spelling it out.

"Nato dove e quando?"

"In ~~Norfolk~~ Port Warwick, Virginia, 14 April 1925."

"Dove ~~Norfolk~~ Port Warwick, Virginia? Inghilterra?"

"The U.S.A." I said.

"Ah, ~~buono~~ bene. Allora, vostro padre? Nome?"

"Alfred Leverett."

"Nato dove e quando?"

"In ~~Charleston,~~ Suffolk, Virginia, ~~South Carolina,~~ U.S.A. I don't know when, exactly. Make it 1886."

"Vostra madre?"

"Oh, for Christ's sake," I said.

"Che?"

"Flora Margaret McKee. San Francisco, California, U.S.A. Put down 1900. Listen, could you tell me when the ambulance is coming if it is and, if not, whether it would be possible to put him in one of those cars or trucks and drive him to Naples? I think he's in a grave condition."

To try to get anything across to him was like casting notes in bottles upon the limitless deep. In his kindly, bland, unruffled fashion he kept scribbling in his ledger, examining my passport and papers while the fierce sun beat down on us and the crowd shuffled and stirred upon the margin of the crossroad like murmurous watchers at some heathen ritual. At its focus, flat on his back, asprawl in sacrificial repose, di Lieto lay with

Figure 4: Page 49 from the printer's copy for *Set This House on Fire.* Styron alters place names and corrects Italian words. The substitution of "Port Warwick" for "Norfolk" is of interest; *Lie Down in Darkness* is set in the fictional city of Port Warwick.

214

~~So, at the tail end of the worst hours I think I have ever known, I found myself hoodwinked, victimized, an unwilling guardian over the squalling litter of a nitwit. Even then I heard them downstairs, scratching and thumping, up to some skulduggery or other. I opened the door behind Poppy in hopes of calling her back, but she was gone; only a soft warm wind, blown through the oaken doors where she had left, played through the dust and the rubbish. Uppermost in my mind, so supremely fixed there now that it was like an obsession, was escape from Sambuco — immediate, headlong, reckless, and by any conveyance possessing legs, wings, or wheels. I was indeed prepared to walk, forsaking luggage and possessions, forsaking everything so long as I might remove myself from this terrible place.~~

I went downstairs and got my luggage together. I could hear the children brawling in a bedroom: to hell with them, I thought, they could take care of themselves. I felt sticky and begrimed; as I sponged myself off in the bathroom I laid out for myself a plan for withdrawal. Money for me at that point was a minor concern; from a schedule I recalled seeing in the hotel lobby I knew the last bus to Naples had left, but I was certain that for the equivalent of ten dollars or so I could easily hire a car and driver to get me there. My boat to America, to be sure, did not leave until five days later, but I felt that it would not be unpleasant to mooch around Naples for a while, revisit the museum, go to Capri and Ischia and Ponza ~~isles I had never seen, which, at this time of the year, would be sunny bowers of perfume and laughter, ripe as Renoir, glorious with maidens from half a dozen lands. Thus I slyly plotted my escape from Sambuco. And although I suffered a twinge of real guilt over running out on Mason (and this despite my conviction that our friendship had been hewn in two before the fact) I put my mind at ease by blandly telling myself that he was beyond help now, that his disposal—I could think of no other word—rested with the police and the investigators and with the protocols of consuldom.~~ As I prepared to go upstairs I remembered the Austin: junk heap that it was, it had cost me thirteen hundred dollars, second hand, and I was not prepared to sacrifice it to the elements or to marauding Italians. But in the end I really didn't care. Perhaps I would wangle out of Windgasser a hundred thousand lire for the wreck—enough to pay for my Naples sojourn; failing that, I would let it stay parked where it was forever, shat upon by pigeons.

And so I started to leave Sambuco.

I did not see Cass at first when I reached the top of the stairs and went back through the living room. He must have come in quietly, or maybe his entrance had been drowned out by the scuffling children: I was almost to the door when, startled, I heard a noise behind me and whirled around to confront him. I didn't know what there was about Cass that made him seem at my first

---

Figure 5: Authorial cuts and revisions on galley 94 of *Set This House on Fire.* Here Styron continues the process, begun in typescript, of making Peter Leverett a more reticent narrator.

But these two photographs—the one with Carole, and the one with Celia—still haunt me; they are as mnemonic as a fragrance, a scrap of music, a familiar voice which has not been heard for many years. I turn back to the first one, trying to extract its mood, comprehend it, place it in time—then all of a sudden (perhaps it's only the memory in turn of the ostrich that does it, or the bedroom full of Swedes) I know what it is and I know what it means. Like one of those trick effects in the movies where for a long instant the scene becomes motionless—a skier suspended in mid-air, a diver rigid in a somersault or a comic pratfall with legs and arms stilled in frozen chaos above the floor—then once again rolls on, this picture suddenly achieves movement; indeed now, with very little effort of the imagination I am able to persuade myself that I am no longer viewing the scene, but am within it as I was so long ago, that my hand moves back just a bit, fidgeting, as, still half-blinded by the flashbulb, I watch Carole's protuberant bulb of a tongue reach Mason's neck and linger there, wet and fluttering, while at the same moment her well-fleshed paw steals forth to unzip his fly. Shades of the divine Marquis! How, after Mason's dilations upon "group interplay" several nights before, it never occurred to me, until it was almost too late, that he had brought me to an orgy, mystified me then as it mystifies me now; I can only say in all honesty that I must have known, or suspected, that it was going to be one, and that deep down I desired orgiastic purgation, too.

Our host that evening, in a large, flossy apartment near Washington Square, was a famous young playwright called Harvey Glansner. Immediately after the war he achieved an astonishing success on Broadway with a play that with great courage, insight, and pity had laid bare, in terms of a lower-class New York family, the neurotic agonies of our time. Then he had had several failures in a row, which in America, especially on Broadway, is the equivalent of the grave. Thereafter, to the distress of many who still saw in him the hope of American drama, his talent had gone to pieces; he took to writing a knotty kind of prose—articles mainly for the small quarterlies—in which he hymned and extolled the then burgeoning signs of juvenile delinquency, psychopaths, pimps, dope addicts and other maladjusted wretches until, finally descending into a sort of semicoherent pornography, he became either unpublishable or unreadable, except by a rather specialized intellectual in-group which applauded any sort of wicked stir, no matter how brainless. He wrote much about the solemnity of the orgasm, its lack and its pain, and its relationship to God. With all of this, he was a gifted writer, even after his fall from Broadway grace, and he might have found more general favor except for the fact that all of his essays gave to sex a reference of horror, criminality, and disease, equate sex with unpleasurableness and you may expect your audience to be obscure, whether your bias is puritan or pornographic. "Like Dante, Harvey's a real hater," Mason said, adding that he was writing a biography of Restif de la called Karl Marx: Giant in Orgasm.

An Interview with William Styron

Michael West / 6 February 1977

From *Island* (Vineyard Haven), no. 1 (1977), 46–63.

William Styron is the highly acclaimed author of *Lie Down in Darkness, The Long March, Set This House on Fire, In the Clap Shack (a play), and The Confessions of Nat Turner,* for which he won the Pulitzer Prize in 1968. But critical acclaim has never come as easily to Styron as has controversy. From his first novel to his latest, novelist William Styron has had to deal with both praise and blame for his treatment of serious themes in elegant language. In the September 1976 *Esquire,* Styron published "The Seduction of Leslie," an excerpt from his current work-in-progress, *Sophie's Choice.*

If Styron's name is familiar to readers of *Esquire* and other periodicals, his face is equally familiar here on the Vineyard where he has spent summers with his wife Rose and their family for twenty years.

On February sixth of this year, I drove to Styron's winter home in Roxbury, Connecticut, where we taped three-and-one-half hours of conversation on a wide range of subjects. The following has been excerpted from that taped conversation, which began with a discussion of the importance of theme in a writer's work.

Island: Do you find the theme emerges as you write the book or do you, for instance, pre-think a theme?

Styron: It can be done both ways. Clearly, if you have a mighty theme, unless you're a mighty writer you're not going to have a mighty book. I really think that what makes so many first novels fail, or makes them uninteresting, is that the writer has not really thought out what he's writing about. He's not trying to give us a fresh, new vision of the world in a fresh, new way. He's going over old ground. He's going over familiar ground because he doesn't really know what that theme is.

217

Island: The themes that have captured your imagination have driven you to complete four novels, if we consider *The Long March* to be a short novel, and I wonder if there are some themes that recur though the stories differ greatly. I am thinking of themes like the struggle of a man or a woman against authority or an authoritarian system, a system of values which seems to oppress.

Styron: Yes, that's been remarked upon before and I think there's some truth in that—a great deal of truth. I have been more or less drawn to human relationships in which there is strong polarity of power and submission, or authority versus subservience, or if not subservience a sometimes unwilling weakness. A long, long time ago, I realized in my own character that, whether I was in the classical sense a radical, I had a very strong streak of rebelliousness in me. And when I was quite young, and in school, or later in the Marine Corps, I realized how powerfully I was repelled by authority myself. I often got into trouble. I never got into major trouble, maybe fortunately, but I had trouble with teachers. And I had trouble in the Marines with authority figures.

I remember especially when I was at Camp Lejeune on KP duty in the mess hall, I was just a buck private, and this was during World War II when I was in training. I still remember the incredible hate relationship I established with the mess sergeant who was, as I recollect, an Italian from New York. His credentials for being a mess sergeant were that he ran a large restaurant in New York. It became a well-known fact that we were at war with each other. This guy was bullying me, and I was just reacting to him. None of the other guys were having this situation. It was just me. I couldn't stand his authoritarian pose. It didn't end up in any particular dramatic crisis or anything, but it always sticks in my mind—the hatred that he had for me and I had for him, and my spurning of his authority.

Along about that time, when I was in the Marines at Duke in the V-12 program, I remember how bitterly I resented a certain mathematics teacher, a woman. She later became a very distinguished educator and I corresponded with her, but that's beside the point. She was teaching mathematics, which I had no interest in whatsoever, and I was determined to read books. I was deeply immersed in the reading that one does at roughly that age.

Island: What were you reading?

Styron: Who knows? I was reading everything at that time. I was reading Thomas Wolfe, Dos Passos, Hemingway, Faulkner. She would catch me over and over reading a book which I shouldn't have been reading behind a mathematics book. She caught me, she threatened me, and from her point of view, quite properly, reported me to the colonel, the Marine colonel who was running the show down there.

And I got in trouble with the Marine gunner who was my nemesis, a very tough character. In those days they used to call them warrant officers. It was before they began to wear those little rectangular bars. He wore a little bomb on his lapel, the symbol of a gunner—a Marine gunner—and he was tough as hell. He put me on report several times.

I'm just bringing these up to show that I always had a very strong anti-authoritarian streak in me. It's a very profound resentment of authority, and I think that has shown up in my work.

Island: Is it authority itself, or is it an attitude that some figures in authority exhibit?

Styron: It might be a duality because there's a part of me, at least at that time, that rather respected authority. After all, I was trying to become an officer myself, and I did become a Marine officer and I rather enjoyed it. It was only a brief period, but I had my little fling with authority. And I recognized that streak in me too—a respect for authority which may be the opposite side of the coin from the rebelliousness that I've often felt.

Whenever there's a new President, I always have presidential dreams. I dreamt that I was in the White House chumming it up with Jimmy Carter not too long ago. And I remember having the same dreams about Eisenhower and Kennedy. Clearly, this is an indication that there's a part of me that very much admires authority. On the other hand, there's some sort of conflict at work, because on the more important philosophical level I think I have always despised authority, especially authority which is used in a malicious, or illegal, or inhumane way.

Island: How old were you when your first novel, *Lie Down in Darkness*, was completed?

Styron: I completed the actual work when I was still twenty-five, and it was published in the fall of the same year when I was twenty-six.

Island: What were you doing in those days? Where were you living?

Styron: I'd been living with some friends up in Rockland County, New York, near Nyack, for the bulk of the writing, a year and a half or thereabouts, and then I moved to New York. I lived on West 88th Street near Riverside Drive. I had no money at all, just enough to get by. I shared an enormous room and a kitchenette with a painter who taught at the New School—a very nice guy—and just struggled along in this place another year until the book was done. Then just about the time it was completed, just as I was heading toward the end, I got this terrible news that I was going to be called back to the Marine Corps. It was the Korean War.

Somehow my publisher managed to wangle a deferment for a few months from the Marine Corps, and, fortunately, because I don't think I would have finished it otherwise. So the last part of the book was written in rather a great frenzy of activity because I urgently had to finish the book. Besides, I thought, who knows? It might be the last book I ever wrote.

Island: Would that last section include Peyton's soliloquy?

Styron: Yeah. It would include most of that. Curiously enough, I wrote the whole book in sequence with one exception: I wrote the whole last part, that baptism scene, before I wrote the soliloquy. It was the only part that was out of sequence. The soliloquy I wrote very rapidly. It took me only about ten days. When I wrote that last word I was finished, and very soon after that, just a matter of days, I had to go to Camp Lejeune, the 2nd Marine Division.

Island: You mentioned that you were sharing an apartment in New York. Were you then studying at the New School?

Styron: I had been . . . I'm one of those people who's not really ashamed of saying that he took Creative Writing. A lot of people think it's a little much. But I don't. I happened to be in Hiram Haydn's class, and he was the one who encouraged me to get this book done. He was at that time in publishing, too. He was a teacher and a publisher. So he had a kind of lock on the book, which was fine. I was glad to have a man who encouraged me and who was also going to publish the book. He was then editor-in-chief of Bobbs-Merrill. So it worked out very nicely.

Island: Who else was in that writing class?

Styron: Well, I can't remember. There were so many faces that moved in and out. I can't tell you exactly who was in the class, but at that time, around the school, Mario Puzo was there writing and another writer named George Mandel, who published several novels.

Island: There was one thing I wanted to ask about *Lie Down in Darkness*. The opening section, which serves to bring the reader rather rapidly into the atmosphere of Tidewater, uses as a vehicle a train ride down to the town of Port Warwick. The peculiar thing about that section is that it is addressed to the reader. But instead of "Dear Reader," it's "You." How did you decide upon using that second-person technique?

Styron: Well, I'll tell you. I confessed it to the man who influenced me, so I might as well confess it to you. It was a direct steal from *All the King's Men*, the beginning of *All the King's Men*, which also uses that "you," the second-person technique, to get the book going. Look back at it some time and you'll see, only it's set in Louisiana, in a car going to Willie Stark's home somewhere in the red clay country of Louisiana.

Now, if mine had been mere imitation, everybody would have noticed it in two seconds. But it wasn't an imitation. It was my taking what Red Warren had done, mainly the use of that "you," and taking his keen observation of what Louisiana was in his time and bringing it to a train ride, that same kind of—not the rhythm even, but just the resonance, the touchstone. So I created something quite original by using this wayback as a model.

Island: I notice in your books that while there is movement in time, let's say present time, there is also plentiful flashback time, so that you travel freely within space and time.

Styron: Yeah. I've always felt some need to do that. I don't know what it is. But again, in this book I'm working on now I do a great deal of that absolute flashing back into time, coming back into the present. I don't know why. It's always impressed me when done properly, as Faulkner so often did, as a very effective device, if it doesn't confuse you or the reader. I've always found this a very powerful use of technique, to draw the attention of a reader into different time compartments.

Island: How did you come to center your first novel on Peyton Loftis? Was the character modeled on someone you knew personally?

Styron: There was a girl in my life at the time. It wasn't a matter or love or anything like that. She had pre-dated my story. I mean, I had known her when I was . . . let's see, I began writing that book when I was about twenty-two. I remembered her from my adolescence, earlier, sixteen or seventeen. But fascinating, a gal who was way ahead of her time. She lived in Virginia and was ahead of her time in the sense that she was "promiscuous" at an early age. Quite good-looking gal. Went to college, went to Goucher, as a matter of fact, then went to New York and became a bohemian. She was almost exactly my age, maybe a year younger. I didn't see her in New York, but I heard the stories about her. She married a Jewish painter and began the drug scene very early. I think she ended up okay. As a matter of fact, several years ago she was on the Vineyard looking really spaced out. No longer in the bloom of youth, I might add, either, but still a very handsome woman.

She, more or less, was the model for this gal. She had a family situation somewhat similar, the father who was the rounder with the pretty mistress. The wife, however, was total invention on my part because I don't think she corresponded with her real mother in the slightest. The family situation was entirely different and, of course, all the basic dramatic events in the book were made up. This girl who I just described to you did not kill herself. So that's about as close to any kind of reality, but it was, quite frankly, based on somebody and some family.

Island: I notice the book was dedicated to Sigrid. Who was Sigrid?

Styron: Sigrid was a girl named Sigrid de Lima who is still very much around. I haven't seen her in years, but she was a girl that I shared this house with up in Nyack, near Nyack, and who was very close to the book and had followed it from its inception. She was one of those people that one has in one's past. I haven't seen her in a long time, I mean, just, you know, like so many people who vanish from your life.

Island: Let's talk about *The Long March.* Does this story derive from a personal episode? For instance, did you have to go on a forced march?

Styron: Yes.

Island: What was that experience?

Styron: Very similar to the one in the book.

Island: You knew someone with a nail in his foot?

Styron: No, I didn't. Mannix was a total figment of my imagination. That part did not really happen. Nor did he really exist. The Colonel is very similar to the Colonel who ran us on this march, and the march itself was very much like the one that we all had to go on, without much exaggeration one way or another. A very, very brutal forced march.

Island: I notice the name of the Colonel is Templeton. I wonder about the choice of his name. Is somehow the idea of a temple associated with authority? You've mentioned the White House. There was a "white house" image, a white house, or white temple that Nat Turner was dreaming about.

Styron: Sure, a white temple.

Island: Is this an echoing of that same symbol of authority?

Styron: Well, I suppose certain aspects of formal religion I have associated with authority, usually very negatively. And it is a theme I want to develop in a novel which I will finish, God willing, after the one I am writing now, one called *The Way of the Warrior,* which I published excerpts from but then put aside. It develops the theme which begins with Templeton, namely, that there is a quasi-religious aspect to military life. I've always thought that the Marine Corps was like a religion to certain people, to certain men. And I try to emphasize in the books I'm writing now how the SS, the German SS, was actually, historically, built by Himmler around the idea of the Jesuits—I mean *consciously* on his part, with the intense loyalty and intense devotion.

Island: That is, the worship of power, a mystique of power, which is built into authority by hierarchy.

Styron: Yeah. And so the religious motif, I think, is very—even the name Templeton, of course, with its connotations. I haven't gone over *The Long March* in a long time, but I think, if I'm not mistaken, that I allude in certain ways to the Colonel as a priestly sort of man.

Island: Culver, the narrator, seems to have a mixed impression of the Colonel as a kind of an obstacle, but at the same time the Colonel comes across as not being particularly inhumane.

Styron: I intended that. That's a fairly early work of mine and I'm still developing that kind of theme, but I'm not a person who necessarily associates military life with evil. That's the reason I was able to see the Colonel, Templeton, as a man of some distinction, of some quality. Obviously Culver doesn't love the Colonel, but has great respect for him.

One of the liberal fallacies—and I use that word advisedly, but it is, I'm afraid, a liberal fallacy—is that the military is unmitigated evil. Especially in the United States. Well, I don't happen to believe it is. It's a necessary aspect of the world we live in. Much of military life is unpleasant, and it goes against the grain of most civilized people. On the other hand, there is much in it that is attractive. Maybe this derives from the fact that I was born and raised in Virginia and I had an uncle who was a general and I lived around military people all my life. Virginia is such a military-conscious state, and I had ancestors who were officers in the Civil War. So, in other words, I don't have this liberal, this famous knee-jerk thing that associates the military profession with fascism or butchery or insensate cruelty or anything like that.

Island: *Set This House of Fire*, it seems to me, is especially interesting from a technical angle. In the first novel, *Lie Down in Darkness*, you use an impersonal narrator. In the second, *The Long March*, the narrator is a by-stander narrator, as in *The Great Gatsby*. Then, in *Set This House on Fire*, there are a pair of narrators, one of whom becomes the major character in the book. Then *Nat Turner*, where it's in first-person, and therefore the narrator is the character. Were you conscious of moving from a third person through a kind of third-person participant into . . . ?

Styron: Yeah. I think it's a perfectly valid way to tell a story. If you can so establish the authority of the second narrator, as to make his experience, again, authoritative, so that the reader accepts the fact that the first narrator can go into his mind, then I think the thing

works. The book has been criticized on many levels, but no one
seems to bother about that, which to me legitimizes the technique.

Island: Were you influenced by other novels. Did you know of
any other novels that had dual narrators?

Styron: Not really. I know the one I'm writing now has a dual
narration—the guy that you read about in that story in *Esquire,* and
the girl, Sophie, who is, as I told you, the heroine. She is, after Peyton, my next female heroine. So I have a dual narration and I think it
works even better, I might add, in this book.

Island: I'd like to move on to the *The Confessions of Nat Turner.* I
remember reading an interview that you did in France published in
the *Southern Review.* You mentioned that the rosebud image in *Citizen Kane* inspired "columbine," the word that Nat Turner spelled out
at the beginning of the memory cycle.

Styron: There was a definite connection in my mind between the
rosebud and columbine. I remember I had something, but I can't tell
you what it was at the moment. The word was not "columbine" but
something like "dogwood."

Island: Which has a bud.

Styron: Yeah. You see, I think I realized that . . .

Island: Too heavily a religious connotation?

Styron: It was too close to rosebud. You see, even if the average
reader would not make that connection, I didn't want myself to make
that close a connection. I didn't want, on the other hand, to drop the
conceit, which I liked, and I just remember going through a little
catalog of flowers in my brain and then suddenly hitting on columbine. It had a nice sound, so I just used it.

Island: At the beginning of *Nat Turner* and throughout the book,
there are a number of references to a dream that Nat has of floating
in a boat in an estuary. He gazes up and sees that white house at the
mouth of the river, a white building which is something like a temple,
but is not a temple. It has no windows, it's smooth and doesn't seem
to be penetrable. Did you conceive that from a dream? Or was that
something that just came out in your writing?

Styron: Well, there are several things that I'm trying to put together about that. I remember my daughter Polly telling me that she
dreamed about a Masonic temple over in Woodbury. I'll show it to
you because it just so happens to be in this new book that Arthur

Miller's wife and Arthur . . . I got it a few days ago. It's all about this
area around here, in Connecticut. It's called *In the Country*. Polly
dreamt about this temple. Here it is, without any windows, you see,
everything closed up, with the columns. And I was fascinated by her
having had the dream.

This was along about the time I was beginning to write *Nat Turner*.
Polly must have been just a little girl, about five or six or seven years
old, something like that. So I put her dream and my own registry of
that temple, plus something else that had haunted me. I'd seen other
temples, other churches, other temple-like buildings all my life and
had been fascinated by the mystery of the structure. Maybe it's Egyp-
tian, but I'm not sure.

Most of what I've written you could torture me and threaten me
with death and I wouldn't be able to tell you just when I wrote it.
Peyton's monologue is an exception, but if you asked me, when did
you write the sequence about the party or one of the parties in *Lie
Down*, I wouldn't be able to tell you to save my life. But I remember
exactly where I was on the Vineyard when I began writing *Nat Turner*
and that passage. It was in a house we rented, just up the beach past
the yacht club, that belonged to Kingman Brewster's mother. We
rented that in the summer of 1962, and I remember sitting down in
the little place in the back where I wrote and setting down the first
words about Nat Turner, never changing a word.

It seemed irresistible to me to have him in this, knowing that he
was going to wake up in jail . . . that he would have this dream of
floating down the river. That just flowed, no pun intended. Then
suddenly I incorporated Polly's vision of this temple, and so it
seemed appropriate. I've been asked about that as often as any single thing in the book. I have had to explain, and I always answer very
simply that it's a mystery. It's a double mystery. It's a mystery why I
put it there, and Nat's a mystery, and that's a mystery within a mystery. Nat doesn't know why it's there, either, you see.

Island: You have written one play, *In the Clap Shack*. What different kinds of problems does writing a play present?

Styron: I hesitate to say this, but I think the drama at this moment
is quite an inferior art form, though I might be mistaken. To me it's
just simply not vital. But this thing cast itself as a play somehow in my

mind. It was going to be a novel, the germ of it, but all of a sudden it seemed to lend itself so beautifully to a stage set.

One of the beauties—though at the same time one of the fatal flaws of writing a play—is the ease with which you can do it, because your use of language is simplified. Obviously, if you're Shakespeare you use your language in it, but nowadays the language . . . You don't have to describe sunsets, getting people in and out of rooms, moods. It is all there in dialog. If you have any ear for speech, which I think I have to some extent, you just put it down, and that makes it very simple just in terms of time. I wrote that play in six weeks.

Island: Compared to your usual rate of production . . .

Styron: Well, it was nothing. It's a blessing in many ways on a certain level. I mean, just the sense of exhilaration you get from being able to have something done, and then also the wonderful community quality later on of putting it on the stage—the actors, the director, as I said, a community venture. It's very inspiring, but you end up with an inferior statement as compared to a novel. Somehow I don't think the times are right for the drama. I don't mean to be condescending. I had great fun writing it. I had enormous fun seeing it put on at Yale. But, it ends up a minor to my mind . . . I'm not ashamed of it, but it is a sort of minor exercise.

Island: How was it received critically?

Styron: Well, Clive Barnes, the "Pope," didn't like it. And, of course, that ruined it. That, in itself, is an indication of how decrepit the modern drama is. When one man by his single statement can determine the success of a play, it's just appalling, beyond belief, and yet there it is. If he had liked it, it would have gone to Broadway. Oddly enough, there were some very friendly reviews. It just wasn't taken very seriously. At any rate, I was not disappointed by anything. I wasn't expecting all of a sudden to turn into a Tennessee Williams.

Island: I know you're thinking about that television extravaganza we've had the last couple of weeks, "Roots," and the book which has accompanied it and all the hoopla that has surrounded the production. What is it called, a media event?

Styron: Media event, right.

Island: Would you say it's more of a media event than a work of art?

Styron: Totally, I don't think there's anything connected with art in the entire thing. It's a media hype.

Island: Then you don't feel that "Roots" was very successful in portraying the true inhumanity of slavery.

Styron: I think it missed the moral dimension of what slavery was about. You can't really be truthful and reduce slavery to random brutality by whites. There was plenty of brutality, but slavery was such a completely human situation in that it was filled with extraordinary other things, love, passion, sacrifice, compassion, understanding. I'm not saying that these existed all the time, but they existed as often as the random brutality.

Island: You're talking from the point of view of the slave owners?

Styron: I'm talking from the point of view of slave and slave owner.

Island: From the point of view of the slave, would there be affection for the master as well as resentment and hatred?

Styron: I know it sounds like the worst old cliché, yet I believe it to be absolutely true that in many cases there was a deep love and affection on the part of slaves for masters. I don't mean to say that this was necessarily always true. Just too much of the record would show that.

Island: Then, in a sense, the attitude of the slave toward the master was not dissimilar to your own feelings about authority. There is some respect and compassion and understanding for a person in authority, and yet at the same time there is strong resentment toward the institution which causes that to be.

Styron: Certainly, yes. And that's what I tried to do in *Nat Turner*—to render slavery in one volume is a tough job, but to get the essence of what it was all about, to show the multi-faceted nature of slavery, to show that it's a political thing, an historical thing. It just wasn't sequence of events in which black people were persistently tortured, raped, mutilated, and so forth.

Island: Could it be that the blacks were looking for an historical romance—rather than a novel about rebellion, authority, the terrible inhumanity of slavery—an historical romance which glorified the slave and the slave's integrity? And wasn't it that it came from a place they weren't looking for?

Styron: It came from the white man. That was the major problem.

If I had been black, that book, warts and all, would have been embraced with hysteric fervor.

Island: If James Baldwin had written *Nat Turner*, for instance.

Styron: If James Baldwin had written it, he would have been apotheosized into Shakespeare. But even if a black man not already known had written it, he would have become the most celebrated black writer in history and the most loved by blacks. I am convinced of that. But they couldn't bear at that particular moment, especially, when they were trying so desperately to find their own identity, to have this white man come along and make what they considered a fabrication.

Island: Do you anticipate that women will take you to task for using a woman narrator in your current work?

Styron: I can't see why.

Island: One thing I have noticed about your work as a novelist, you don't hesitate to put yourself into psyches that you couldn't possibly have experienced or inhabited.

Styron: Well, that doesn't bother me in the slightest because if women do that, they are just being silly as they have recently been about so many things.

Island: Such as?

Styron: Criticizing men for almost anything that doesn't follow their propagandistic—

Island: You're speaking of radicals—

Styron: Yes, mainly. This ludicrous thing they recently did with the *American Poetry Review*. Picketing, calling *American Poetry Review* racist and anti-feminist because it didn't publish such-and-such a quota of black writers and such-and-such a quota of women, which is the most dreadful form of fascism.

Island: Quite clearly, *APR* had women involved from the beginning.

Styron: Of course, Muriel Rukeyser.

Island: Diane Wakoski.

Styron: But the idea of imposing a quota system as if everything all of a sudden has to be 20% black because they represent that much of the population, 50% women because they represent . . . as if talent were not the only criterion. It is totally inexcusable when an editor hasn't the right to choose poems on the basis of their aesthetic merit and that alone. It has nothing to do with sex or race, it has to do with one's gifts. I think it's the most dreadful thing I've ever heard of. It was in the *New York Times* about a week ago. Adrienne Rich, being the ringleader of the pickets.

Island: I want to talk about books for a second, if we can shift into that. What books and writers continue to mean the most to you?

Styron: A great deal of poetry of the Elizabethan period, Shakespeare, John Donne. A great deal of modern poetry, Whitman, Emily Dickinson. And, in the present time, people like Roethke, Auden, Eliot, Lowell.

Island: How about novelists?

Styron: Well, there again, the standard—Melville, Faulkner, Hemingway, Fitzgerald, and certainly Thomas Wolfe, and Tolstoy, Chekhov, Flaubert, but almost no English writer since 1900.

Island: I wonder why that is.

Styron: I don't like the English spirit . . .

Island: What is it about the English spirit?

Styron: Camp. It's frivolous, evasive.

Island: Who would be the great English novelist then?

Styron: Thomas Hardy, I think.

Island: Thomas Hardy, not Dickens.

Styron: Well, Thomas Hardy coming after Dickens. I'd include Dickens among the pantheon. I really make one exception to the English writers, and that is I admire Orwell, although he wasn't a novelist. I have absolutely no use for Graham Greene.

Island: What about Americans? Of course, the American writing experience is relatively short. I guess there have been about two hundred years for novels to emerge . . .

Styron: We've done rather well for a primitive country in terms of our literature.

Island: You've mentioned Faulkner and Hemingway, and so forth.

Styron: Yes. It's a little early to say about the ones following that. I don't like to knock my contemporaries, and I generally refuse to do it, but I think that it was quite wrong for Bellow to get the Nobel Prize when Nabokov did not.

I think Bellow is a good writer, but vastly over-rated. For Nabokov not to have gotten it was scandalous, just on the simple grounds that he was sick and a lot older, a man of enormous achievement. But I don't give that much of a damn about the Nobel Prize anyway, insofar as it symbolizes what people think about excellence, often erroneously.

Island: How do you think your work differs from your contemporaries?

Styron: I know only one thing, that I've gone my own way and I've never followed any trends. I've been trying to say what I wanted to say in the way I wanted to say it, taking my own time and doing it generally slowly, not really caring about turning a book out every year like some writers, people like Updike who seem to have a compulsion to be on the scene all of the time. And I'm just doing what I've got to do. Usually tackling very ambitious themes . . .

Island: Increasingly ambitious . . .

Styron: Yes, but it's something I don't shrink from because it's the only way—taking one's vision, which is comprised of a story on the crudest level, but a very necessary level, and adding to it the philosophical weight of what one wants to say, then making it all go together in the form of, usually, a long but I hope not bloated novel. This book I'm working on now will be quite long, but it won't be half as long as *Gravity's Rainbow,* or something like that.

Island: I've noticed in the *Esquire* Capote pieces that a number of writers, not to mention celebrities and socially prominent people, are portrayed rather mercilessly by Mr. Capote. Yet somehow you have escaped his acid wit. Do you have any idea why this is?

Styron: I know Truman. I don't know him very well but I've known him over the years, and we always got along. I like him, he likes me, we like each other's work, appreciate our mutual problems, and so I think that's the reason. It's a personal, mutual respect.

Island: He's a good person to have respect you, given the kind of pen he wields.

Styron: You wouldn't want to get on his list, so to speak.

Island: What is the setting of this new novel? The piece that I read in *Esquire* was set in New York.

Styron: Yes, that's right, in Brooklyn. In general, the story begins with myself, who I call by nickname, being fired from his job at McGraw-Hill in the summer of 1947, just out of college, and going to Brooklyn to live in a rooming house where the narrator meets a couple, a Jewish boy and a very beautiful Polish girl. It turns out the

Polish girl is not Jewish, but has been in Auschwitz and is a survivor of twenty months in Auschwitz. Basically it's an attempt to deal with just that. It's an attempt to deal with Auschwitz.

Island: Were there a lot of non-Jews in those concentration camps?

Styron: About one million at Auschwitz out of four. The statistics are blurred, but if you are talking about the non-Jews who died in exactly the same way as the Jews, in the gas chambers, two and one half million Jews and about one million non-Jews. All this is on the historical record. Oddly enough, this is information that does not seem to bubble to the surface. It's not in the public mind.

But what mystifies me, and it's very hard to express, is that we are all of a species, you and I and all of our ancestors, we came from the same womb, the same source and we are in effect brothers. But all the horror and suffering, aside from natural disasters which there is no way to explain, are caused by man, by our own species, acting in evil ways toward himself. It's a very simple, but a very complex equation. Nature is indifferent. You could say much of the evil that we feel is a product of irrational nature, disease, let's say cancer. There's no way of explaining it. It happens, and it's evil. And an earthquake, you could say, is a kind of indifferent evil, or a flood. These things are part of the natural scene, but, basically, the unhappiness and the things we all consider to be evil derive from ourselves.

We who are supposed to be brothers are the authors of the pain and oppression of the world. And it's a mystery, because one would think that, theoretically, a species such as we are with our capacity for love and goodness and friendship, which we all have, most of us, unless we're crazy, so often are mechanized and twisted through society, politics, through a thousand different ways, into causing evil and suffering. It's a mystery but I think that's what a writer has to deal with. And I have. For instance, my friend Fuentes, who knew Malraux very well, quoted something of Malraux's which he typed out for me. I'm thinking of using it, it's such a strong statement, as an epigraph for this book I'm writing now, which goes in translation: "I seek the crucial region of the soul where absolute evil opposes brotherhood." It's a very strong and moving statement and I find it very sympathetic to my own ambitions, to my own artistic desires, and it is apposite to the theme of the book I'm presently writing. So I'd like to use it as one of the epigraphs to the book.

Island: Have you a provisional title for this book?

Styron: I have a working title and I think it's probably going to be the final title. It's called *Sophie's Choice.*

Creators on Creating:
William Styron
Hilary Mills / 1980

From *Saturday Review,* 7 (September 1980), 46–50. Copyright © 1980, Saturday Review magazine. Reprinted by permission.

Since 1951 when he was awarded—at the very early age of 26—the Prix de Rome of the American Academy of Arts and Letters for his first novel, *Lie Down in Darkness,* William Styron has continued to challenge the moral and intellectual complacency of readers throughout the world with his provocative novels. His fourth, *The Confessions of Nat Turner,* won a Pulitzer Prize in 1968, and his new novel, *Sophie's Choice,* published in June 1979, was on the hardcover bestseller list for 47 weeks and won the American Book Award for Fiction in May, 1980.

He spends his summers in an expansive and gracious home on Martha's Vineyard, where he lives from spring to fall with Rose, his wife of 27 years, his four children, and two dogs. There he talked about the themes in his work, his habits, and the process of creation.

Q: In your first novel, *Lie Down in Darkness,* you wrote about a woman's madness partly from a woman's point of view. In your novel *The Confessions of Nat Turner,* you wrote about a slave rebellion from a black slave's point of view; and in your new novel, *Sophie's Choice,* you write about the Holocaust from a Polish Catholic's point of view. Why did you choose to write about these subjects and do you see any connections between them?

A: I suppose the pathos of the victim has always been a central consideration in what I've written—the victimization of people by life or by other human beings, sometimes even to the extent that it has to do, at its most extreme, with slavery. That's always been some sort of guiding theme and has always seemed to me to be a very important artistic theme—what other people do to each other in the guise of idealism or of passion or of zealotry, whatever.

Q: When *The Confessions of Nat Turner* came out at the height of the black separatist movement in the late sixties, it received some very severe negative reaction on the part of blacks. I understand you and your family received bomb and kidnapping threats. Were you expecting any kind of negative reaction to *Sophie's Choice* and did it affect what you wrote?

A: I was, to be honest, somewhat worried that it would be misconstrued by the Jewish readers but I found, to my pleasant surprise, that it wasn't. I thought there might be some objections to a goy attacking the question of the Holocaust and to the notion that for almost the first time you had a major character in a literary work who was not Jewish and who was a victim of the Nazis, which of course is true of Sophie. She's not a Jew, she went to Auschwitz, and she is a victim. I had to say to myself from time to time that this is not the pattern, that Jews were the major victims, but I also had to face the fact that there were other victims and I was determined to put that down. I think it's a great tribute to the honoring of truth by Jews in general that there has been no objection to this.

Q: When you're writing a new novel do you find that you are consciously competing against yourself, against your previous works, trying to make the new one better?

A: No, I don't think so. You try to do your best, but I think it's a fallacy that people must create better and better works. It would be terribly romantic, almost foolishly so, to think that. The only thing you can expect—and the only thing that can be expected of you—is to create a work which adheres to your own high standards. It should be like a plateau in which there is, one feels, a relatively high level of performance. It's got to have the same intelligence, the same artistic integrity, the same direction, and all that, but it would be impossible to hope that each work would be better than the last.

It's like Beethoven's symphonies. One loves them all without feeling that any particular symphony is greater than the other, although one might have one's favorites. But you always recognize the grandeur of the spirit that informs all the music.

Q: What was the original inspiration for *Sophie's Choice?*

A: It was a kind of revelation, a dream, in which I woke up one spring morning after having been in this funk over a book I was involved in—namely a book about the Marine Corps that I'd been writing for several years and which was proceeding slowly without much inspiration. I sensed I had dreamed a vision of a girl named Sophie whom I remembered from Brooklyn in the postwar years. She was a very vivid image in my mind and in my dream. When I woke up I lay there for quite a long time with a sense that (and I don't mean to sound fancy or imply that this was a psychic experience because it wasn't), but I realized I had almost been given a mandate to write this book. I saw the whole thing plain: the idea of combining Sophie's story with a story I had heard of another victim of the camps who had to make a choice between her children—all this seen through the eyes of a young man. It was almost as if the story was outlined.

Q: Why did you choose to make the book partly autobiographical?

A: I realized that this was very important in order to make this story as seductive as I could make it, as dramatically compelling. I had to back off and give the reader—from the very first page—a sense of who was talking, which is a very good dramatic device and an old-fashioned one, but one that if done properly almost never fails. It's at the heart of storytelling and is the art of the novel—to establish oneself with a great authority as the narrator who's going to tell you a very interesting story, but who has not gotten around to telling you the story yet.

A good example of this device is *Moby-Dick* where Ishmael goes through a long, wonderfully comic episode in New Bedford right before he gets you on the ship. He establishes the right to dominate your attention. I didn't do this with anything so obvious as *Moby-Dick* for a model, but just used a device that has been used many, many times.

All of this developed within weeks. I knew roughly what I was going to do with the book the day I set the first words of it down, which was the day I woke up with that dream. There are a lot of things that came later, such as Sophie's background and the development of the camp itself—the Auschwitz theme—all of that developed much later. That's part of the discovery that I had in the novel. Whereas on one level there were many things I saw immediately about the ultimate culmination of the book, there were many other things that I had to let grow organically as I went along.

Q: Did you make any notes on future developments?

A: I made some but I keep very few notes. I had a page of very small handwritten notes, which I posted on the wall of my studio in Connecticut and which I also brought with me here to the Vineyard. But they were mostly notes to remind myself to read this and that or to remember this and that.

Q: Once you started to write that first day after the dream, did you then write consistently everyday?

A: I tried to maintain a consistent schedule but I couldn't really. For one thing, I had to break off early in the book and go to Poland. I realized I was going to be deficient unless I did go.

Q: What other research did you do for the book?

A: I had read a lot about the concentration camps, but I had not read any detailed scholarly stuff. There was some invaluable material I got at Auschwitz, namely two books. One contained the autobiography of the commandant and the other was a series of depositions and confessions by various SS officers who had served at Auschwitz. I read them in detail and realized at that point that it would be essential to my story to make Sophie have a relationship with the commandant, which she eventually did.

I also realized that in order to make Sophie really complicated and give her other dimensions, I couldn't make her just a victim. That was very essential to the dynamism of the story. If she was just a pathetic victim she wouldn't be very interesting; but to put her in juxtaposition with the commandant—not really as a collaborator by any means but as a person who in desperation is acting in an unconventional way vis-a-vis the Nazis, trying to masquerade as a collaborator—this would give her a larger dimension.

Q: Once you returned from Poland did you continue to write everyday?

A: Yes, I've always tried to work everyday when I'm in the course of a specific work. I try to write four hours each day but often it's three hours or two. I start in the midafternoon and try to work through six or seven.

Q: Have you ever had writer's block?

A: Yes I have. I wish I were one of those totally unblocked writers. In fact, it was writer's block that was bothering me about the novel I was writing before *Sophie*. I was blocked not because I couldn't write, but because I had an insufficient understanding of my material. I now realize pretty much what that understanding is and I'm no longer blocked about it, but in effect you might say that I began *Sophie* as a kind of release from the tensions and difficulties I was having on this other book.

Q: Can you describe the way you felt when you were blocked?

A: Blocking is one of those despairing moments when you're drowning. You have no connection with your material and also you don't want to write. Something in you causes you to refuse to write. With *Sophie* I never had these blocks. I had very great trouble in making the material work—architectural problems—but no moment when I said I can't write.

Q: Twelve years went by between the publication of *Nat Turner* and *Sophie*. Were these architectural problems with *Sophie* part of the reason it took so long to finish?

A: *Sophie* took four-and-a-half years to write and, given the book's length and difficulty, I would say that was a fairly good schedule. People tend to add on the years that I didn't publish.

Q: How long does it take to write a page generally?

A: When it's going well I can write a page in 15 minutes. When it's going hard I can take two hours.

Q: Do you type or write in longhand?

A: I write in longhand in pencil on yellow legal pads.

Q: Do you ever cross out or rewrite?

A: I try to interline. I have a great respect for my own calligraphy in the sense that I like to write clearly because it frightens me to think that the typist won't be able to read the manuscript, because I don't type myself. So I try to write very clearly. Instead of crossing out I usually erase and, as I said, I do a great deal of interlining.

In general my technique has almost never varied in that it is an accumulation of pages which I will never change in a major way. I don't write a first draft and then go back and dismantle it. I write very painstakingly from page one. It's like building a brick wall from the ground up.

Q: Have you ever ripped up an entire page?

A: Oh many times, oh sure. I've written many pages and para-graphs that I've thrown away entirely.

Q: Do you ever show or read manuscript pages to anyone while a work is in progress?

A: Just to my editor Robert Loomis. I read about two-thirds of *Sophie* to Bob while it was in progress and he was the first to read the whole typewritten manuscript.

Q: Where do you usually work?

A: I have a little studio in the back of my house in Roxbury, Con-necticut, and a similar one here in the Vineyard.

Q: Do you tend to read other contemporary novelists while you're at work on a book?

A: I don't read many of my contemporaries for various reasons, but I did read Walker Percy and Phil Roth while I was at work on *Sophie.*

Q: Which novelists would you say have seriously influenced your work?

A: I don't think I can say, there's such a multiplicity. At one time I thought it was mainly Faulkner, but there were so many others really, as various as Flaubert and Tolstoy, Scott Fitzgerald and Thomas Wolfe.

Q: Do you see yourself as part of a literary generation?

A: I don't really know and that always bothers me. I've always read with amusement those profound articles or reviews that usually list four or five novelists as being the leading novelists of our time, and I've never been included in the list. It doesn't bother me one way or the other except I'm always amused that someone would theorize about who are the great writers of our time. I don't think there's any possible way you can determine until a certain amount of time has passed.

I have absolutely no doubt—I will say this without modesty be-cause I don't think modesty is involved—that in 40 years my work will be read with at least the same interest as anyone who is living contemporaneously with me. I simply have no doubt.

Q: In *Sophie's Choice,* you talk about the decline of the Southern novel and the rise of the Jewish novel after the war and how torn you were between these two traditions when you were writing your

first novel. Would you say there are any new literary movements
happening now, and do they affect the way you think about your
work?

A: Writers are far more independent of literary movements than
one might imagine. I do think the most pernicious effect on literature
in our times has been what I call academic criticism—the bloodthirsty professors and third-rate academic minds that have tried to
define literature in our time. They've been intellectually despicable,
intellectually negligent, and intellectually stupid. I detest the proprietary nature of this criticism, the idea that only a certain form of writing
is valid—in this case post-modernism. I'm talking about the works of
John Barth, William H. Gass, Thomas Pynchon, Barthelme and so
on. Whereas John Barth is a writer I admire for many of his works, I
hate the idea that post-modernism is exclusively the only form of
writing.

Q: Would you call yourself a Southern novelist?

A: No, I would not call myself a Southern novelist. I would call
myself a committed American novelist who happens to write out of
an awareness of his Southern roots and Southern heritage, but I do
not wish to consider myself a "capital S" Southern writer.

Q: In a recent interview, John Irving extolled the virtues of a
bourgeois lifestyle for creative writers. You've been married to the
same woman for more than 25 years, have four children, a large
house in Roxbury and in Martha's Vineyard. Do you think this external stability has helped you get on with your work or do you find it in
some ways confining?

A: I think it's been a stabilizing and important influence. I could not
have lived in Bohemia or lived the life of a renegade or a pariah, but
I think my works have been nonetheless revolutionary in their own
way and certainly anti-establishment. I have had in my little study in
Connecticut all these years that famous line from Flaubert tacked to
my wall: "Be regular and orderly in your life like a Bourgeois so that
you may be violent and original in your work." I believe it.

Q: A friend of yours, Robert Brustein, fondly mentions in his new
book, *Critical Moments,* that you became increasingly intolerant of
the outside world—meaning friends and family—the summer before
Sophie was finished. Why do you think this was?

A: I don't remember that I was any more intolerant than usual, but
you do live in two different worlds when you are writing and it's often

hard to decompress and get back into the world of cocktail parties. I'm very antisocial at times. I almost never go to a cocktail party— ever. Right across the board. I would go to a dinner party if I knew it wasn't too big. I'm not a hermit.

Q: Do you tend to socialize a lot with other writers?

A: I don't make a point of it, but I know a decent amount of other writers and from time to time I see them.

Q: Do you prefer their company?

A: Not necessarily. On the other hand, writers share a community of interest. I certainly don't shun the company of other writers. I don't know a vast number of them but I do know a few: Philip Roth, Arthur Miller, Peter Matthiessen. James Jones was a very good friend. One of my best summer fraternizers is Art Buchwald.

Q: In your novel *Set This House on Fire,* the protagonist points out that most creative people are oral. Why do you think this is and has it plagued you?

A: I don't know if we're more oral than other people. I like to drink but I don't drink to excess. I have, however, drunk more in the past than I do now.

Q: Do you find drinking helps your work in some way?

A: It's always been a help to me. I've never written a line in my life while I'd had a drink, but in terms of its ability to relax you and to allow you certain visionary moments when you're thinking about your work, I think it's very valuable. Let's say a day is finished and you've put in some good hours of writing and you're still perplexed about the next day. Just to be able to have a few drinks and to think in this released mode often gives you very new insights.

Q: You must have known a few writers who have drunk to excess.

A: Oh sure, there have been many writers who have killed themselves with booze and that's to be devoutly avoided. But I think in general alcohol has been a liberating influence when handled properly for writers and other creative people. As one gets older one simply can't drink as much. But a drink still stimulates me.

Q: Your friend James Jones once told a young novelist that as soon as he finished a book he should start working on another one or otherwise the ensuing publicity would distract his ego in one way or another. Have you started on the next book yet or have you taken some time out to bask in the limelight after *Sophie's Choice?*

A: I don't really believe Jim's edict. I don't believe it's a necessarily true one. It was fine for him. The limelight hasn't been at all unpleasant, but I have started back on the Marine book.

Q: Would it be fair to assume it's about some sort of victim?

A: Yes, it's about a victim of the military establishment and of militarism in general.

Why I Wrote *Sophie's Choice*

Michel Braudeau / 1981

From *L'Express,* 28 February 1981, p. 76. Reprinted with permission.

When his first novel, *Lie Down in Darkness,* was published, William Styron, born in Virginia in 1925, was compared to Dostoevsky and Faulkner. His next four novels, *Set This House on Fire* and *The Confessions of Nat Turner* among them, gave him worldwide fame. His audience is constantly increasing among critics and the general public, sometimes at the cost of controversy. His undeniable courage and "guts" have opened for him the doors to the "Pantheon" of American letters in his lifetime. With *Sophie's Choice*—published in the U.S. in 1979 and scheduled for publication next week by Gallimard in an excellent French translation by Maurice Rambaud—Styron has taken on the most dangerous and vast subject among his works: Auschwitz. Stingo, the narrator, is twenty-two and aspires to become the "James Joyce of the South" when, in 1947, in a Brooklyn boarding house, he meets Sophie, thirty, a Polish survivor of Auschwitz, and her lover Nathan, an American Jew. The complex relationships between Stingo and this sadomasochistic couple will lead him to write, as did Styron, a life of Nat Turner, the black slave whose revolt shook the American South a hundred and fifty years earlier. Stingo will also discover the heart of modern darkness, the camp at Auschwitz which has been called "the anus of the world." On his twelve-acre farm in Roxbury, Connecticut, where he has been living for the past twenty-seven years, Styron calmly watches the rising sales of his book, which remained for more than forty weeks on the *New York Times* bestseller list. Michel Braudeau went there to interview him.

E: Why did you settle in Roxbury?

WS: Because living in a city like New York is incompatible with my taste for tranquility.

E: Do your royalties allow you to live independently?

WS: You know, I don't do badly from a material point of view.

E: You don't publish that often.

WS: Yes, but sales have been very strong each time. Nearly two million copies of *Sophie's Choice* have been sold, the paperback edition included. That adds up to a lot of money, also to a lot of taxes. I earned $700,000 from a work on which I spent five years. That's what a good doctor makes.

E: To what extent are the plot of *Sophie's Choice* and the character Stingo autobiographical?

WS: Stingo is not just the product of my imagination. Like him I was a reader in a publishing house, McGraw-Hill, for a few months. It was a boring and mediocre job among very pompous people. Like him I stupidly refused the manuscript of *Kon-Tiki*, by Thor Heyerdahl, which became an enormous bestseller. And like him I was dismissed for my casual attitude. Because I refused to wear a hat. It was ridiculous. I have never worn a hat except when I was in the Marines, and I was not going to start just to please them. Also because I made soap bubbles in the hallways. Like Stingo I was in love at a very young age with a certain Maria who, much later, committed suicide in a bizarre way: she drove her car from a pier into the sea. And the episode of my mother's death is also accurate, as is my feeling of guilt.

E: Did you, like Stingo, inherit a sum of money equal to the proceeds from the sale of a slave by your great-grandfather?

WS: No, that's an invention. I don't feel guilty in the least when it comes to slavery.

E: What about your family?

WS: My family owned slaves, but I don't believe that guilt can be transmitted through generations. On the other hand, one fact has made me sensitive and attentive to the subject: my great-grandparents had slaves, and I still have the list of the people they owned. Long lists of names, often biblical names like Reuben, Jacob.

E: How long did this last?

WS: Until the Civil War, about 1860. I remember that my grandmother had two young slaves, Lucilla and Lucinda, whom she liked very much and for whom she used to knit socks. And I always heard my grandparents talk about the "Brunwsick Boys," those young slaves who, in the spring, were sent to Brunswick, Georgia, to collect turpentine in the pine and loblolly forests when the sap rises in the trees. Five or six months later they would come back to North Carolina, to the small town where my father and my father's father were born. The return of the Brunswick Boys, who were hired out like farm machinery, was always the occasion for great celebration. Horrible tales also circulated constantly, like the one I relate in the novel, of blacks accused of having looked at a white woman "indecently" and consequently being tortured to death. The practice of lynching lasted for a very long time. In 1936 there were a hundred and fifty lynchings in the United States, and in the South, in Alabama, ninety percent of the victims were blacks. This continued until the beginning of the civil rights movement in the fifties.

E: In your novel you allude on different occasions to the difficulties you encountered after the publication of *The Confessions of Nat Turner*, a first-person narrative in which you tell about the revolt of a black slave in 1831.

WS: The book came out at the end of 1967, and you must remember that we were at that time at the height of the black revolution. Cities like Newark, Detroit, Los Angeles were on fire. I was attacked, of course. They said I had perverted history. Blacks called me a racist.

E: Except for James Baldwin.

WS: Yes, Baldwin was on my side, along with a few others. But a book entitled *William Styron's Nat Turner: Ten Black Writers Respond* was published. It was the first time in this country that an entire book was devoted to an attack on a novel. And without analyzing it in detail. I was a racist and that was that.

E: Did you defend yourself?

WS: No. My novel stood on its own. Historians defended me. A Marxist like Eugene Genovese—who may well be the best historian of the South—undertook to defend me in the *New York Review of Books* by refuting all the charges at great length. As for myself, I had a clear conscience.

E: What led you to write *Sophie's Choice*, which isn't a noncontroversial work either.

WS: Several things. First a book I read after the war, *Five Chimneys* by Olga Lengyel, a Hungarian doctor who survived Auschwitz.

She tells how, through ignorance, she let her children be led to the gas chamber. Had she said that they were older than they were, they might have been kept alive to work. Then the story of a gypsy woman who, like Sophie, was ordered by the Nazis to select which of her children was to be put to death.

In the late forties I moved in a boarding house in the Flatbush area of Brooklyn, precisely where my novel takes place. It isn't New York. It's more like Neuilly, a kind of Nowhere. One fine morning, at the doorstep, I met a young blond woman, superb, older than me but still young. Her English was a bit hesitant. A number had been tattooed on her arm. We took a few walks together. She had come back from Auschwitz and was in love with a man with whom she lived above me (I derived the character of Nathan from him). He was a nice man, really, and quite inoffensive. One night she gave a party and invited me. I remember going upstairs and seeing her, so beautiful, sitting at a table loaded with everything imaginable: turkeys, hams, sausages, ice cream of various sorts. And I, who knew she had come back from Auschwitz. . . . That's all I remember. Shortly thereafter I had to leave the boarding house. I was broke and went to live elsewhere, in Rockland County.

E: We are still far from the novel.

WS: I'm getting to it. In 1977, I had been writing a book about the Marines, "The Way of the Warrior," for two and a half years when I began this one. One morning I got up—it seems difficult to believe but that's the way it went—it was a beautiful day, the temperature ideal. I had slept well and in my dreams I had seen Sophie again, with her tattoo in the Brooklyn boarding house. I said to myself: "Drop the Marines, she is your novel. You are going to tell what this woman lived through, the choice she had to make, and you'll begin with the life of an unknown writer in New York." And I did not leave that project for five years. Still, abandoning one novel for another was a strange decision to make, a gamble. In a way Sophie imposed herself upon me.

E: Did the Sophie of Brooklyn write to you after the book's publication?

WS: No. Not a word from her. But I did receive a rather astonishing letter: "You seem to be describing a woman I knew in Brooklyn in 1949," wrote my correspondent. And that's what is fantastic: I knew

the real Sophie in 1949 and not in 1947 as I wrote in the novel.
What makes me believe that the man wrote the truth is what he
adds: "This woman lived in an apartment on Caton Avenue." Now, I
mentioned that street only once in passing at the end of the book,
without giving it much importance, so I'm sure that this man was not
inventing. He continued: "I knew that woman and together we went
to Jones Beach just as you mentioned it; her name was Sophie."

I went nearly mad reading that honest, sincere letter, which gave
another incredible detail: "After lying on the beach, I couldn't find the
car I had rented in the parking lot. She became angry. I didn't have
enough money to take her out. I didn't call her for a week and one
day *she* called me. She was in tears because of her boyfriend and
she said to me: 'Guess what he did to me? He strangled the cat.' And
she was crying. . . ." Exactly the kind of thing Nathan could have
done. And this man asks me if, perchance, I had not taken the same
type of twisted mind as a model.

E: And the real Sophie . . .

WS: . . . was called Sophie, of course. And has never written to
me. Perhaps she has died, disappeared.

E: Or else does not read novels?

WS: When I knew her, she was absorbed in *Manhattan Transfer,*
by Dos Passos. In two years my book has been very widely circulated. She may possibly have read it. I don't know.

E: So, the Sophie of your novel is Polish, Christian, and raised in
an educated, middle-class, seemingly liberal environment. How does
she arrive at "hating the Jews passionately"?

WS: She does not hate them, at least in the beginning, and I really
don't believe the character to be antisemitic. She must sometimes
play that role because she works in the house of Höss, the commander at Auschwitz. I know, role-playing and truth, all that's ambiguous. She also has outbursts of antisemitism against Nathan when
he rejects her. In any case, I didn't intend to paint her white as snow.
You must consider the antisemitism of her environment, of her father,
and, to be honest, of Poland at that time. One cannot conceive of
someone totally untarnished by antisemitism within that context, any
more than one can imagine someone in the American South entirely
free of racism based on color. If my book must send a message—and
I'm not sure that it should—it is that antisemitism such as infected the

whole of Europe can end up making anyone a victim, even someone not Jewish, like Sophie.

E: What about Nathan? You portray him as a Jewish intellectual, brilliant, very gifted and fascinating. Then we learn that he is a drug addict, that he's mad. Isn't that a rather easy and vague way of explaining his behavior?

WS: In an "optimistic" hypothesis I could have made him a very compassionate individual, understanding, marvelous. Which he is to a certain point. Someone very tender, capable of boundless generosity and of a great deal of wit, or else Sophie would not have been in love with him. But had he been just that, a great guy, and had they had many children, there simply wouldn't have been any novel.

E: But by making him a madman, didn't you glide over his psychology?

WS: I wanted him to be Sophie's destiny, her last executioner. The process of Sophie's destruction began at Auschwitz; Nathan completed it in Brooklyn.

E: What do you think of his statement, "As a Jew I consider myself an authority when it comes to anguish and suffering"?

WS: Nathan says this at a time when his sense of humor is particularly lacking. Ordinarily he is too ironic to say such a thing. Let us say that, in this scene, he is in a pompous phase. I also wanted to underline the fact—and I hope not to appear too caustic in saying this—that in the United States we live practically in a Jewish atmosphere. My wife is Jewish, my friends are Jewish, and American culture tends to be Jewish in a rather odd way which has not been totally elucidated. In spite of that, there are times when this complacent idea seems to appear: namely, that the monopoly on suffering is somehow held by the Jews. With my book I would like to make people see that though the Jews were by far the principal victims of the Holocaust, there were others: the Armenians, the Gypsies, also the Poles. To ignore the existence of these victims—even if it is certain that the Jews suffered more than the others—is to minimize the Nazi horror. It is to underestimate dangerously its totalitarian dimension.

E: Is that why you made Sophie a Christian?

WS: Precisely. As a Jew she would have been but one more victim, and there wouldn't have been a novel. She had to be a Christian.

E: In another scene in the novel, Sophie's friend, the resister

Wanda, argues with a Jewish member of the Resistance in the War-saw ghetto, who speaks to her of "our precious legacy of suffering."

WS: This expression, somewhat ridiculous to my mind, was really used by a Jewish writer, Saul Bellow, for whom I have the greatest admiration. But still, I don't see how anyone's "legacy of suffering" can be in any way "precious" or glorious. Moreover, there is a trace of privilege in such an expression which drives me to say: the Jews suffered more than anyone else during the Holocaust period. Post-script: they are not the only ones to have suffered.

E: How do you explain the title, *Sophie's Choice?* Did she have only one choice to make?

WS: Of course not. First through her lies, then through her con-fession, one discovers several states in her evolution, in her tragedy, several levels of horror, with a choice at each level. To be for or against the Nazis, for or against the anti-semites. To be a member of the Resistance or not. Finally to choose to live or to die. Not forget-ting the choice she must make to save only one of her two children. As Hannah Arendt wrote in *Eichmann in Jerusalem,* by putting you in such a position, the Nazis made you the executioner of your own children, which is perhaps the ultimate form of evil.

E: You distinguish between two kinds of evil?

WS: More accurately I denounce the romantic image of evil as violent and melodramatic. As Simone Weil wrote: "Imaginary evil is romantic and varied, whereas true evil is dark, monotonous, spare, boring." It is the evil of the Nazis, hideous, monotonous. Everyone, including those in the schools, should be made to read, as they are Salinger's *Catcher in the Rye,* the confessions written by Rudolf Höss, the commander of Auschwitz, during the months which pre-ceded his trial and hanging so as to understand the banality, the mediocrity, the true nature of evil. I also maintain that an error is made by imagining that the military alone is capable of pure evil, often represented as being aggressive, exciting, and orgastic. True evil, the evil at Auschwitz, was mainly the work of civilians. Among the SS in Auschwitz, all segments of German society were repre-sented: doctors, carpenters, postmen, and so on. Heinrich Himmler was a poultry farmer.

E: On this question of evil you cite George Steiner, with whom you feel some affinity.

WS: Yes. In "Post-scriptum," a text in *Language and Silence,*

Steiner makes a striking remark about the concept of time. He notes the fact that millions of people were being exterminated while in New York other men were sleeping, making love, going to the movies. For Steiner, as for me, there is something inconceivable there. Evil, as it was unleashed at Auschwitz, is of such a nature that it seems to exist on another temporal scale; as if there were some equivalent of the "black holes" in space. It is only an idea, of course, a way of answering an impossible question.

E: Did not the Nazis also have to create "defenses" for themselves so as to be able to continue exercising evil?

WS: Hannah Arendt makes note of this very pertinently. The problem of the Nazis was suppressing not so much their consciences as the "animal pity" that any man feels when witnessing someone else's pain. Their "trick" consisted in reversing the situation. Instead of pitying the victims they spoke of the horror of having to bear such a spectacle. It is what Höss does constantly: he complains about his own pain, his burden, his headaches.

E: You show another type of SS, Dr. Jemand von Niemand, the officer who forces Sophie to choose between her daughter and her son. He is both more human and more monstrous.

WS: That one still has kept a sense of Good and Evil. It may be because of his past as a believer. Before studying medicine he would have liked to take holy vows. In fact I stole this idea from Walker Percy, who is a more philosophical writer than I am: the only way of making God real in a world He has deserted is to commit the most horrible sin conceivable. Who knows whether to affirm one's capacity for sin is not as positive an act in the eyes of God as a supreme act of life—Albert Schweitzer's work, for instance.

E: As you describe them, the Nazis are not complete atheists.

WS: Indeed not. Most of them believed in some vague God but, after all, perhaps animals also believe in God. On the other hand, all Nazis denied Christ.

E: We arrive at Dostoyevski's idea: "If God is dead, everything is allowed."

WS: I'd rather say that for the Nazis, denying Christ's existence meant the possibility of committing any crime.

E: Were you attacked by the Jewish community after the publication of *Sophie's Choice* as you had been twelve years earlier by the black community for your portrait of Nat Turner?

WS: Fortunately, no. To be frank, I expected some very negative reactions. After all I was a "goy" and I touched on a quasi-taboo subject. Elie Wiesel and George Steiner had said that this must not be talked about, it's sacred. And I who am not Jewish, who have not known the camps, dared to enter this secret temple. In the book I have explained why I granted myself (and any human being) the right to speak about the Holocaust. Only one Jewish writer has attacked me. He makes three points: first, he regrets that Sophie is a Christian and not a Jew. But I have already answered that. Second, he believes that the image I gave of Nathan was that of the demonic Jew, whom all Gentiles fear, which is absurd. Third, I was supposed to have shown the sexually desirable aspect of a mutilated person, which is stupid. If Nathan and Stingo desire Sophie, it's really not because she has come back from hell but simply because she is a superb woman. No one took these arguments seriously.

E: It seems a relief to you.

WS: I knew very well that I was grappling with an enormous subject which could explode in my face at any moment. This may seem a bit vain, but the fact remains that on all important points, those I felt I absolutely had to deal with, Auschwitz or Occupied Poland for example, I received no fundamental criticism. This allows me to think that in a certain way, in some desperate way, I mastered my theme. I knew that if someone could point out, "You're making a grave error there; such a thing did not exist at that particular time," then the whole book would fall apart. And no one would have missed the opportunity to corner me. But here it is. There are no small errors either, and I'm proud I was able to be precise in this book. I'm proud to have spoken the truth. It gives the book some authority.

E: You barely touch on the question of antisemitism in the United States except parenthetically, at the beginning of chapter 6, when you speak about Nathan's brother who is an officer in the U.S. Navy.

WS: Antisemitism does exist in the United States, of course, although it has never taken the extreme forms you have known in Europe. It has existed notably in the Navy, where Jews have never been welcomed, especially in the officer class. It was different during World War II: the Navy needed doctors badly and many Jews were doctors. They did their best on both sides to forget the Navy's antisemitism. Only one Jew, Admiral Rickover, the father of the nuclear submarine, was admitted in the officer corps. But even he lived in a sort of intellectual ghetto where he spent all his energy on his project.

E: American antisemitism is not mentioned often, aside from the Navy.

WS: It has always existed, but on a rather small scale.

E: Because the first victims were the blacks?

WS: Yes, and because the Jews succeeded in doing here what they had accomplished in nineteenth-century Germany.

E: Do you consider yourself to be antisemitic?

WS: In America any Wasp is raised, as I was, with a certain dose of antisemitism. For me it was never virulent, but there was that feeling that it was better not to associate with them, even if they were O.K. There have always been "Jewish jokes" about their alleged stinginess. But the same can be said about all the other ethnic groups, the Irish, the Scots. And God knows what the Poles have been subjected to with those horribly offensive, obscene "Polish jokes." Of course, every three months or so you read in the paper that swastikas have been painted on the walls of a synagogue or that a Jewish cemetery has been desecrated. I don't think it is of great import. There is no place on earth, pre-Hitler Germany included, where the Jews have more successfully achieved the equilibrium between identity and assimilation. In this society there is no area to which they don't have free access.

E: What about the South?

WS: Jews might even be respected there more than elsewhere. If this seems strange and rather unpleasant, let's say that the reason may be that southerners already had the blacks as scapegoats. But I mostly think that southern Protestants have always felt very close to the Jews because of the Bible, of the Old Testament, which is a source of wisdom for them also.

E: You designate Auschwitz as the ultimate example of a western-style slave society. Which?

WS: In fact, none. Auschwitz can be compared to nothing. Slavery in the South, even at its worst, did not have this rational, absolute aspect. In the South, a slave was someone often treated with genuine human respect. Even the least scrupulous masters always had to take into account the fact that the slave represented a tool, an investment. In the Antilles of the eighteenth century, there were European masters who let their slaves die on the job. But that's an exception. With

Auschwitz, what is new—and Richard Rubenstein showed it with great accuracy—is the concept of the "absolute superfluity of human life," which authorizes mass extermination.

E: How did you obtain your information about Auschwitz? Did you speak with survivors?

WS: No. I preferred not to meet any and instead to stick to my intuition.

E: Did you read specialized works? Did you visit the camp?

WS: Yes, I went to Auschwitz. I felt it as an imperious need as soon as I began writing this book. I had to see. I've read many things: Höss's autobiography, Tadeusz Morowski's volume of short stories, *This Way for the Gas, Ladies and Gentlemen,* which is remarkable. At Auschwitz itself there is some kind of bookstore where they sell books about the camp in English, French, German, Russian, Polish. Some were written by members of the SS, others by prisoners. Before dying, members of the Sonder Kommando (the Jews who worked at the upkeep of the gas chambers) wrote their wills, hid them in bottles, and buried them next to the crematoriums. They have been unearthed and are shown on the very spot.

E: This visit weighed heavily . . .

WS: Yes. Because these testimonies authenticated everything. I had come to Auschwitz by train because I wanted to make the same trip as my heroine, in the same season, at the end of March or the beginning of April, to absorb the landscape. I went to Krakow, a beautiful city where the United States has a consulate because there are so many Poles with family in the Midwest that exchanges are constant—and the vice-consul took me to the camp. I spent a long day there. A horrible visit, beyond anything believable. Several days later in the plane from Warsaw to Vienna I was still in a state of complete emotional shock, as in a coma. I understood to what degree the trip had been necessary. How absolutely necessary it had been to my perception of history to have seen the place, those barbed wires, those fences, those barracks, all those things one cannot believe even when seeing them.

E: How were you able to decide to write on such a subject, in spite of everything?

WS: Perhaps because of the Malraux sentence which I used as an epigraph. It was my friend Carlos Fuentes who called my attention to this sentence from *Lazare:* "I seek that essential region of the soul where absolute evil confronts brotherhood." It seemed to me that if I could reach this area, this moment, I could try—as much as was in my power—to elucidate one of the major mysteries of the history of twentieth-century man. It seemed that if I could develop a metaphor to represent this "confrontation," if I could recreate this moment of absolute evil under some form plausible to the reader, taking my own capabilities and the imperfections of art into account, then I would be taking up Malraux's challenge; I would be doing what every writer must try to do.

E: Why have you written only five books in thirty years?

WS: I write little and slowly, like my master Flaubert. I produce hardly more than three or four pages a day. I'd like to go faster, but you know Faulkner's definition: to write a novel is placing oneself in the position of a one-armed carpenter trying to build a chickenhouse in the middle of a hurricane. That's where we've all gotten.

E: Somewhere in your novel you mention the disillusionment all writers encounter in their maturity. Still, you must have had some motivation for undertaking such a work.

WS: I simply wanted to point out how difficult it can be to start writing. Starting is so boring. It calls for so much work, so much effort and pain. In a letter to his publisher, Joseph Conrad explained that every time he'd open the door to his study, see his work table and white sheets of paper, he was close to bursting into tears. Real tears, you know, tears of anguish, of true suffering for having to sit down again and stick to it, again and again and again.

E: The biographical notice in the paperback edition of your novel says that the author, "after having worked in publishing, went in pursuit of the Great American Novel." What do you think?

WS: I'm not the one to say whether I caught it.

E: *Sophie's Choice* is an example of a great "European novel."

WS: So I've been told. Except by the Russians who, reviewing my book, wrote, "It's a true Russian novel."

E: You will be translated into Russian?

WS: Yes. My translator is a wonderful woman. She comes straight from the K.G.B., but her translation is excellent. Six months ago she said this novel would be the greatest American success in Soviet literary history. I have no reason to question it, since she is K.G.B. We spent three hours together editing very carefully through the love scenes, which she found crude. She kept repeating: "Our people are very human; of course we behave the same way as your people . . . but . . . but it is against the law."

E: What do you plan to write after *Sophie's Choice?*

WS: I'm going back to my book on the Marines. It will deal with American imperialism in the course of our century and with guilt. It is no small subject. But it will be a short book.

E: You seem to believe in the role of literature, contrary to Sartre.

WS: Sartre was wrong. For me, if literature cannot change the world in a radical way, it can, all the same, penetrate deeply into human consciousness. Millions of people can read, and I believe that a book can work on their consciences. As a writer I have no other goal. The letters I receive are proof enough that I have succeeded.

William Styron

Stephen Lewis / 1983

Transcription of an interview broadcast by the Canadian Broadcasting Corporation in 1983; text published in *Art out of Agony: The Holocaust Theme in Literature, Sculpture and Film* (Toronto: CBC Enterprises, 1984), pp. 171–90. This published text included passages from *Sophie's Choice*, inserted between the questions and responses. These passages have been omitted from the reprinting below.

When Styron and I shook hands, his first words were, "I'm told you're a socialist." "Yes," said I. "So am I," he responded. And from that moment on, the interview proceeded with preternatural ease.

Even though Styron has experienced stunning artistic success, there's not a hint of egotism. Every subject was met forthrightly, with no affected, weighty musings. Styron is neither dogmatic nor equivocal—just open and direct. He gave several years of his life to *Sophie's Choice;* it reflects his deepest convictions.

SL: *Sophie's Choice* was an astonishing and overwhelming success in every sense. How do you account for that?

WS: I'm not really sure. I think certain books seem to coincide with the *Zeitgeist,* with the spirit of the time. And I think that, at the simplest level, *Sophie's Choice* coincided with a deep and troubled interest in the Nazi period and the Holocaust. In certain ways, ever since World War Two, we have been thinking about the Nazis and the camps and the Holocaust in general, but I think it came to a crescendo in the late 1970s, when my book was published. The book appeared, after all, only a year after that rather sensational and not terribly good television programme, *Holocaust.* In the years preceding the late 1970s there just was not enough general consciousness of what had gone on. Finally the accretion of fact, and the sense of the horror, just grew and grew.

SL: Is that what happened to you as a novelist? Is that what propelled you?

WS: I have been interested in the subject ever since the years right after World War Two, when I was in college. The subject fascinated me even then. Although there was not much literature on it then, that changed as time passed. But even then, there was a book, a fascinating book called *Five Chimneys,* by a woman victim of Auschwitz, a survivor who had been a doctor. It is not a terribly literary book but it is a very skillful and graphic description of Auschwitz. I had it in the back of my mind through the period from World War Two until the mid-seventies, when I began to write *Sophie's Choice.*

SL: Did you read a lot of survivor literature?

WS: I read a certain amount. The odd thing about the Holocaust is that there is a sameness to the accounts, which prevents one from having to read a vast number. There was also a kind of ultimate horror. Once you have absorbed a few of the details, you don't need to absorb a great deal more.

SL: There is a view that says, first, that only survivors should attempt to recreate the Holocaust in literature or film; and second, that any attempt to recreate it necessarily diminishes the event. Were you worried about any of that as you wrote?

WS: No. Of course, I was perfectly aware of the argument in favour of silence, and also the argument that says that anyone who is not a survivor is incapable of rendering the story. I simply don't agree with either of those points of view. I realized I was treading on very delicate ground, and I did not want to rush into it in any haphazard way. I knew there was a risk, but at the same time I balked at the idea that, as horrible as it was, the Holocaust was some sort of sacrosanct area that could not be treated. I especially balked at the idea that someone who was not there was incapable of dealing with it. If that is true, then it is true for all experience. It would have prevented our greatest Civil War novel from having been written. *The Red Badge of Courage* was written by Stephen Crane, a man who was never within a hundred miles of a battlefield, and yet it remains our most powerful document about the combat side of civil war.

SL: Elie Wiesel and his colleagues would presumably argue that the enormity of Auschwitz and of the Holocaust was qualitatively different. Against it, even evocations of the Civil War are diminished.

WS: I certainly understand that aspect of the argument. And for that reason, I approached the subject with as much humility as I could muster. I realized that I was dealing with something totally unusual, not an ordinary catastrophe, but an exceptional catastrophe of universal scope. Even so, I could not be persuaded that this should prevent someone from dealing with it.

SL: Did you deal with it because of the creative impulse of the novelist, or because you wanted the world to understand what had happened and what the implications were?

WS: Some of both, I think. I don't know which component loomed the largest in my reckoning when I started the book. I was haunted by the central metaphor, which is the choice. In the book I mentioned, *Five Chimneys,* the author, Dr. Olga Lengyel, did not have to make the choice that Sophie had to make, but she did lose her two children because of a miscalculation. She was trying to protect them, but she made a miscalculation. I can't remember exactly, but I think she said that one of the children was younger or older; at any rate, they both went to the gas chamber. That demonstrated to me the unbelievable, haphazard horror of the Nazi tyranny. Then in the 1960s I read Hannah Arendt's book, *Eichmann in Jerusalem.* Somewhere in the text, she mentions, in passing, a gypsy woman who was forced to make that choice, in other words to become the murderer of one of her children. That struck me between the eyes, and I made the link between Olga Lengyel and that woman. I suddenly realized that this had to be the metaphor for the most horrible, tyrannical despotism in history, that this was a new form of evil, an evil so total that it could cause a woman to murder one of her own children. That was the central guiding, motivating factor behind writing *Sophie's Choice.*

SL: Yet the question of choice was endemic to the entire Holocaust experience. It was not unusual. It was true of all ghetto life, all the deportations. Families were often given only three meal tickets for five, and they had to choose who would live and who would die within the family structure. Kids were constantly being separated that way. But I take it that it was so visceral for you that it seemed to sum up the evil incarnate?

WS: Yes, it's almost a poetic metaphor, in a gruesome way. It summed up the absolute totalitarian nature of this evil, which we really had not seen, certainly in civilized society, since history began to be recorded. It seized me so poignantly that I was compelled to write a book about it. I also connected it with something that had happened to me: I went to Brooklyn, in the late 1940s, and met a young—older than I was, but nonetheless young—woman who had been a survivor of Auschwitz, and who had a tattoo on her arm. Her name was Sophie.

SL: Was she Polish and Catholic?

WS: She was Polish and Catholic. Oddly enough, I got a letter not too long ago from a woman who had been in that same house at roughly the same time. She reminded me that Sophie looked a bit like Ursula Andress, which indeed she did.

SL: In your essay, "Hell Reconsidered," you express the view that the world must know that the Holocaust was not merely a Jewish phenomenon, but that it embraced many others.

WS: People like Elie Wiesel have resisted this idea, with some justification, I think, because of the way it has been presented to the world. I don't think for an instant that anyone can object to the fact that Jews, quite properly, say that they were the chief victims. Indeed they were; there is simply no doubt about it. In fact, I think it can be argued that the phrase "the war against the Jews" describes what the Nazis were doing to a great extent. It was an overriding obsession.

SL: Wiesel said, "Not all victims were Jews, but all Jews were victims."

WS: Yes, I think that is true. But I am troubled nonetheless by a certain ungenerosity that does not allow the understanding that there were, indeed, not just thousands, not hundreds of thousands, but millions of non-Jews who died just as horribly as the Jews, although perhaps not as methodically. It has to be remembered that the population of Auschwitz at any single time was largely Gentile, not Jewish. The Jewish victims were being exterminated, to be sure, and the non-Jews were dying in their own particular way, which is to say that they were slaves who were being starved to death, and they died just as verifiably as those who went to the gas chamber. This has bothered me; it has bothered even people like Simon Wiesenthal, the leading Nazi hunter of our era. He is on record as saying that he is troubled by the fact that "the six million" seems to be proprietary. He says, "I always insist that we talk about not the six million Jews but the ten million, or the eleven million or whatever number of people, Jews and non-Jews, who were direct victims of the Nazi terror." I think that there should be a kind of codicil or postscript or some banner floating along with the Jewish banner, saying, "We also died."

SL: Is Sophie your codicil?

WS: In a sense. I certainly didn't write the book to make a message. To be quite honest I have been very moved by the reaction on the part of so many Jews who accept Sophie for what she was, and who also accept the fact that the book never fails to demonstrate that the Jews were the chief victims and that Sophie's own father, who was a rabid anti-Semite, was a necessary instrument for this horror. I have tried to use Sophie not in any sort of agit-prop way to say that others died, but to demonstrate quietly that there were more than a few Poles who were caught in the same sort of agony as the Jews.

SL: I did an interview recently with Yaffa Eliach, who has written a book, *Hasidic Tales of the Holocaust*. And when I questioned her about Sophie, she asked how many Polish Catholics stood on that platform at Auschwitz and had to make that choice, compared to the vast numbers of Jewish mothers who stood on that same platform.

WS: If one wishes to speak numerically, no one could ever argue with the fact that the Jews were the chief recipients of the horror. I don't think there is any argument about that. But it seems to me if one Polish child suffers direct agony at the hands of the Nazis, this is an indication of what the Nazis were up to. It wasn't just one little Polish child: there were literally hundreds of thousands, even millions of Slavs who suffered. To be sure, they did not suffer the direct extermination process, but they died horribly of disease, torture, starvation, medical experiments, and so on. My point is quite simple: they should be put somewhere into the record.

SL: What did you think of the film of your book?

WS: I thought the film was a remarkably faithful adaptation of the book. I thought it did a splendid job, in a linear way, of representing the book. At the same time, the film necessarily had to commit rather enormous sins of omission, and much of the book was not in the film. I regretted that, but that is implicit in the making of movies. It would have been a ten- or twelve-hour movie if it had tried to reproduce the complexity of the book.

SL: In failing to reproduce the complexity of the book, does it do the subject-matter an injustice?

WS: No, I don't think so. I think the great virtue of the film is that it extracted the essence of the book, the central story. The message of the book was retained. Of course, it could not contain any of the purely philosophical points that were made, but I thought it did an awfully good job of capturing the basic outline.

SL: You did? I thought it was a betrayal of your book, if I may be direct about it. I felt that the inability to convey what Auschwitz was, what those seething platforms were, what the crematoria were, constituted a betrayal. Apart from all of that, I thought: here's a writer who has intellectually and aesthetically established the nature of the evil and along comes a film crew and violates it.

WS: Well, I certainly had no feeling of happiness over what the film failed to do. There were so many vast areas of the book that were not even suggested. I sensed a terrible sort of emptiness in myself after I had seen the film. But my feeling of deeply qualified approval does have to do with the fact that I thought it caught the essence of Sophie's horror, of Sophie's agony. And did it rather well through the extraordinary performance of Meryl Streep. Knowing the films as I do, I think it could have been totally parodied, totally ruined, but I don't think it ruined the book.

SL: You talked of *Holocaust,* the TV series, in your essay "Hell Reconsidered." You called it soft-headed vulgarity and slick footage. But you would feel, I take it, that even a film that ultimately trivializes the event is better than no film at all.

WS: I would say so. Naturally it is difficult to be objective about the difference between the movie of *Sophie's Choice* and a television programme like *Holocaust.* But despite my lack of objectivity, I think I would have to say that the movie of *Sophie* is a far more honest attempt to capture the essence of the Holocaust than the television series was. I felt that there was a severe dishonesty in the television series, but I did not feel that there was any dishonesty in Pakula's approach to the film. I felt it failed on many levels, but that if there was honesty in the book, he replicated that honesty to some degree. Therefore, to answer your question, yes, I feel it is better to have a frail and faulty version than to have nothing at all. Despite the caveats you've just mentioned, there have been a lot of people who probably would not read the book but who leave the movie feeling that they had learned something or were moved in some way.

SL: Does it concern you that for the lumpen proletariat *Sophie's Choice* is the Holocaust? It is the single most vivid evocation that society has embraced in a combination of literature and film in recent memory. Therefore, isn't it a little worrisome that the book has so much greater fidelity than the film?

WS: You're right. One could possibly be left with the impression, if one were unsophisticated, that the film is the Holocaust. The book explains in much greater detail that the Holocaust was far more complex.

SL: You achieve, in the book, an extraordinary combination of fact and art, if you will forgive the separation. You use Höss's material. You use Steiner's. You use established works to give authenticity and an intellectual frame. Was that a difficult process?

WS: For me it wasn't so much difficult as necessary. I felt that I had to draw upon what insights had been provided by people much more knowledgeable than I about the period. I felt that I had to do my homework. I wanted to be as absolutely accurate as I could about my facts and figures, and I've been pleased that I've had almost no major objections from people who might be expected to make objections, scholars of the period and so on. This is not to say that I wanted in any sense to over-research the book. I think books that are overly researched smell of the library and, therefore, don't work. So I was very careful. I read, I think, just enough. I read Steiner, I read Hanna Arendt. I read survivors' documents. But I imagine the total number of hours I spent in reading was very modest.

SL: D. M. Thomas also went back to one survivor's account to give authenticity that couldn't be achieved, he felt, by interposed description.

WS: Yes, I think that that was very wise. One has to obey one's instincts if one is writing a novel; it's a mysterious process, but you have to obey your gut feeling rather than your head sometimes.

SL: There is in your book, as in Thomas's, a lot of sexuality, some would say eroticism.

WS: Given the nature of the relationship between Sophie and Nathan, I think I would have been remiss had I not tried to explore the sado-masochistic eroticism that existed. Sophie and Nathan were possessed by some sort of demons that caused them to devour each other, and that involved a great deal of erotic lunacy. After all, they did kill each other, and they had to come very close to the brink. As a metaphor, death and love have always been entwined in literature. The death wish and the procreative wish have often been so closely connected you can't separate them. That was essential to me, and to the relationship between Sophie and Nathan. I might add, parenthetically, that it is one of the things that I think was totally lost in the movie. There was some sort of timidity, almost, which prevented the movie from touching on that very important area of the relationship between Sophie and Nathan. It vitiated the whole ending, to my mind, because there is no premonition, as you get in the book, of why and how they're going to die together, by mutual suicide, by poisoning, not even a hint of that in the movie.

SL: The Holocaust theme is a theme of such darkness that, in those books that deal with it, the sexual relationships are bleak and self-destructive and almost pornographic themselves, as though in some wretched way they were a mirror of the event.

WS: You are making a connection between the quasi-pornographic, almost brutal sexuality and the pornography of violence, which, of course, was rampant at Auschwitz. And I think that, possibly consciously or unconsciously in trying to outline the sexual connection between Sophie and Nathan, and the violence of it, I was indeed trying to connect it to the brutality of Auschwitz. I mean, after all, he kicks her, breaks her rib, he urinates on her. This was a mirror of the kind of the thing that was going on at Auschwitz daily.

SL: Has the book yet been translated?

WS: It has been translated into, I think, twenty-two languages. In France, it is now the best-known serious American novel since World War Two.

SL: Do you get different responses from different cultures?

WS: In a curious way, it's the little things that interest me. For instance, I've not been allowed to be published in Poland—largely because of the fact that I bear down fairly heavily on Polish anti-Semitism. Some of the Polish actors, when the movie was being made in Yugoslavia, were warned officially that they could not come back to Poland if they played in the movie. In the Soviet Union, part of the book has been translated, to great fanfare, but they've put an official block on it for some reason. And it has been published in Hebrew, and I've received quite a few letters from Israel about the book, all of them favourable. The summer before last, I received a rather wonderful telephone call from Tel Aviv from a woman who just wanted to say how much she liked it.

SL: It's immensely gratifying as a writer, isn't it, when those spontaneous things happen?

WS: Yes, that makes one feel very good.

SL: One last question. Your works all deal with individual suffering in historical terms—what might be termed the continuing slavery of humankind.

WS: Yes. A form of human domination seems to be a constant in human history. Part of the message, if there is such a thing as a message, in *Sophie's Choice* was that the Nazis actually got everyone. They got the Jews first and foremost and most specifically, but anything so deadly, anything so utterly consummately filled with evil has to have at least a residual effect on everyone else. This seems to me the chief weakness of the totally proprietary notion of the Holocaust by Jews. Just the magnitude of the venture had to cause suffering that was universal.

William Styron: The Confessions of a Southern Writer

Georgann Eubanks / May 1984

From *Duke Magazine*, 71 (September–October 1984), 2–7.
Reprinted by permission.

"I remember, after I had graduated, when I was living in West
Durham on Sixth Street, right off the Duke campus, behind the
Women's Auditorium, I had a little apartment, a room I shared with
friends. I had a dog. I hadn't written a word except a few student
things. I remember I was reading—as one does at that age—reading
like a condemned man, like there was nothing else in life, and I made
the Women's Library my preserve. I would just read all the time. I
was word-drunk.

"I remember saying to myself, 'I'm going to be a writer. If these
people can write, *I* can write. If I live long enough, don't suffer some
awful disease, if life goes on in some reasonable equilibrium, I'm
going to be a writer and a pretty good writer.' I remember vividly the
moment I said that to myself. There was so much passion boiling up
in me, I knew I could not be deterred."

The year was 1948. Surrounded by the teeming silence of the
library, a young man from the Tidewater region of Virginia had
landed upon what was to be the germ of his personal story. He had a
vague idea of the plot he wanted to unravel for himself—he, the
determined protagonist called to an ambitious work: to write, to write
well, to be known for it, to become an accomplished storyteller.

Today, William Styron ('47)—the architect of that resolute vision
which has resulted in countless essays and five novels, with a sixth on
the way—sits back in his chair at the Durham Hilton on Erwin Road,
pulling vigorously at a black cigar as big around as the neck on his
bottle of Moosehead Beer. Occasionally, between sips of the drink,
he blows a mighty cloud of smoke toward the ceiling. Styron, at 59,
is back in Durham to receive the 1984 Duke Distinguished Alumni
Award at commencement. He speaks without reservation about the

progress of his career, the business of books, the drive and the terror behind his own very private creative process.

"For me, starting a novel is like starting a plantation. Before the earliest signs are out, there is a lot of planting and hoeing and traveling around to the seed salesmen. It evolves very slowly and sometimes very haltingly. I admire writers who have it all worked out and seem to churn them out organically. I find I'm always in a state of extreme unhappiness. I wish I were one of those spontaneous writers who could let it determine itself. But it doesn't seem to work that way for me."

Long periods have elapsed between the publication of Styron's novels. But ever since his first book appeared in 1951, readers and critics have hung on Styron's every word, anxious to follow the course of his life and career, smitten by the elegant rhythms in his voice and vocabulary, impressed by the depth and intensity of conflict he brings to what he labels the "few large themes that I've explored and I'm still exploring."

Defying the English teacher's dictum which suggests only immature writers rely on autobiographical material for their fiction, Styron has always carried a thread of himself through his works, drawing on his personal experiences—as a child troubled by a difficult home life (*Lie Down in Darkness*, 1951), as a Marine caught between World War II and the Korean conflict (*The Long March*, 1953), as a scholar studying abroad (*Set This House on Fire*, 1960), as a Southerner growing up on the edge of the cauldron which gave rise to the civil rights movement (*The Confessions of Nat Turner*, 1967), as a would-be writer living in Brooklyn (*Sophie's Choice*, 1979).

A Southern sensibility continues to inform Styron's writing, though he has lived for the last thirty-odd years with his wife, poet and Amnesty International activist Rose Burgunder, in Roxbury, Connecticut. As Robert Penn Warren wrote, William Styron "was born at almost the last moment when it was possible to get, firsthand, a sense of what old-fashioned Southern life had been, or to hear, actually, the word-of-mouth legends about it." He may be one of the last among a handful of living writers, including Warren, Eudora Welty, Walker Percy, and Duke's Reynolds Price, who can justifiably be classified as "Southern writers" in the tradition of Wolfe and Faulkner. (Styron covered Faulkner's funeral for *Life* magazine in 1962.)

"I've always had a sense of the uniqueness of my Southern roots. I identify strongly with my father's side of the family, which is ancient. The family goes back in Virginia and North Carolina as far back as you can go in this country, practically—to 1635, the Southern equivalent of the Mayflower. I have a very strong attachment to the South as an idea. But I'm skeptical about the South any longer as a reservoir or fountain of peculiar artistic achievement, for obvious reasons. The Old South has disappeared—the aspect of it that made it so compelling and dramatic as a source. The enormous tension between the races and the intense parochialism and sense of family roots, community, and religion—these things have become the victims of attrition.

"I wouldn't go so far as to say that the South is dead as a source, but I don't think you can say there will be a continuum of Southern literature as we have known it. Younger writers like Barry Hannah and Bobbie Ann Mason do capture a flavor of the South, but I don't know if it makes much difference any longer, whether the voice is so distinctive as to make it peculiarly Southern anymore."

Styron's lament is, in part, a lament on the coming of the plasticized, homogenized, and bureaucratized society. From our differences springs our strength, he suggests; from our differences springs our richness as a culture. "The culture of the South has come to resemble the culture of the North. I watch television and I see the survivors of tornadoes here in North Carolina and they don't sound like people from the North, of course." He smiles. "And yet, they are participating in cultural activities that their parents and grandparents couldn't have conceived of. For instance, they go to Burger King. They have interstate highways that take them rapidly to Washington or New York, or they get on a Delta plane and go. And all of this didn't exist as recently as when I was growing up. But now it's commonplace to feel an interrelationship with the North, and I think that makes a difference."

Styron grew up in Newport News, Virginia. His mother died of cancer shortly after his fourteenth birthday, and he was sent away to an Episcopal prep school near Saluda, Virginia. Two years later, he enrolled as a freshman at Davidson College. But the Marine Corps had different plans for the young Bill Styron. As part of the V-12 officer training program, he was transferred to Duke in 1943. World

War II was in full swing. Although not happy about the transfer, he
soon discovered a reason to change his preconceived notions about
Duke as a country club for disappointed Northerners who could not
make the grade in the Ivy League. His discovery was Duke professor
of English William Blackburn.

"He was far and away the man who made me become the person
I became. He saw in me whatever potential I had to be a writer,
which is important because, at that age especially, even though you
have the fire burning in you, you might not really feel that you've got
it. 'It's a delusion on my part,' you say to yourself. What's so valuable is to have someone come along like Blackburn and say, 'Look,
you really have it!' That's the important thing. That's the function of
the mentor."

Long interested in the terribly crucial, somewhat mystical relationship between mentor and pupil, Styron was himself a participant in a
Yale University study on the subject. Labeled "The Seasons of a
Man's Life," the study was run by the psychology department and,
Styron says, is still widely read in psychology courses some ten years
after its completion. He was among the twenty to thirty anonymous
subjects interviewed. "One of the facts that emerged was that on
every level—whether you were a brick layer, a streetcar conductor, a
doctor, or a writer—somewhere along the line there was a mentor
who contributed to your success. In every case there was some person, not a parent, who was almost essential to one's smooth development into maturity, someone who gave the vision and the
idealism necessary to excel."

Styron finished his studies at Duke after a two-year hiatus in the
Pacific with the Marines. He never saw combat. After graduation and
an unsuccessful bid for a Rhodes Scholarship (Blackburn nominated
him), he left Durham for New York City and worked at McGraw-Hill
for six months before being fired for "general inattention." He returned once again to Durham, reading voraciously in the old library
at Duke and keeping in touch with his mentor across campus.

Styron didn't light for long. Frustrated with his earliest attempts at
writing, he moved to Brooklyn. At the insistence of Hiram Haydn at
the New School in Manhattan, he finally began in earnest to tackle
the long process of writing a novel. The rest is the stuff of which
important literary biographies are made.

For *Lie Down in Darkness*, Styron won the Academy of Arts and

Letters' *Prix de Rome*. The book is the poignant story of a young woman from Tidewater Virginia whose homelife is so unhappy, her parents' relationship so tumultuous, that she ultimately commits suicide. It is an astute study of how the ingrained gentility of Southern families—their propensity toward politeness and "good manners"—can mask a terrible inner hostility which must eventually erupt. Following the brilliant success of *Lie Down in Darkness,* Styron went to Paris. There he helped found the *Paris Review* along with friends George Plimpton, Peter Matthiessen, Harold Humes, and others. The legendary magazine was a product of the postwar literary fervor created by expatriates living in the same section of Paris where the "lost generation" of World War I (Hemingway, Gertrude Stein, Sartre) had lived and written and talked about books into the early hours of the morning. While in Paris Styron wrote a novella, *The Long March.* His third book, *Set This House on Fire,* followed eight years later to splendid European reviews, though the reception in the United States was, at best, lukewarm.

When *The Confessions of Nat Turner* was published in 1967, Styron walked away with a Pulitzer Prize and straight into a raging controversy. *Nat Turner* is the historically-based portrait of a black man from Southampton County, Virginia, who led America's most significant slave revolt. The revolt took place in 1831 only miles from the home where Styron grew up. Both literary critics and civil rights activists blasted Styron for having assumed the narrative persona of a black man, depicted in the book from childhood to his imprisonment after the failed insurrection. The uncanny timeliness of the novel was not deliberate; the theme reflected Styron's long-held fascination with this bit of Tidewater folklore. "I had been thinking about Nat Turner since I was a child," he says. Beyond probing the psyche of the central character, *Nat Turner* examines, as a contemporary reviewer put it, "the whole institution of slavery, the master-slave psychology, the wellsprings of racial hatred, and the degrading effects—on both blacks and whites—of a declining agrarian economy." For his part, Styron told the Southern Historical Association that exercising "the liberating imagination" rather than dwelling on "useless fact" best served the novelist's purpose: "I supplied [Turner] with the motivation. I gave him a rationale. I gave him all of the confusion and desperations, troubles, worries."

Publication of *Sophie's Choice* in 1979 brought another round of harsh criticism. Again, Styron was tackling a huge chunk of history; and again, some critics insisted that the author was too far removed emotionally from the material—from the horrors of the Holocaust, in this case—to handle it adequately. Styron, in fact, had predicted the flak he would receive during an interview with Duke *Archive* editor Michael Stanford ('78) in 1977: "When *Sophie's Choice* comes out it will probably be an event, and that's both good and bad, but you can't do anything about it. It's sure going to get the same sort of fusillade as *Nat Turner*. Rabbis, Poles, ex-Nazis—they'll all be after my hide." Hide intact, a serious Styron nods wearily at the now-familiar mention of these attacks. He reaches to his forehead to push back a thick crest of gray hair. "I have been exposed to a great deal of criticism for all my work, and I'd like to think that criticism of the harshest sort is almost a tribute. There have been very few writers of any stature who have not been subjected to a great deal of abuse and almost hysterical criticism.

"Reviews ultimately are things you have to be very leery of taking too seriously. *Sophie's Choice,* regardless of its defects, has had a very broad impact. My agent in London just talked to me the other day. She says the paperback in England is doing something almost no American novel has ever done. It's getting close to half a million in sales, which is almost unheard of. In France, the hardback has sold over 200,000 copies. Now, I've never felt that sales themselves are a criterion of excellence. We know too many novels in which that becomes a ridiculous benchmark. But I think the book, ultimately, made no major errors in its use of history. And, as a result, it gives a kind of new view of what happened during the Nazi period which people have found very compelling."

Shrugging off criticism is easy for Styron. So is avoiding the writer's temptation to second-guess himself. "Of course, there is no novel that, if you look back on it, you probably wouldn't want to tinker with. If I were a sculptor and if my statue was not public property, I could be honing away certain parts of it, polishing it. But in the end, I don't think there is anything to any large degree which I would like to alter."

Sophie's Choice—the story of a Polish woman who survived Auschwitz—is an enormously complicated narrative which required that Styron digest reams of research material. In 1975, when the idea struck, he had already spent nine years—off and on—working on another novel, *The Way of the Warrior,* a "fictional memoir" based on his experiences in the Pacific in World War II. That story was proceeding at a snail's pace when Styron awoke from a dream one morning with the vision of Sophie, a character based on a woman he had met briefly while living in Brooklyn.

"The title and the ultimate vision of the book came almost instantaneously." Styron snaps his fingers. "I knew exactly the overall plan: that it would be about a young man coming to Brooklyn, meeting a young woman who, by degrees, would reveal that on such-and-such a day in Auschwitz, she had to choose between her children.

"When I told Bob Loomis ['49], my editor at Random House, that I was starting *Sophie's Choice* after I had already told him I was deeply into this other novel, I thought he'd have a heart attack. He said, 'You mean . . .?' And I said, 'Yes, it's now 1975, and I've just started a novel called *Sophie's Choice,* and I don't know when it's going to be finished.' It was four years—a total gamble on my part— before the book came out in June of 1979. I might have been crazy. It might have been total junk!" Working the cigar in his mouth, Styron laughs with the unrestrained thrill of a gambler who won the sweepstakes. "The architecture of the book, as it turned out, was very difficult to put together, very mysterious."

With *Sophie,* Styron is still enjoying his greatest commercial success. "Did you see the movie?" he asks with earnest curiosity. Although he had little involvement in the making of the film, aside from some suggestions about the script, Styron liked the celluloid version and has declared it a "valid translation" of the book. "I think I was as well served as anyone who's written a complicated novel." Styron told a *New York Times* reporter, "I think Meryl Streep's performance is the best performance I've ever seen by an actress in the movies."

Styron calls himself "pragmatic" when asked the relative importance of whether people saw the film or read the book first. (The book was in its tenth printing when the film hit the theaters.) "That was a very interesting example of cross-pollination. I don't know how many serious readers of the book the movie picked up. The book and the movie together—it doesn't matter which came first, as long as people read the book."

Popular acceptance of this Styron-styled "large theme"—a theme as sweeping and menacing as the Holocaust—isn't strange to the author who cloaked it in fiction and delivered it with force. It's not a matter of readers, or movie audiences, wanting to feel depressed; it's a matter of their wanting to develop understanding. "The book does have some kind of reverberation. There are certain works that touch some kind of nerve universally, that gather together all the anxieties that people feel. The Nazi period was a world cataclysm from which we're still recovering. I was gathering the psychological residue from that period, and the novel was the first attempt by an American to deal with it as part of the general experience as opposed to the accounts written by the survivors of the Holocaust."

Now Styron is back slogging through the steaming jungles of the Pacific, trying to fashion the novel he left behind for Sophie. "I've only gotten into it very recently—since Christmas—to be able to tell you what it's about." What it's about is "the last military engagement in World War II and the last man who died in combat, that is, outside of the bombs that were dropped on Japan." Styron's last man, the last warrior, he describes as "a tremendously attractive young man, a Yale graduate, a very appealing person intellectually, but a complete snob and reactionary, a member of the Northern, monied, WASP establishment. And opposed to him is the narrator, who is something of a repeat of the autobiographical narrator of Sophie's Choice—in the crudest description, a Southern liberal.

"The book ends when the atomic bomb drops. That is crucial to the development of the story: the narrator's life is saved because of the atomic bomb, directly. This is the sort of fact that begins to get lost in the mists of history: that there were people like myself who probably wouldn't be here if the atomic bomb had not been dropped. Had I been lucky or unlucky, depending on your point of view, to be, let's say, as little as six months older, I would probably have been, instead of at the edge of the action in Okinawa, in the action at Okinawa. A lot of people have forgotten the two-month battle, 12,000 American dead, for one little hunk of real estate. I might have very well been among them."

As Styron puts it, the book is "an examination of the futility of war. A young man, 17 or 18, finds himself totally helpless, a pawn in some huge military apparatus. He didn't ask to be involved in this. He's completely helpless. That's what I'm trying to get at." Styron is clearly on a roll talking about this book-to-be, after all the years of struggle. His passion is in his posture. He leans forward as if telling a happy secret. "It is not only an examination of war but also of class in America, of the strange angers and hysterias that have made us the nation we are. It's an examination of wealth, an examination of liberalism versus reactionary oligarchy as exemplified in these two characters."

Does Styron plan to have the South symbolically "win" this time, since it is the Southerner who survives? "No," he says emphatically. "I did not contrive to have the reactionary die because of its symbolic effect. I think this is one of the residual themes left over from the Civil War. It has to do with a sense of attitudes. It's incredibly complex because the South has developed its own monied class, has produced its own wealth, its own class values. You can no longer say that the South is a populist, downtrodden nation facing the adversary of the rich, vibrant North. The South is rich in its own way. It's complex and I don't want to oversimplify it, but part of the adversary relationship here is between these two characters. The Northern character is not evil, he's just part of a way of life. It's Newport, North Shore, Long Island. It has a lot of bigotry, anti-Semitism—especially since I'm placing it thirty years ago at the end of World War II, when these attitudes were more dramatically apparent."

A large theme within a large theme—William Styron's metier, his "plantation." He paints a big picture, sweating over every word. Usually at night, alone, commanding only a pencil and a pad of yellow foolscap, he has chosen to plow in his imagination the fertile ground of those peculiarly dramatic and emotion-laden junctures in human history, "where human beings are a hair's breadth away from catastrophe."

Now thirty-six years beyond those quiet days of reading and rumination in the library at Duke, Styron shows a seasoned perspective of the craft of writing that is less giddy, more somber, even forbidding. "Writing is an awful profession, it really is. I sometimes wake up in a sweat and ask myself, 'Why did I become a writer?' It's like a progressive, slow, terminal disease. It can't get any better.

"It seems like it would be a lesson one would learn around the age of 20 or thereabouts that what you're doing is *confronting the unknown*. There's this blank paper. It's a corridor, it's a white corridor

with no resonances, with no shadows, and down you go—Plunge!—
for several years, trusting to your intuition, to whatever knowledge
you've got, whatever ingenuity you can summon. But no one's there
to tell you that you might run into a dead end, and there's no way
out." He slaps his small hand on the table. "The amount of faith you
have to have in yourself is considerable—especially in this country
where the critical standards are so vicious. There is a terrible thing in
American writing which calls you to task, asks you to exceed yourself
every time. It's the Hollywood syndrome. You can't sit down and just
say, 'Well, today I'm going to write something else, and it will have its
own level, and it's not going to be the *Divine Comedy* or *War and
Peace*. It's going to be something else.' All the American writers I've
known and talked to frankly admit they have been haunted by this—
our success motif. I'm getting over that fear, but there's always a
residue of it in the back of my mind.

"I suppose if I were an athlete, I would like to be a mountain
climber, climb Everest. For me these things are like climbing mountains. I don't think there's anything mean or shabby about that kind
of ambition. You give it every bit of your power, and every now and
then you reach an impasse, go up the wrong path, and have to start
another route. I'd rather be a failed ambitious writer than a mediocre
writer who has tried nothing."

Though he sounds miserable, he's not. Scatch the surface of the
frustration, and beneath it you find the optimist with a strong belief in
the nobility of his profession. "Plainly, it would be a wonderful thing if
more Americans were literate and attentively so. They don't happen
to be. I'm still rather pleased that we are saved to the degree that we
are by the fact that we do have a small but very lively minority of
people who care, and that people *do* read and writers do have some
kind of influence."

As a writer who has not shied from the most complex questions
confronting humanity, the darkest of themes, what he has called "the
catastrophic propensity on the part of human beings to attempt to
dominate one another," Styron finally admits his hope for the ultimate survival of the species.

"I think we're going to muddle through. I think the terror of the
race to our own annihilation is so great that we're going to find some
kind of answer. But I think people like Reagan exacerbate the horri-

ble insecurity that already exists so much that sometimes we get very close to deep trouble. And again, this is what I'm trying to illustrate in my books. The ultimately transcendental and important thing about art is its ability to do anything—that's the definition of art. It can deal with any experience—past, present, or future—so long as it works, so long as a significant number of people accept it as working."

For William Styron, it works.

Index

A

Absalom, Absalom! (Faulkner), 30, 54, 87, 134
Adventures of Augie March, The (Bellow), 151
Adventures of Huckleberry Finn (Clemens), 109, 126, 143
Aeschylus, 111
Algiers Motel, The (Hersey), 105
Algren, Nelson, 64, 112, 168
All My Sons (Miller), 166
All the King's Men (Warren), 133, 140, 157, 221
Amistad, 151
Anderson, Bob, 164
Anderson, Sherwood, 38, 103, 146, 154
Andress, Ursula, 259
Andreyev, Leonid Nikolaevich, 15
Anna Karenina (Tolstoy), 37
Aptheker, Herbert, 88, 100, 106
Arendt, Hannah, 249–50, 258, 262
Armies of the Night (Mailer), 155, 157
Auden, W. H., 110, 230
Austen, Jane, 36

B

Baldwin, James, 56, 82, 99–100, 103–04, 112, 157, 245
Barber, Sam, 163
Barnes, Clive, 227
Barth, John, 240
Barthelme, Donald, 240
Baum, L. Frank, 39, 109
Beat Movement, 16, 29
Bellow, Saul, 27, 63, 151, 153, 201, 230, 249
Benito Cereno (Melville), 92
Bennett, Lerone, 135
Bergman, Ingmar, 159
Berlin, Isaiah, 115
Bernstein, Leonard, 163
Bettelheim, Bruno, 198
Blackburn, William, 9, 49, 110, 177, 268

Blake, James, 168
Blake, William, 12
Blow Up, 182–83
Bobbs-Merrill (publisher), 4, 7, 221
Bosch, Hieronymus, 19
Braque, Georges, 186
Brautigan, Richard, 158
Brecht, Berthold, 184
Brewster, Kingman, 226
Brontë, Emily, 35
Brown, H. Rap, 104
Brown, John, 84–85, 116, 195
Brustein, Robert, 208, 240
Buchwald, Art, 241
Burgunder, Rose, *see* Styron, Rose Burgunder
Burroughs, William, 54
Butor, Michel, 25, 28
By Love Possessed (Cozzens), 63

C

Cabell, James Branch, 4
Cable, George Washington, 12
Caldwell, Erskine, 3
Calisher, Hortense, 17
Capote, Truman, 3, 16, 64, 112, 155, 231
Carmichael, Stokely, 104
Carter, Jimmy, 219
Catch-22 (Heller), 158
Catcher in the Rye (Salinger), 112, 249
Cather, Willa, 154
Change of Mind, A (Butor), 25
Cheever, John, 112
Chekhov, Anton, 15, 164, 230
Christie, Agatha, 109
Citizen Kane, 196, 225
Civil War (American), 24, 44, 58, 67, 105–06, 111, 116, 154, 191–92, 224, 244, 257
Clemens, S. L. (Mark Twain), 4, 17, 97, 103, 109, 126, 143, 144, 152
Commager, Henry Steele, 125
Confessions of Nat Turner, The (Styron), 31, 43–48, 55–58, 66–108, 114–44, 157,

161, 165, 170–71, 173–74, 191–99, 209–
10, 224–26, 228–29, 234–35, 238, 245,
266, 269
Conrad, Joseph, 8, 36, 38, 254
Copeland, Aaron, 163
Corry, John, 188
Cowley, Malcolm, 38–39, 54
Cozzens, J. G., 63
Crane, Stephen, 257
Critical Moments (Brustein), 240
Crucible, The (Miller), 171–73, 179–80

D

Dante, 119, 128, 274
Davidson College, 110
de Lima, Sigrid, 222
de Maupassant, Guy, 15
de Musset, Alfred, 15
de Vries, Peter, 152
Death of a Salesman (Miller), 171, 181
Deer Park, The (Mailer), 112
Defoe, Daniel, 109
Del Duca (publisher), 23
Dickens, Charles, 14, 41, 230
Dickinson, Emily, 110, 230
Divine Comedy, The (Dante), 274
Donne, John, 20, 110, 230
Dos Passos, John, 12, 17, 30, 219, 247
Dostoevski, Feodor, 17, 19, 112, 250
Doubleday (publisher), 168
Douglass, Frederick, 45, 125
Dreiser, Theodore, 146, 152
Drewry, William S., 68, 79, 88–89
Duberman, Martin, 173
Duke University, 4, 6, 9, 38, 49, 110, 218,
265, 268

E

Easy Rider, 182, 185
Eichmann in Jerusalem, (Arendt), 249, 258
Eisenhower, Dwight D., 26, 219
Eliach, Yaffa, 260
Eliot, T. S., 27, 97, 110, 230
Elkins, Stanley, 112, 128
Ellison, Ralph, 81, 103–04
Emerson, R. W., 154
Epstein, Jason, 147

F

Faulkner, William, 3, 6–7, 11–13, 17, 21, 24,
26–27, 30, 36–38, 53–55, 63, 71, 81, 87,

95, 103, 105, 111, 120, 122, 126, 134,
152, 154–55, 219, 221, 230, 239, 254,
266
Faust, Irvin, 152
Fellini, Federico, 159
Fielding, Henry, 187
Finnegans Wake (Joyce), 13
Fire Next Time, The (Baldwin), 157
First Circle, The (Solzhenitsyn), 113, 157
Fitzgerald, F. Scott, 12, 14, 17, 30, 51, 110–
11, 154, 179, 224, 230, 239
Five Chimneys (Lengyel), 245, 257–58
Five Easy Pieces, 185
Flaubert, Gustave, 12, 13, 15, 30, 111–12,
230, 239–40, 254
Forrest, Bedford, 126
Forster, E. M., 13–14
Fowles, John, 186–87
French Lieutenant's Woman, The (Fowles),
186
Freud, Sigmund, 18
Friedman, Bruce Jay, 152
From Here to Eternity (Jones), 16, 36
From Shakespeare to Existentialism (Kauf-
mann), 61
Fuentes, Carlos, 232, 253

G

Gaddis, William, 112
Gass, William H., 240
Gayle, Addison, Jr., 151
Genovese, Eugene, 106, 108, 112, 138, 173,
245
Gide, André, 112
Gill, Brendan, 63
Gilman, Richard, 107
Ginsberg, Allen, 56
Glasgow, Ellen, 4
Godard, Jean-Luc, 184
Goering, Hermann, 198
Gogol, Nikolai, 15
Golding, William, 158
Goldwater, Barry, 149
Gone with the Wind (Mitchell), 39, 139
Gorki, Maxim, 15
Grass, Gunter, 157
Gravity's Rainbow (Pynchon), 231
Great Gatsby, The (Fitzgerald), 51, 224
Greene, Graham, 230

H

Hadrian's Memoirs, 62
Hamilton, C. V., 136

Hamlet (Shakespeare), 118
Hannah, Barry, 267
Hardy, Thomas, 230
Harris, Joel Chandler, 105
Hasidic Tales of the Holocaust (Eliach), 260
Hawthorne, Nathaniel, 15, 152, 154
Haydn, Hiram, 7, 49–50, 177, 206–08,
    220–21, 268
"Hell Reconsidered" (Styron), 259, 261
Heller, Joseph, 87, 158
Hemingway, Ernest, 27, 30, 33–38, 42, 54,
    110, 154, 179, 183, 219, 230, 269
Henderson the Rain King (Bellow), 201
Henry IV, Part One (Shakespeare), 129
Hersey, John, 105
Herskovits, Melville, 47
Herzog (Bellow), 63
Heyerdahl, Thor, 244
Hicks, Granville, 26
Higginson, Thomas Wentworth, 106
Himmler, Heinrich, 249
Historical Novel, The (Lukács), 122
Hitler, Adolph, 252
Hook, Sidney, 148
Horney, Karen, 19
Höss, Rudolf, 249, 253, 262
Housman, A. E., 113
Howe, Irving, 122
Hugo, Victor, 15
Humes, Harold, 269
Huxley, Aldous, 110

I

Ibsen, Henrik, 164–65
In Cold Blood (Capote), 112, 155
In the Clap Shack (Styron), 226–27
In the Country (Miller/Morath), 226
Irving, John, 240

J

Jackson, Andrew, 103
James, Henry, 15, 146
Johnson, Lyndon, 149
Jones, James, 16, 36, 41, 241
Jones, LeRoi, 56, 140
Jonson, Ben, 110
Joyce, James, 4, 6, 12–13, 54

K

Kaufmann, Walter, 61–62
Kazan, Elia, 176–77
Kennedy, John F., 26, 149, 219

Kerouac, Jack, 29, 64, 158
Keyes, Frances Parkinson, 95
King, Martin Luther, 99
Knowles, John, 158
Kon-Tiki (Heyerdahl), 244
Krafft-Ebing, Baron Richard von, 19
Krantz, Bertha, 208–09

L

Language and Silence (Steiner), 249–50
Lardner, Ring, 152
Lasch, Christopher, 101
Last Analysis, The (Bellow), 153
Lazare (Malraux), 254
Leavis, F. R., 166
Lee, Robert E., 130, 142
Lengyel, Olga, 245, 257–58
Lewis, Sinclair, 4, 152
Liberal Imagination, The (Trilling), 110
Lie Down in Darkness (Styron), 3–7, 11, 13,
    15, 18, 23–24, 49–54, 61, 111, 151, 155,
    197, 199–201, 206–08, 219–24, 226, 234,
    266, 269
Light in August (Faulkner), 11, 21, 30
Lolita (Nabokov), 157
Long, Huey, 125, 140
Long March, The (Styron), 20, 23, 52, 187,
    218, 223–24, 266, 269
Loomis, Robert, 174, 206, 208, 239, 271
Lowell, Robert, 27, 230
Lowry, Malcolm, 111
Lukács, Georg, 122–24, 131–32, 138

M

McCarthy, Mary, 159
McCullers, Carson, 17
Macdonald, Dwight, 63
McGraw-Hill (publisher), 6, 111, 231, 244,
    268
McLuhan, Marshall, 157, 160
Madame Bovary (Flaubert), 12, 112
Mailer, Norman, 16, 64, 65, 112, 153, 155,
    157
Malamud, Bernard, 151
Malcolm X, 98–99, 140–42
Malraux, Andre, 141, 232, 253–54
Man with the Golden Arm, The (Algren), 112
Mandel, George, 221
Manhattan Transfer (Dos Passos), 247
Marine Corps, 52, 187, 236, 246
Marlowe, Christopher, 12, 17, 110
Marryat, Frederick, 109
Marx, Karl, 100

Mason, Bobbie Ann, 267
Mason, F. Vanwyck, 95
Matthiessen, Peter, 241, 269
Maugham, Somerset, 18, 38
Melville, Herman, 92, 103, 113, 154, 230, 236
Menninger, Karl, 19
Michaels, Leonard, 152
Miller, Authur, 27, 166, 208, 225–26, 241
Milton, John, 119, 128
Mitchell, Margaret, 39, 139
Mobile (Butor), 25
Moby-Dick (Melville), 236
Morath, Inge, 225–26
Morison, Samuel, 125
Morowski, Tadeusz, 253
Morris, Willie, 168–69
Mr. Midshipman Easy (Marryat), 109
Myer, Howard, 106

N

Nabokov, Vladimir, 157, 230
Naked and the Dead, The (Mailer), 16–17, 112
Nathan, George Jean, 166
New School for Social Research, The, 49, 177
Nicholson, Harold, 30
Nixon, Richard M., 155
nouveau roman, 25
Nozaka, Aikyuki, 113

O

O'Connor, Flannery, 154–55
O'Neill, Eugene, 166
Orwell, George, 110, 230
Other Voices, Other Rooms (Capote), 16

P

Page, Thomas Nelson, 12
Pakula, Alan, 261
Percy, Walker, 155, 239, 250, 266
Perkins, Maxwell, 36, 179
Phillips, John (J. P. Marquand, Jr.), 169
Phillips, Ulrich B., 128
Picasso, Pablo, 186
Plimpton, George, 178, 269
Podhoretz, Norman, 64, 113, 156
Pornographers, The (Nozaka), 113
Porter, K. A., 63
Portnoy's Complaint (Roth), 161
Poussaint, Alvin, 136

Price, Reynolds, 266
Proctor, Jim, 185–86
Proust, Marcel, 22, 115, 195
Pushkin, Aleksandr, 122, 124
Puzo, Mario, 221
Pynchon, Thomas, 231, 240

R

Rahv, Philip, 26, 166
Random House (publisher), 151, 174, 208–09, 271
Ransom, John Crowe, 55, 110
Reagan, Ronald, 274
Recognitions, The (Gaddis), 112–13
Red Badge of Courage, The (Crane), 257
"Red Leaves" (Faulkner), 54
Renoir, Jean, 159
Remembrance of Things Past (Proust), 115
Rich, Adrienne, 230
Rickover, Hyman, 251–52
Robespierre, Maximilien, 195
Robinson Crusoe (Defoe), 109
Roethke, Theodore, 230
Romain, Gary, 47
Roots of Heaven, The (Romain), 47
Roth, Philip, 112, 152, 161, 239, 241
Rourke, Constance, 119
Rowe, Kenneth T., 177
Rubenstein, Richard, 253
Rukeyser, Muriel, 229

S

Sadism and Masochism (Stekel), 19
Salinger, J. D., 17, 23, 26, 64, 112, 150, 158, 249
Sanctuary (Faulkner), 21
Sartre, Jean Paul, 255, 269
Schweitzer, Albert, 250
Scott, Sir Walter, 122–23, 144
Seasons of a Man's Life, The (Levinson), 268
Seize the Day (Bellow), 153
Sentimental Education (Flaubert), 13
Separate Peace, A (Knowles), 158
Set This House on Fire (Styron), 20–25, 28–30, 53, 57–59, 179, 205–06, 211–16, 224–25, 241, 266, 269
Shakespeare, William, 12, 110, 118, 125, 129–31, 227, 230
Shaw, Irwin, 41
Ship of Fools (Porter), 63
Solzhenitsyn, Aleksandr, 113, 157
Sophie's Choice (Styron), 197–202, 204,

231–39, 241, 244–64, 266, 269–72; movie version, 260–61, 271
Sophocles, 17, 111
Sound and the Fury, The (Faulkner), 13, 54, 71, 81, 103
Southampton Insurrection, The (Drewry), 68, 88–89
Spenser, Edmund, 110
Spock, Benjamin, 148
Stanford, Michael, 270
Stein, Gertrude, 38, 269
Steiner, George, 249–51, 262
Stekel, Wilhelm, 19
Stendhal (Marie Henri Beyle), 122
Stevens, Wallace, 27, 110
Stowe, Harriet Beecher, 171
Streep, Meryl, 261, 271
Styron, Paola, 225–26
Styron, Rose Burgunder, 205, 208, 266
Styron, William
  as southern writer, 11–12, 14, 21, 29, 43, 104–05, 149–55, 240, 267
  critics and reviewers, 15–16, 25–26, 30, 55, 107–08, 164–68
  death of the novel, 155–57
  Jewish intellectuals, 148–49, 152–54, 250–52
  narrative technique, 21–22
  on pornography, 160–61
  status of writers, 26, 64–65, 244, 273–74
  writing classes, 9, 32–39, 107, 176–78
  writing habits, 6, 9–10, 31, 41–42, 50–51, 80, 203–216, 238–39

T

Tate, Allen, 26, 55, 110, 115–16
Thackeray, W. M., 117
Thelwell, Mike, 98
Thin Red Line, The (Jones), 41
This Way for the Gas, Ladies and Gentlemen (Morowski), 253
Thomas, D. M., 262
Thoreau, H. D., 154
Tin Drum, The (Grass), 157
To Have and Have Not (Hemingway), 42
Tolkien, J. R. R., 158
Tolstoy, Leo, 15, 37–38, 122, 132, 183, 187, 230, 239, 274
Trilling, Lionel, 110, 148
Trollope, Anthony, 187
Turgenev, Ivan, 15

Twain, Mark—*see* Clemens, S. L.
"Typhoon and the Tor Bay" (Styron), 8–9

U

Under the Volcano (Lowry), 111
Updike, John, 231

V

Valery, Paul, 4, 51, 112, 170
Van Dine, S. S., 109
Vesey, Denmark, 98
von Niemand, Jemand, 250
Vonnegut, Kurt, 158
Voznesensky, Andrei, 113

W

Wakoski, Diane, 229
Wallace, George, 141
War and Peace (Tolstoy), 132, 274
Ward, Geoff, 169
Warren, Robert Penn, 3, 27, 95, 113, 116, 120, 122, 133, 140, 154, 157, 221, 266
Watts, Richard, 164
"Way of the Warrior, The" (Styron), 204, 223, 246, 271
Webster, John, 19
Weil, Simone, 249
Welty, Eudora, 3, 266
Westmoreland, William, 130
Whitehead, Robert, 173–74
Whitman, Walt, 230
Whittlesey House (publisher), 111
Wiesel, Elie, 251, 257
Wiesenthal, Simon, 259
Wilbur, Richard, 27
Wilcock, John Hart, 90
Wilde, Oscar, 114
Williams, Tennessee, 27, 227
Wilson, Edmund, 26, 55, 166
Wizard of Oz, The (Baum), 39, 109
Wolfe, Thomas, 3, 22, 36, 110, 179, 219, 230, 239, 266
Woodward, C. Vann, 112
Woolf, Virginia, 107
Wright, Richard, 103
Wuthering Heights (Brontë), 35

Y

Yeats, W. B., 110, 119